Connecting High-Leverage Practices to Student Success

Melissa and Wendy first and foremost dedicate this book to their mentors—individuals who led the field in co-teaching. We stand on the backs of giants, and our giants are Lynne Cook, Marilyn Friend, and Peggy King-Sears. We are indebted to you.

Melissa would like to dedicate this book to her husband, Chuck. I am so grateful for all the wonderful things that have emerged through our lifetime of collaboration. Thank you for your constant support and encouragement.

Wendy would like to dedicate this book to her husband, Donald Anderson. D, you are thoughtful, kind, loving, incredibly supportive, and a great collaborative partner. Other than your weirdly obsessive love of backpacking, you're perfect.

Connecting High-Leverage Practices to Student Success

Collaboration in Inclusive Classrooms

Melissa C. Jenkins

Wendy W. Murawski

CORWIN

FOR INFORMATION:

Corwin

A SAGE Company

2455 Teller Road

Thousand Oaks, California 91320

(800) 233-9936

www.corwin.com

SAGE Publications Ltd.

1 Oliver's Yard

55 City Road

London EC1Y 1SP

United Kingdom

SAGE Publications India Pvt. Ltd.

Unit No 323-333, Third Floor, F-Block

International Trade Tower Nehru Place

New Delhi – 110 019

India

SAGE Publications Asia-Pacific Pte. Ltd.

18 Cross Street #10-10/11/12

China Square Central

Singapore 048423

Vice President and
    Editorial Director: Monica Eckman

Publisher: Jessica Allan

Content Development Editor: Mia Rodriguez

Editorial Intern: Lex Nunez

Production Editor: Tori Mirsadjadi

Typesetter: C&M Digitals (P) Ltd.

Proofreader: Sarah Duffy

Indexer: Integra

Cover Designer: Candice Harman

Marketing Manager: Olivia Bartlett

Printed in Canada

Library of Congress Cataloging-in-Publication Data

Names: Jenkins, Melissa, author. | Murawski, Wendy W., author.

Title: Connecting high-leverage practices to student success: collaboration in inclusive classrooms / Melissa C. Jenkins, Wendy W. Murawski.

Description: Thousand Oaks, California : Corwin, [2024] | Includes bibliographical references and index.

Identifiers: LCCN 2023015896 | ISBN 9781071920817 (paperback) | ISBN 9781071920824 (epub) | ISBN 9781071920831 (epub) | ISBN 9781071920848 (pdf)

Subjects: LCSH: Group work in education. | Inclusive education. | Teaching teams.

Classification: LCC LB1032 .J43 2024 | DDC 371.3—dc23/eng/20230426
LC record available at https://lccn.loc.gov/2023015896

This book is printed on acid-free paper.

23 24 25 26 27 10 9 8 7 6 5 4 3 2 1

Contents

Note from the publisher: The authors have provided video and web content throughout the book that is available to you through QR (quick response) codes. To read a QR code, you must have a smartphone or tablet with a camera. We recommend that you download a QR code reader app that is made specifically for your phone or tablet brand.

About the Authors

Melissa C. Jenkins, PhD, is an assistant professor of special education at the University of Mary Washington in Fredericksburg, Virginia. She brings over 18 years of public school experience to her role as a teacher educator, having worked in Virginia public schools as a special education teacher, instructional coach, and central office administrator. Melissa is dedicated to helping educators bring high-quality, inclusive practices to schools. She loves speaking and writing about collaborative practices, early mathematics intervention, and positive behavioral support. When not working, Melissa enjoys practicing yoga to find literal and figurative balance in life. She also takes great joy in big and small adventures with her family.

Wendy W. Murawski, PhD, MBA, MEd, EdS, is the executive director and Eisner Endowed Chair for the Center for Teaching and Learning at California State University, Northridge, where she is also a full professor in the Department of Special Education and the director of SIMPACT Immersive Learning. Dr. Murawski is the national past president of the Teacher Education Division of CEC and an internationally known speaker and author, presenting in Europe, Asia, Africa, and North America. She has published extensively around inclusive education, co-teaching, collaboration, and Universal Design for Learning, to include 18 books and numerous chapters, blogs, and peer-reviewed articles. She is the CEO of 2TEACH® and 2TEACH GLOBAL (www.2TeachLLC.com), two educational consulting companies dedicated to promoting inclusive education around the world. In her personal life, Wendy enjoys curling up in front of a fire with her cat Monkey on her lap, her dog Honey at her feet, her husband Donald making dinner as she reads a book while sipping merlot and being texted sweet messages from her college-bound son, Kiernan. This scenario actually happened . . . once.

Foundations of Co-teaching and Collaborative Teaming

Introduction to Section I

Foundations of Co-teaching and Collaborative Teaming

///

Every year, we continue to learn more about what works and what does not work for our diverse group of students. We use research to guide us, sharing strategies with our colleagues and trying out new techniques to meet the constantly changing needs of our classes. Veteran and novice teachers alike seek guidance for how to integrate important frameworks and practices, as each school year and each group of students is unique.

While clever techniques and Pinterest-worthy ideas abound, teacher educators caution current and future educators to be wary of simply trying to be "fun" without using approaches based on research or evidence. Teacher educators are not alone in their emphasis on the need for scientific evidence over anecdotes or impressive pictures. Federal laws, including the Every Student Succeeds Act (which replaced the No Child Left Behind Act) and the Individuals with Disabilities Education Improvement Act (IDEA), actually require teachers to use practices grounded in research. This brings us directly to this book.

Sharing ideas and collaborating with others to get better and to meet students' needs is, in itself, an evidence-based practice. In this text, we describe the research demonstrating why collaboration results in improved teaching quality and thereby improved student outcomes (Ronfeldt et al., 2015). Obviously, though, the content of what is shared between teachers also matters. Thus, we focus this book not merely on ways to collaborate through teaming or co-teaching, but also on the practices we learn through that collaboration. After clarifying key terms like high-leverage and evidence-based practices, we make a case for how collaborative activities can connect these practices and the outcomes we desire for students.

Focus, Framework, and Format of Text

This book is grounded in the principles of inclusive education. Within that broader emphasis, this text focuses on using co-teaching and collaborative teams to bring high-leverage practices together within a multi-tiered system of support to meet the needs of *all* learners.

To create our framework, we have chosen the four areas of practice from the 22 high-leverage practices for special education. These four clusters are collaboration, instruction, assessment, and social emotional/behavioral skills (McLeskey et al., 2017). In our view, collaboration is central. Co-teaching and collaborative teaming can only be accomplished when it is present. Collaborative assessment and instruction that embed high-leverage practices and evidence-based practices lead to positive student outcomes in academic and social emotional/behavioral skills.

Our tone is intentionally informal. While we make sure to give credit for key concepts and research by using citations and quotes, we generally strive to use a conversational tone. We will talk to you, the reader. To avoid confusing "him/her" pronouns, we choose instead to use "they/them/their" as a singular.

Recognizing that readers are themselves as diverse as the students with whom they interact, we tried to create a book that can be read in the order that is most meaningful to each individual. Chapters have been formatted into three sections. The first one, *Foundations of Co-teaching and Collaborative Teaming,* provides guidance for developing the fundamental elements of co-teaching, including discussions of partnerships and parity, roles and responsibilities, communication and co-planning, as well as co-teaching and collaborative teaming models. Those who feel competent in these areas may choose to skim the first section and to focus on the second and third sections, which offer more strategies. However, reading the first section will ensure that readers and the authors are using the same terminology and have the same expectations throughout the text.

The second section, *Collaborating for Academic Success*, offers detailed guidance (with examples) for using high-leverage and evidence-based practices for assessment and instruction to address academic standards and goals. Similarly, the third section, *Collaborating for Social, Emotional, and Behavioral Growth*, provides numerous descriptions and examples of these practices for assessment and instruction to address social emotional learning and behavioral goals. The second and third sections can be read in any order. Those most interested in strategies related to behavior or social emotional learning may want to read the third section first and move back to the second section when they are looking for more ideas to enhance academic outcomes for their learners.

Throughout the book, we emphasize the crucial role of collaboration. Collaboration is certainly not a new concept in schools. In fact, "collaboration is a ubiquitously championed concept and widely recognized across the public and private sectors as the foundation on which the capacity for addressing complex issues is predicated. For those invested in organizational improvement, high-quality collaboration has become no less than an imperative" (Gajda & Koliba, 2007, p. 26). If we accomplish our objectives, this book will help you connect your understanding of how to use co-teaching and collaborative teaming to apply high-leverage and evidence-based practices in a multi-tiered system of support—all for the benefit of students in an inclusive environment! While seemingly complex, the examples and vignettes provided throughout should make each reader feel empowered to reach out, collaborate, and engage in more effective inclusive practices.

Key Terms

To get the most out of this text, certain terms and concepts need to be clarified so that both readers and authors are on the same page. First and foremost, this book is written from an **inclusive education perspective**. But what does this mean and how does it relate to collaborative teaming and co-teaching, our topic of focus? For us, **inclusion** is a philosophy, not a particular practice or set of skills.

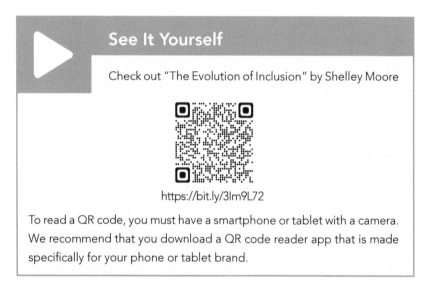

See It Yourself

Check out "The Evolution of Inclusion" by Shelley Moore

https://bit.ly/3lm9L72

To read a QR code, you must have a smartphone or tablet with a camera. We recommend that you download a QR code reader app that is made specifically for your phone or tablet brand.

It embraces the belief that all children have the right to be taught in the general education classroom and participate in activities with their nondisabled peers of the same age or grade level. Our philosophy of inclusion recognizes that this practice may not be easy and may require adaptations, assistance, and modifications to the setting or materials, or even content. Above all, we emphasize the fact that these adaptations are both doable and worth it. To promote this belief system, educators will need support from one another and from the families of students with whom they work. Collaboration supports educators in transforming inclusive philosophy into inclusive practice. (To learn more about the history of inclusive schools, see Shelley Moore's video linked in the "See It Yourself" box above.)

We continue to mention collaboration and co-teaching, so it behooves us to define these two key terms as well. While most individuals know the general definition of **collaboration**, its meaning in this text is focused on the sharing of mutual goals, responsibilities, resources, and accountability between educators and other educational stakeholders, such as families and students. Collaboration is a style of interaction, not a step-by-step process. Two or more educators who share the goal of including students with disabilities in more general education activities for improved academic, behavioral, or social emotional outcomes can collaborate to help realize this goal. These educators might participate in larger group meetings that involve other adults or even the students themselves, or they might merely consult with one another. They might invite others who have specific expertise to join for focused collaborative sessions, or they might engage with one another daily through co-teaching. If these interactions are based on open and active communication, trust, respect, and shared expertise, then each of the scenarios above would qualify as collaborative.

Co-teaching is a specific collaborative practice with a more refined definition. While many teachers have heard of co-teaching, we find that most have experienced something we would call "in-class support" as opposed to true co-teaching. True co-teaching happens when two or more professional educators co-plan, co-instruct, and co-assess (Murawski, 2010); it is not enough for them to be merely present in the same classroom together or to collaborate in general. Simply being in the same room does not qualify as co-teaching! Co-teaching certainly does require collaboration and the elements that define it—shared goals, accountability, responsibility, resources, and expertise, as well as trust, respect, and strong communication skills. While collaboration can occur in myriad examples, co-teaching is focused on what occurs in the shared classroom between two professionals. These two individuals can come together to co-teach just one lesson (e.g., a school psychologist comes in to co-teach a lesson on self-care with a general education third-grade teacher) or a unit (e.g., a school nurse comes in to co-teach a unit on health and sex education with a general education health teacher).

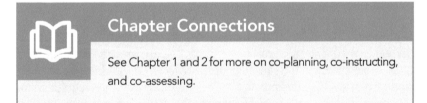

Chapter Connections

See Chapter 1 and 2 for more on co-planning, co-instructing, and co-assessing.

More often, however, co-teaching exists in American schools in the form of a general education classroom teacher sharing the class with a special education teacher for an hour, a class period or two, or even a full day. More information on what co-planning, co-instructing, and co-assessing can entail is provided in future chapters.

There are a few other key principles and practices that require review prior to moving on to our explanation of how collaboration and co-teaching can help serve as a connection to, and enhancement of, inclusive education. Table SI.1 (Section Intro) offers an at-a-glance reference for many of the key terms and concepts that permeate this book. In fact, they are so important, we will offer a similar table in each of the three section introductions for your convenience!

TABLE SI.1	Principal Concepts Related to Collaboration in Inclusive Education
RESEARCH-BASED PRACTICE	**DEFINITION**
Collaboration	Collaboration is a style of interaction, not a step-by-step process. It requires the sharing of mutual goals, responsibilities, resources, and accountability between educators, education stakeholders, families, and students. Collaboration can occur between two individuals or within larger groups.
Co-teaching	Co-teaching requires two or more professionals to co-plan, co-instruct, co-assess, and co-reflect. Educators can collaborate to co-teach one lesson, one unit, or an entire school year. Key elements for successful co-teaching include time for planning, professional development, use of multiple co-instructional approaches, parity, and administrative support.
Multi-Tiered Systems of Support	Multi-Tiered Systems of Support is an evidence-based framework designed to meet the needs of all learners through data-driven instructional delivery across three tiers of support. Multi-Tiered Systems of Support include academic and behavioral strands. The strands focus on data collection to identify areas of need for staff development and student learning, to promote proactive universal supports, and to systematically intensify intervention for students.
Response to Intervention	Response to Intervention is a strand of Multi-Tiered Systems of Support that traditionally focused on intervention for academic skills. The framework and terminology emerged from special education requirements for intervention before initial evaluation. However, the framework evolved to create a system in which educators provide early intervention to students as soon as academic concerns become evident, regardless of whether the child may require special education (U.S. Department of Education [USDOE], 2007a).
Universal Design for Learning (UDL)	UDL is a framework for planning, instruction, and assessment that promotes equity and inclusion. UDL is centered around three guidelines that can be applied across grade levels and content areas (CAST, 2018). These include multiple means of engagement, representation, as well as action and expression. The integration of UDL concepts is intended to promote accessibility across phases of instruction for all students and reduce the need for multiple forms of individualized differentiation.

Much of this book focuses on how collaborative teaming among adults (and students in some instances) will help make the connections needed to implement high-leverage and evidence-based practices. **Evidence-based practices** are strategies that have proven to be effective based on objective evidence—most often, through educational research or metrics of school, teacher, and student performance (Gaines & Murawski, in press). To be considered evidence-based, a practice is expected to be effective in real-world classroom settings, not just under research conditions. Such practices exist across content areas and for students at different developmental levels. The standards that must be met to qualify a practice as evidence-based are rigorous. In fact, some say these requirements are so rigorous that it is nearly impossible to meet the criteria in special education due to the complex diversity of student and educational settings (CEEDAR Center, 2014). We embed many of the agreed-upon evidence-based practices into examples and vignettes throughout this book.

Similarly, **high-leverage practices** are research-proven techniques that are effective in improving student learning and behavior (McLeskey et al., 2017). These practices are of value to all educators seeking to meet the needs of diverse learners in inclusive settings (Ball & Forzani, 2011). They can be used across grade levels, ages, and content areas. There are 19 general education high-leverage practices, introduced as **[GE_HLP#]** in this text, with # replaced by the corresponding number. They were developed by the TeachingWorks program at the University of Michigan and are applicable to all students. Students with disabilities may require additional considerations. Thus, the 22 high-leverage practices in special education, **[SE_HLP#]**, were developed by a variety of educational experts and published by McLeskey and colleagues (2017).

Dive Deeper

Visit TeachingWorks to learn more about the general education high-leverage practices.

bit.ly/40ZmTr9

High-leverage practices for students with disabilities can be found here:

bit.ly/413gnQc

Links to the websites where you can find all these strategies are provided in the Dive Deeper box. We have also included the high-leverage practices with connections to specific collaborative strategies in Appendices A and B of this book. A goal for this book is to highlight how collaboration between professionals, students, and family members can integrate the high-leverage and evidence-based practices to meet the monumental challenge of inclusive education. As Gaines and Murawski (in press) write, "robust, effective schoolwide collaboration is neither a luxury nor a passing fad. Rather, it is the very foundation upon which effective, inclusive, and organizationally adaptable schoolwide communities are cultivated and maintained" (p. x). Collaboration connects high-leverage and evidence-based practices to contribute to student success.

Collaborative Teaming

1

In the introduction to this section, we defined collaboration as a style of interaction and co-teaching as multiple professionals co-planning, co-instructing, and co-assessing the same group of learners. We also emphasized that merely placing two or more educators in the same room does not qualify as either collaboration or co-teaching. Co-teaching is a service, and one that is rendered differently based on the individuals providing the service. Collaboration is also a difficult-to-quantify interaction, but it is certainly easy to know when it is *not* happening. In an inclusive school environment, some educators may co-teach and others may not, but all need to be collaborating. Collaborative teaming occurs at department meetings, grade-level activities, co-planning sessions, Individualized Education Program (IEP) meetings, School Site Council meetings, parent–teacher organization gatherings, and more. When multiple individuals gather to achieve a common goal, collaborative teaming is in place. And, simply put, *relationships do matter* when it comes to collaboration.

Building respectful relationships—with colleagues, family members, specialists, and students—is a general education high-leverage practice **[GE_HLP10]**. Respectful relationships foster a positive classroom and school culture and lead to a more inclusive environment for all. Once relationships are established, collaborating parties can use self-awareness and communication skills to identify clear roles and establish responsibilities, leading to a sense of parity between participants. While Chapter 3 will go into more detail on how to establish specific roles and responsibilities, the current chapter emphasizes how collaborative teaming can help **establish a consistent, organized, and respectful learning environment [SE_HLP7]** for our colleagues, our families, our students, and ourselves. By creating organizational structures and norms to aid in smooth and effective collaborative teaming, we can ***organize and facilitate effective meetings with professionals and families*** **[SE_HLP2]**, thereby demonstrating our commitment to true collaboration and inclusion.

Before we jump right in, it behooves us to define what we mean by **collaborative teaming**. Collaborative teaming is happening when two criteria are met: (1) multiple individuals get together with the common goal of solving a mutual problem and (2) they are willing to share expertise, resources, and accountability while communicating respectfully and trusting one another. Knackendoffel (2005) emphasized that collaborative teaming is a process, not a specific model of service delivery.

Collaborative Teaming Beliefs

1. All participants in the collaborative relationship must have equal status (parity).

2. All educators can learn better ways to teach all students.

3. Educators should be involved continuously in creating and delivering instructional innovations.

4. Education improves when educators work together rather than in isolation.

5. Effective collaborative relationships involve people who see themselves on the same side, working toward positive outcomes for students.

Source: Knackendoffel (2005, p. 1).

Collaborative teams may involve two educators (e.g., co-teaching), multiple educators (e.g., department meetings), teachers and special service professionals (e.g., grade-level meeting with a speech teacher), or educators and families (e.g., IEP meetings). As Dr. Margaret King-Sears and colleagues (2015) explained:

> Collaborative teaming is not used in schools that strive to practice inclusive education merely because education laws and regulations require it. Collaborative teaming is so central to inclusive schooling that it can be viewed as the glue that holds the school together. It is through collaboration that the educational programs and special education supports for individual students are planned and implemented. (p. 5)

In this chapter, we first discuss the concept of **parity** as it relates to collaboration and the way individuals work in teams of two or more to build those relationships. Think of parity as a feeling of equality between individuals. Research has identified a lack of parity as one of the key barriers to true collaboration between educators (Ghedin & Aquario, 2020), as well as between educators and families (Fallah et al., 2020). As part of our conversation around parity, we address issues that may arise when trying to engage in collaborative teaming with a variety of partners, to include special service providers, administrators, families, paraprofessionals, and others. Next, we identify how teachers' self-awareness of strengths, challenges, values, and biases can impact collaborative relationships and lead to improved parity—or serve as a barrier to it! Through a better knowledge of self, potential collaborating partners can recognize what they bring to the interaction, what they need or want from their partners, how to identify when those needs are not being met, and how to make appropriate adaptations. Finally, we describe elements required for educators to build, model, and engage in respectful relationships as they participate in collaborative teams.

The Role of Parity in Collaborative Relationships

Diversity and various frames of reference add value to the collaboration. If each member of a team were to have the same skills, interests, and areas of expertise, there would be little value added by additional participants. Members of a collaborative team, or teachers in a co-teaching partnership, need to feel valued for the unique perspectives or skills they bring to the table. For example, in an IEP meeting, a speech pathologist may share their expertise related to expressive language, while an administrator is able to describe components of the master schedule that may impact students' academic elective options. In a department meeting, team members may share an affinity and talent for their subject, but still have different perspectives and skills they can contribute when designing lessons. Families who are asked to share information about their children so teachers are better able to integrate areas of interest will feel valued and know they are positively impacting their children's education. This feeling of parity means that each member sees their contribution is necessary and valuable. Bringing in different but complementary areas of expertise is exactly what is needed for strong collaborative partnerships. When one member of a team feels superfluous, invaluable, or secondary to another team member, the parity between team members is lost. Note that parity does not require collaborators to do the same thing or the same amount, it is a *feeling* that all are equally valuable and engaged in the work at hand.

Parity Issues With Families

When collaborating as a larger team involving home and school, a lack of parity is often identified between parents and educators. The literature is replete with examples of family members who felt demoralized, patronized, humiliated, disrespected, and condescended to by educational team members (Fallah et al., 2020; Kelty & Wakabayashi, 2020).

If families feel unwelcome in the school environment or feel that the opportunities provided for them to collaborate are not inclusive of diverse family types, they may not see the collaboration offer as genuine. Family members may feel judged if their manner of communicating or collaborating is different from that of school personnel. Certainly, other factors, such as poverty, language, family structure, transportation, and technology, can also negatively impact family engagement and collaboration if educators are not responsive (Hindman et al., 2012). Despite numerous barriers, the research also continues to find that when families and school personnel do collaborate—often for activities such as IEP or Student Study Team meetings—the benefits far outweigh the struggles (e.g., Fallah et al., 2020).

Chapter Connections

See Chapter 8 for more on how a community liaison might enhance collaboration between educators and other stakeholders.

Parity Issues With General Educators

General education teachers report feeling confused and unimportant during IEP meetings where special education professionals take the lead, often using jargon that is inaccessible to anyone outside the field of special education (Fallah et al., 2020). Each member of an IEP meeting is there because they bring a unique perspective on how to support the student; to alienate anyone during these meetings by not establishing practices that ensure parity is to miss the whole point of the collaboration. General educators are valuable contributors to collaborative meetings because of their knowledge of standards and curriculum, familiarity with age-expected social and academic development, and relationships with students and family members. It is important that administrators and special education professionals highlight this knowledge and encourage general education teachers to be active members of special education/intervention team meetings. General educators can also be helpful in calling out jargon or asking questions about technical aspects of special education meetings. In all likelihood, if a general education teacher doesn't know what a test score or acronym means, someone else at the table is also unfamiliar with the concept. When professionals ask questions of each other and family members, they acknowledge the expertise that others bring to the table and deepen the collaborative engagement.

The strategies provided in the following list are offered to help ensure that all team members feel equally valued and included.

Strategies to Enhance Parity on Collaborative Teams

- Create name cards for team meetings that include community or family members. Position the name cards outward so everyone can see names and titles.

- Design posters identifying norms for collaborative meetings and place them in conference rooms. Review norms with new teams and team members.

- Develop table tents with the agenda or typical process for team meetings to ensure all members are aware of how the meeting will progress. Review at the beginning of each meeting.

- Just as teachers do with student cooperative learning groups, consider identifying specific roles within collaborative groups to ensure everyone feels valued and engaged. These may include facilitator, reporter, recorder, timer, materials manager, tech support, jargon catcher, welcomer, and so on.

- Ask the "jargon catcher" to help clarify terms so no one has to be embarrassed if they are unfamiliar with acronyms or internal slang. Do this at the beginning of each meeting so it is a familiar and expected practice.

- Use DoodlePro, Calendly, or another app to schedule meetings that are convenient for all members. Be sure to include paraprofessionals and additional support personnel for meetings in which their roles will be discussed. Students can also be included, especially in meetings about themselves!

Parity Issues With Related Service Providers

Collaboration with related service providers has its own barriers and issues. Related service providers include individuals such as school psychologists, speech-language providers, occupational and physical therapists, adapted physical education teachers, mobility and vision specialists, social workers, nurses, and behavior coaches. While each of these individuals has their own unique area of expertise that they might bring to an inclusive classroom—and a teacher would be lucky to have them—most are spread quite thin across a school district. As schools become more inclusive, more of these providers are beginning to offer their services through collaborative, push-in, or even co-taught models, as opposed to the more common pull-out, clinical application

(Zimmerman et al., 2022). When teachers witness the strategies and cues these experts use with students, they are more likely to apply those same skills in the future, even with students not yet identified as having specific special educational needs.

One strategy for building communication and collaboration between related service providers and classroom teachers is to add consultation time to the IEP so providers can schedule regular and consistent time in the classroom. For those who are still providing more pull-out services to students, a baby step toward increased collaborative teaming is for service providers and teachers to create a shared communication notebook (hard copy or digital). A notebook could house comments by the service provider following sessions with students and allow teachers to ask questions or seek suggestions for better meeting students' needs in the classroom. Because teachers interact with students in more settings and for longer periods of time, service providers can also learn more about the students and their behaviors by communicating with teachers, thereby reinforcing the feeling of parity between both parties.

Parity Issues With Paraeducators

By definition and title, paraprofessionals are not credentialed or certified educational professionals. Thus, there is no expectation of parity between teachers and paraprofessionals. Paraprofessionals typically have little to no formal training in education; however, veteran "paras" may have extensive experience in working with a student or group of students. Many also get to know students on a more personal level, learning students' strengths, interests, communication styles, family dynamics, and culture, at a level that teachers should value. Thus, communication, collaboration, and teaming can and should still occur between paras and teachers, despite the lack of formal parity. When teachers demonstrate respect and communicate clearly with paraprofessionals, everyone benefits. For enhanced teaming, teachers should determine paras' knowledge of content and students, the strengths they bring to the classroom, and their own beliefs and values.

Dive Deeper

Seeking training opportunities for paraprofessionals? Check out the free, on-demand training on high-leverage practices designed specifically for paras at

bit.ly/41d0J4S

Teachers and paras who will share a classroom, even if only for part of the day, need to find time to communicate what that dynamic will look like. There are times when a paraprofessional's beliefs about the best way to work with students or families does not align with the teachers' perspectives. This issue needs to be addressed proactively and clearly to minimize confusion and possible resentment. Communication notebooks are a positive, effective, and efficient way for collaborative teams to write short notes to one another throughout a day; these may stay between a teacher and a para or, when specific to a student, even include family communication. Scheduling quick checks can also give paras and teachers the opportunity to review upcoming activities, discuss plans, answer questions, talk about a particular student, share a strategy, or look at data. When possible, we encourage teachers to seek training opportunities for the paraprofessionals with whom they work; the more professional development they receive, the more collaborative teaming will ultimately be possible!

Self-Awareness

As mentioned, collaborative teaming is most beneficial when all individuals on the team bring their unique skills and perspectives, and when they feel valued for those distinctive traits. While both internal (e.g., active listening skills) and external (e.g., posters of norms on the wall) structures can be in place to support parity, educators are more likely to make use of those structures when they have a strong sense of self-awareness. For example, if you know you tend to interrupt others, that knowledge alone will help you improve your communication skills and take a breath before interrupting again. We've all experienced the person who was not self-aware and clearly did not pick up on social or communication cues. How often do you want to get into conversations with that person? We are guessing not very often!

Richardson and Shupe (2003) tell us that increased self-awareness includes understanding how "students affect our own emotional processes and behaviors and how we affect students" (p. 8). Wait. What? Students impact our emotions and behaviors? We are professional educators! Aren't we always in charge of how we feel, what we say, and what we do? Go ahead. Take a moment to laugh. Obviously, Richardson and Shupe recognized that not only do others impact our emotions and behaviors, but also we need to do the work to figure out exactly what our triggers and reactions are, and why we respond the way we do. While these authors focused on the impact of students on teachers, we would apply this need for self-reflection to work with colleagues, administrators, and families as well. By getting in touch with one's own feelings, strengths, challenges, values, and behaviors, educators are better equipped to work with other adults on collaborative teams. In fact, while Murawski (2003) introduced the co-teaching definition as "co-plan, co-instruct, and co-assess" two decades ago, recently "co-reflect" has been frequently added to the definition (Conderman & Hedin, 2017; Dubeck & Doyle-Jones, 2021).

Identifying one's strengths and challenges as a collaborator requires true reflection and honesty with oneself. While it may be relatively easy to point out strengths like "I'm really good at math" or "I put a lot of time into lesson planning," it may be more difficult to acknowledge other strengths such as "I regularly employ active listening skills," "I'm funny," and "I put my phone away during collaborative planning meetings." Yet these are strengths that need to be acknowledged, celebrated, and shared! Strengths do not need to be specific only to content expertise. In fact, there is a wide array of areas in which teachers may want to consider strengths, including general pedagogical knowledge, curriculum knowledge, pedagogical content knowledge, knowledge of learners, knowledge of educational contexts, as well as knowledge of educational ends, purposes, and values (Rytivaara et al., 2019). Family members bring their knowledge about their child, at home and in the community, while related service providers offer an insight into specific fields of expertise. Paraprofessionals too bring a unique insight, often interacting with students on a different level than teachers do. Beyond these areas, individuals also possess personal attributes that can be considered strengths when collaborating; they include communication skills, trustworthiness, dependability, humor, commitment, and flexibility, among other characteristics.

As much as we prefer to be strengths-focused, engaging in self-reflection requires taking a hard look at areas for improvement. Personal challenge areas can be difficult—but are essential—to identify:

> Although teachers need to learn how to recognize signs of emotional distress in their students, it is equally important to acknowledge that teachers' own personalities, learned prejudices, and individual psychological histories have helped shape their attitudes and responses to certain behaviors. (Richardson & Shupe, 2003, p. 9)

Being able to honestly share personal challenges with oneself and those with whom you are trying to collaborate will lower barriers, make collaboration more effective, and ultimately make you a more responsive educator. Consider identifying any potential triggers or pet peeves you may have and sharing those proactively and diplomatically with potential team members.

Self-awareness also extends to acknowledging one's values and biases related to classroom culture. What practices are sacrosanct to you? What would be difficult for you to get rid of? Sharing a classroom during co-teaching means that partners need to be forthright about what is important to them, while still being open to the idea of letting go of control and developing new shared norms and ways of doing things. The ability to bring in multiple voices, teaching styles, and perspectives is paramount to collaboration. Ask yourself: Are you holding on to certain practices out of fear, habit, preference, or because you truly believe in them? If the latter is the case, be prepared to share your values with your collaborators.

Being able to communicate about one's values will help partners avoid offending one another, mitigate negative effects of bias, and allow for more open feedback. When preferences or practices relate to one's culture, language, or background, sharing those values assists others in understanding and appreciating where you are coming from, especially if they do not share your culture (Aceves & Orosco, 2014; Richards-Tutor et al., 2016). Awareness of different cultures and how they can impact collaborative relationships also applies to collaboration with families. When school teams acknowledge strengths of families and build on them, they increase the amount of available supports at school, at home, and in the community (Kelty & Wakabayashi, 2020).

To be able to **_organize and facilitate effective meetings with professionals and families_ [SE_HLP2]**, educators need to recognize that what is considered an "effective" meeting for one family may vary from what is considered "effective" by another, and both may differ from what is considered "effective" by the school personnel. Asking team members at the beginning of a meeting (or even prior to it!) about their goals helps collaborating team members find commonality and use the time efficiently so all participants walk away pleased.

Relationship Building for Collaborative Teaming

Individuals who share resources and accountability as they work together to achieve shared goals exemplify collaboration. To the layperson, collaboration is—in a nutshell—teamwork. It is evident when we cheer on our favorite sports teams ("Go Manchester United!") and when we watch a well-organized group of baristas get us our chai lattes in record time despite long lines ("Thank you, Starbucks!"). We know there is a significant amount of behind-the-scenes collaboration when we attend a well-run conference, concert, or other event. And, just as we know collaboration has occurred when everything runs smoothly, we are equally aware when collaboration breaks down. Successful collaborative relationships, or a lack thereof, are almost always due to two linked factors: **communication** and **role understanding.** We address both here but go into more detail on roles related to co-teaching in Chapter 3. These two factors are not the only ones impacting the success of collaborative teams. Other critical competencies include mutual trust and respect, conflict resolution skills, willingness to collaborate, a positive attitude, and more (Suter et al., 2009).

Using Strong Communication Skills

The literature across multiple disciplines links open communication with positive outcomes, while communication failures are linked to negative, and sometimes even harmful, outcomes (Suter et al., 2009). Both informal and formal communication skills are key to successful collaboration and may encompass a wide range of strategies and purposes. Solis et al. (2012) remind us that, when engaged in collaborative consultation, interpersonal skills that need to be practiced include active listening, empathy, assertiveness, questioning to gain information, and negotiating an outcome that is mutually beneficial. The application of these skills can help co-teachers share information regarding their preferred teaching styles, philosophies, and classroom expectations; negotiate roles that each person prefers; discuss which co-teaching model might best meet their students' needs; manage conflicts; and take turns sharing ideas and concerns.

Developing Team Norms

One of the first actions that teams should take, whether they are a co-teaching team or a larger collaborative body (e.g., a grade-level team or parent–teacher–student association), is to **identify norms [GE_HLP5]**. Norms help to establish a shared purpose for the collaboration, ways to interact and communicate, techniques for managing conflict, as well as reinforcement of shared accountability, resources, and ownership of the situation. Basically, team norms are principles that the group agrees to use for their interactions or to determine the way the group operates.

Example of Transdisciplinary Team Norms

1. Respect the shared expertise of all team members. Each team member brings unique knowledge about a discipline, child, and/or interaction in the classroom. Team members should listen to each other's expertise and value it.

2. All children in the classroom are the responsibility of all team members. Children learn from all adults in the classroom, all adults share accountability for child outcomes, and all adults celebrate all children's accomplishments.

3. Team member role assignments should be clear and flexible.

4. A conflict resolution process will be developed and used. When a conflict occurs, team members will be asked to consider differing perspectives and support the team in modifying their consensus to move the collaboration forward.

Team norms help **establish a consistent, organized, and respectful learning environment [SE_HLP7]**. Transdisciplinary teams are made of individuals who collaborate and agree to cooperate across their fields, sharing roles, expertise, and consulting with one another throughout the process. Transdisciplinary team members are comfortable with the concept of role release, helping another team member learn your role if it will benefit students. The following list offers an example of team norms used by a transdisciplinary team.

Giving and Receiving Feedback

Giving and receiving feedback openly is a key aspect of successful communication and can greatly impact collaboration. Yet these are not intuitive skills. Educators do not always know how to adequately give feedback to peers. Moreover, they often lack the ability to receive constructive feedback, frequently feeling judged or evaluated. When teachers spend a significant time in their own classrooms, or "silos," it can be hard for them to open up to outside ideas, opinions, and criticisms, even when those are intended to be constructive. Educators also tend to have different perspectives shaped by their cultural and personal backgrounds as well as their professional ones. To emphasize these differences, we often tell teacher educators: "General educators are taught to see the forest: How can I take this third-grade class and prepare them to be fourth graders? Special educators are taught to see the trees: What does Eli need to improve his reading comprehension skills?"

These differing frames of reference result in messages that may cause anxiety, frustration, anger, or embarrassment. In this respect, Hackett et al. (2021) note:

> These apprehensive feelings may be internalized and prevent the guest or host [special or general education teacher] from feeling comfortable, regardless of messages voiced. Accounts of the shared experiences can be radically different for several reasons including communication barriers, cultural norms, or feelings of being the outsider. (p. 118)

Murawski and Lochner (2018) suggest that team members who share common goals create a community of practice, develop team norms, and use a *2+2 model* of giving and receiving feedback, wherein each team member offers two suggestions for improvement as well as two areas of strength to one another.

Building Role Understanding Across Tasks

The special education high-leverage practices encourage educators to **establish a consistent, organized, and respectful learning environment [SE_HLP7]**. By keeping this goal in mind, collaborators can identify tasks that will help to establish such an environment. For team meetings, this may include creating a checklist of actions to be taken, including warm welcomes, introductions, and ensuring the meeting is well-run and jargon-free. A template for the agenda can be created so that meetings are organized and all participants know what to expect. Accepted positive behaviors and team norms might be posted on a table tent, laminated, and set out during meetings for all to see. While general transdisciplinary team norms, such as those described above, are foundational to role understanding, the Check It Out callout box here displays a table tent that might be created to set guidelines for specific behaviors during a team meeting.

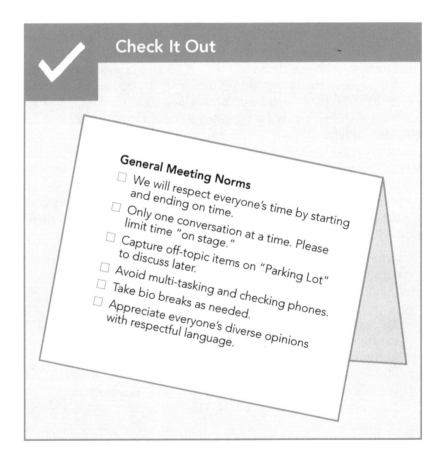

Check It Out

General Meeting Norms
☐ We will respect everyone's time by starting and ending on time.
☐ Only one conversation at a time. Please limit time "on stage."
☐ Capture off-topic items on "Parking Lot" to discuss later.
☐ Avoid multi-tasking and checking phones.
☐ Take bio breaks as needed.
☐ Appreciate everyone's diverse opinions with respectful language.

Being able to talk about what organization, structure, and respect look like in a shared class can help co-teachers recognize their differences and determine roles. Co-teaching pairs may want to collaboratively identify what each member sees as a consistent, organized, and respectful environment. For example, one teacher may feel strongly that lecture notes should be made accessible via the class website. The other teacher may not feel as strongly about it but, in an effort to maintain a consistent environment, will agree that these notes can be posted for the shared class as well as for a section that is not co-taught. While the first co-teacher takes on the role of capturing and posting the lecture notes, the second may take on a different role, such as obtaining various forms (e.g., Audible, hard copy, graphic novel) of a book they are about to read in class. Negotiation and compromise will be required often when collaborating and, in a co-taught class, both teachers should be able to use their strong communication skills to do so.

Establishing Mutual Trust and Respect

While the definitions of collaboration and co-teaching are fairly clear, the practices vary based on the contexts in which they are applied. Regardless of the specific context, professional relationships are key to successful collaboration and co-teaching. Sometimes, people just "click" with one another—and sometimes they do not. This concept of "clicking" falls under the broad category of personal characteristics. While structural aspects of collaboration are important (e.g., time, staffing), the personal aspects appear even more critical. These include compatibility, attitudes, behaviors, culture, and communication styles (Ghedin & Aquario, 2020). Those who need to collaborate do not always have to be best friends. However, it is difficult to collaborate with someone you do not trust or respect, or with whom you cannot communicate. When colleagues get to know one another beyond the superficial level, their mutual trust and respect can grow. ***Building a respectful relationship* [GE_HLP10]** and ***environment* [SE_HLP7]** are critical for strong collaborative teamwork.

Even when partners do not agree, they should do their best to respect one another's differing opinions. This effort entails using strong communication skills when differences are discussed, negotiated, and used to reach a compromise, or even when they are acknowledged and avoided. When trust is present and relationships are strong, disagreements and conflicts can even strengthen collaborative teams. One of the primary purposes of collaboration is to benefit from different perspectives, opinions, and frames of reference; to ignore or silence this diversity would minimize its potential benefits. Taking time to build trust and respect in a collaborative team, whether that team is composed of many individuals or two co-teachers, is worth the time spent. The strategies offered in the following list offer ways for team members to build trust and respect as they improve communication skills and establish strong relationships.

Strategies for Respectful Relationship Building and Communication

- Spend time at meetings talking about what "safe and brave spaces" may look like. A safe space is one that doesn't incite judgment regarding differences, while a brave space is one that recognizes differences and encourages respectful dialogue to build understanding around those differences.

- Start each collaborative team meeting with a statement like the following one: "This meeting is intended to be a psychologically safe event, where we give one another the benefit of the doubt when taking risks. We will avoid all embarrassment, ridicule, and shame so that we can engage, connect, and learn from one another." (More information on psychological safety is provided in Chapter 3.)

- Administrators can set aside 10 minutes at each faculty meeting to have "brag time." Select 10 faculty at random to stand up and "brag" about themselves for one minute. The goal is for them to share their skills, expertise, experiences, and interests with colleagues. No one is allowed to be humble or say anything negative about themselves. Learning more about the skills of colleagues (e.g., Who speaks Farsi? Who used to be a professional skateboarder? Who can code HTML?) builds respect, communication, and collaboration. This may also lead to possible co-teaching pairings!

- Colleagues who will co-teach in the next semester or school year are encouraged to complete Murawski and Dieker's (2004) SHARE worksheet. This resource encourages educators to consider their expectations and preferences regarding the planned co-teaching relationship. After completing the worksheet individually, the team meets to share responses and determine where they may need to compromise, or discuss how to operate their shared classroom.

- Special educators can create a school blog or newsletter to share strategies for differentiation, accommodations, and modifications. These resources can be disseminated to families and to general education colleagues. Such blogs and newsletters will help others

> recognize the value that special educators bring to collaborative teams or co-teaching situations.
>
> - Proactively establish communication plans with co-teaching teams, paraprofessionals, related service providers, and other collaborators. Consider selecting times for communication, sharing how to give/receive feedback, and planning how to deal with disagreements. This is also a good time to discuss how to share with one another if participants do not feel psychologically safe.

Dealing With Conflict

Even in an excellent relationship, conflict will occur due to disagreements, incompatibility of perspectives, and differences of opinion. While ineffective communication skills can certainly exacerbate a bad situation, conflict doesn't always have to be destructive. In fact, research has identified benefits for individuals who collaboratively problem solve to address conflict and grow from the interaction (Greer & Dannals, 2017). Collaborators' goal should be to communicate, negotiate, and come to a consensus that respects differences of personality, culture, training, or opinion (Suter et al., 2009). Most people do not seek out conflict, but we also know that it really cannot be avoided. If team members have not taken the time to identify the purpose for collaboration, establish norms, delineate roles, or communicate through challenges, a conflict between them can get worse, adding stress to the relationship and preventing the team from functioning well (Steele et al., 2021).

One potential source of conflict is when educators have differing opinions to share with families. For example, if co-teachers disagree about accommodations to be provided to a student in their co-taught class, they often feel the need to come to a consensus before discussing those accommodations with the student or their family. Team members, in education and other fields, often want to present a cohesive and unified opinion when interacting with families (Suter et al., 2009). However, we must remember that families are part of the team and should be allowed to participate in the problem-solving process, even when there are potential disagreements. In fact, the purpose of meetings is to discuss ideas and reach a consensus about the best option. Parents need to hear pros and cons of different options so they have a voice in the decision making. In our experience, these discussions elicit true collaboration among team members and often produce new and powerful ideas.

Being Willing to Collaborate

Willingness to collaborate is more than merely a desired characteristic. It can make a significant impact on the efforts of a team. In 1993, Anderson et al. proposed "willingness to collaborate" as a communication trait and a concept, creating a Willingness to Collaborate Trait scale. Their study defined willingness to collaborate as "active communication involvement with another during the process of decision making. Conceptually, this means a willingness to participate in decision making but also includes a willingness to negotiate and be assertive" (p. 4). They found, not surprisingly, that interpersonal communication competence was a strong predictor of willingness to collaborate. Consider how the opposite may be true. A family member or educator who lacks strength in interpersonal communication skills may struggle or be reluctant to participate in a collaborative team, not because they do not believe in the goals of the team but because of low comfort with the communication required to be a part of that team. Ensuring that all members have time to process, ask questions, and participate equally will help ease those who are uncomfortable in collaborative situations. While a positive attitude and desire to work together will go far in ensuring that a collaborative team is successful, other skills, such as listening, turn-taking, and oral communication, also play a role.

Different team members' willingness to collaborate may impact others' participation. In many instances, a school leader or administrator will be a group member. While this individual is a leader in many capacities in the school environment, within a collaborative team they are supposed to share with the other members an equal role and voice. This dynamic can be sometimes difficult to navigate. However, research has found that school leaders who demonstrate willingness to collaborate and communicate inspire other team members to do the same (Karadimou & Tsioumis, 2021). School leaders can positively influence team processes, strengthen teams' self-esteem, and play an essential role in building a collaborative climate (Tschannen-Moran & Gareis, 2017).

Summary

Collaborative teaming occurs between educators, family members, and students for the purpose of creating a **consistent, organized, and respectful learning environment [SE_HLP7]**. It takes concerted effort to build the **respectful relationships [GE_HLP10]** that result in effective teams. Self-awareness and strong communication are among the interpersonal skills essential for developing parity. Structural supports, such as **norms and routines for work [GE_HLP5]**, and **well-organized collaborative meetings with professionals and family members [SE_HLP2]** are also crucial features.

Co-teaching Models

2

Nothing is more indicative of a strong—or weak—co-teaching team than what is observed in the classroom when students are present. A team may get along well, and may even plan well together, but the rubber hits the road when they get in front of their shared class. It is when students observe parity—or a lack thereof. It is when students are engaged, motivated, and learning—or not. It is when teachers take advantage of the fact that there are two of them—or it is when an observer would reflect that the class was led by a teacher and an active, or even passive, paraprofessional. It is during these observations that an outsider might see two collegial professionals working seamlessly to provide differentiated and universally designed instruction for all learners—or two teachers doing what one teacher might have done alone with their own class.

By now, most educators and administrators know that simply putting two educators in one room does not equal co-teaching. Teachers need time to discuss how they will share responsibilities, meet students' needs, put their egos aside, and find time to co-plan, among other tasks. Another major requirement is to understand the various models for co-instruction, in terms of content, logistics, and environment. Breaking students into small groups provides a much-needed reduction to student–teacher ratio, but there are considerations for effective grouping. Does the special educator know the content well enough to teach it? Will students be homo- or heterogeneously grouped? Will small groups occur in the same classroom or are there additional spaces for breakout groups? How long will the group work take? How will the co-teachers manage time, space, and noise? How should they set up the classroom? How do students learn the behaviors needed to work in small groups? And the list goes on.

Co-teaching gurus Drs. Lynne Cook and Marilyn Friend did not introduce the concept of co-teaching in 1995 and then ask teachers to figure out what a shared classroom might look like. They provided very clear, concrete depictions of approaches, or models, of co-teaching so that those willing to collaborate would know how they might engage learners without stepping on one another's toes. Their five co-teaching approaches have been the foundation upon which all other approaches have developed.

In subsequent editions of their best-selling textbook *Interactions: Collaboration Skills for School Professionals* (Friend & Cook, 2021), they added a sixth approach, breaking One Teach–One Support (OTOS) into One Teach–One Assist and One Teach–One Observe. We believe that OTOS sufficiently captures both assisting and observing. (We know from a personal conversation with Lynne Cook that she believes so as well.) Thus, in this book you'll note that we refer to the original (and, as we argue, the best) five co-teaching approaches. Over the years, others have added to the literature by providing alternative options for co-instructional approaches; however, we believe that none of the additional options are truly new. We give respect to Lynne and Marilyn for their insight and the unique contribution they made to the field by introducing the initial five approaches.

Discussing each one of them, we will highlight how they can be used to integrate classwide peer tutoring (CWPT) into the inclusive classroom. The following box provides important background information about CWPT.

Focus on an Evidence-Based Practice: CWPT

CWPT has been identified as an evidence-based practice by the What Works Clearinghouse (U.S. Department of Education [USDOE], 2007b). The general premise behind CWPT is that students are paired and designated as "tutor" and "student." Tutors ask questions and provide feedback based on their peers' responses. Students are taught how to be supportive tutors and how to reinforce learning through repetition. Points are awarded by the teacher(s) for tutoring appropriately and for correct responses.

In addition to being an evidence-based practice, CWPT also incorporates high-leverage practices related to grouping students. Specifically, it provides an intentional structure for **setting up and managing small-group work [GE_HLP9]**. Working with smaller groups allows teachers to better engage their learners. This approach is also great for conducting formative assessments to check for understanding, differentiate students based on these data, and build skills as needed. The field of special education specifically encourages teachers to **use flexible grouping [SE_HLP17]**. The emphasis on *flexible* grouping demonstrates the need for educators to recognize the diversity of students' needs on a regular basis. Each student has a different neurodevelopmental profile, so groups must be dynamic, rather than static. Flexible grouping also helps to avoid the stigmatization that may occur when groups are created based on ability level or, worse, disability label.

One Teach-One Support

As its title indicates, OTOS is simply when one educator takes the lead on instruction while their partner moves into a support role. The most common approach to co-teaching (Hanover Research, 2012), it is also the approach that is considered the least effective (Hang & Rabren, 2009) in terms of student outcomes. While this model requires the least amount of collaboration and co-planning between teachers (King-Sears & Jenkins, 2020), it also results in the least amount of differentiation for students and interaction between teachers. OTOS is not entirely unhelpful. There are times when the ability to divide roles this way is invaluable: one teacher conducts direct instruction with a whole class while their partner observes the interaction and gathers data for IEP goals or other decision making purposes. There are also times when only one teacher's voice is needed; the other educator in the room can use proximity control and circulate to help with class management.

The key to successful OTOS is to make it purposeful, strategic, and planned (Karten & Murawski, 2020). Too often, OTOS appears to be a default option for co-teachers who have not planned their collaboration well (King-Sears & Jenkins, 2020). This is what it often looks like: The general education teacher comfortably takes their place in front of the class, sharing a lesson that they might have led in multiple other classes, co-teaching or not. Meanwhile, the special educator frequently becomes a helper. As the special educator circulates, they quietly answer questions of students willing to get their attention. This teacher may also take the role of a student, raising their hand to ask questions on behalf of young people unwilling or embarrassed to draw attention to themselves. While these actions can be beneficial to students, it is difficult to explain to administrators in charge of the budget how they are different from actions that could have been taken by less well-educated, and much less well-paid, paraprofessionals. On the other hand, when teachers co-plan their lessons together, they may choose to use OTOS to collect data, manage materials efficiently, or have one teacher model note taking on the whiteboard, Smartboard, or screencast.

Applying CWPT to OTOS

Let's apply the OTOS co-teaching approach to CWPT. Using this approach, one teacher could remain as the lead of the class, providing directions to students and tutors. This teacher would act as a time-keeper and monitor the overall noise level and interaction of peer teams. The other teacher, in the support role, could circulate among teams holding a clipboard to write down points for the teams' participation and responses. Students would be spread out around the room, working in pairs as they reinforce math facts, spelling, vocabulary, social skills, reading fluency, or new content knowledge.

Team Teaching

Because co-teaching involves working as a team, the co-teaching approach named Team Teaching is often used synonymously with co-teaching. However, while co-teaching is the umbrella term (remember our three pillars of co-planning, co-instructing, and co-assessing?), Team Teaching is but one of the five co-teaching models originally identified by Cook and Friend (1995). Team Teaching, like OTOS, is what is known as a "whole-group approach." Students remain in the large classroom setting while teachers interact differently with them. An outside observer seeing OTOS in action might incorrectly assume that there is a teacher and assistant working in the room. However, an observer seeing Team Teaching in action might be enamored with the dynamic interaction between the two teachers and watch for longer than intended.

Team Teaching involves two educators essentially sharing the stage. That stage may be at the front of the room, or it might be the entire classroom. A less dynamic use of Team Teaching might involve both teachers circulating, providing feedback to students, helping with behaviors, and answering questions. A more exciting use of the approach would have both teachers grabbing students' attention at the beginning of a lesson with a roleplay or funny interaction between the two.

For example, an "intro" to a lesson—otherwise known as an "anticipatory set" for those of you using lesson-planning lingo—might involve one teacher introducing a concept and the other teacher interrupting to disagree. As students watch wide-eyed, their teachers respectfully but vigorously present evidence to support their own views. Students might be asked to vote or choose sides, getting them engaged in the topic. Using Team Teaching, co-teachers might opt to model social skills or the use of lab equipment; they might debate the merits of solving a math problem in two different ways, allowing students to choose which group they'd like to join to learn the technique they prefer. Team Teaching allows co-teachers to exchange jokes, establishing a strong culture of respect, parity, humor, communication, and collaboration in front of their shared class.

Chapter Connections

See Chapter 3 for more on relationship building and communication.

While Team Teaching can indeed be dynamic, consider the following factors. To be comfortable together in front of a class, co-teachers need to respect one another, be willing to let go of complete control, have strong verbal and nonverbal communication skills, and celebrate one another's strengths; they also need to be aware of, and considerate of, one another's weaknesses or areas of vulnerability (Rodrigues, 2013). In addition, using this approach too often means that students continue to remain in a whole-group setting. No matter how engaging their co-teachers may be when using this approach, a whole-group setting means less differentiation, less student–teacher interaction, and, quite simply, too much seat-time. Also, if an outside observer were to peek in and see co-teachers merely going back and forth with their comments or PowerPoint (e.g., "You do slide one and I'll do slide two"), the observer may see this dynamic not as an exciting play but as something similar to a tennis match. Simply going back and forth with content not only may bore or confuse students, but it also misses the entire purpose of Team Teaching—real interaction between teachers for the purpose of engaging students!

Applying CWPT to Team Teaching

Let's consider how the Team Teaching approach could work with CWPT. Using Team Teaching, both educators share instruction and activities with the whole class. Thus, co-teachers would start the CWPT activity by modeling what is expected of the students. One co-teacher would take the role of a tutor and the other one would be a student. They might provide both examples and non-examples (e.g., "That's your answer? Really? That's dumb."). After making sure that students understand the technique, the teachers may jointly identify teammates. As students begin to work together, both teachers circulate, offering feedback, giving out points, and documenting progress. As students continue to tutor in pairs, co-teachers may meet on the side of the room, sharing their data and determining next steps.

Parallel Teaching

Like parallel lines, Parallel Teaching involves two groups next to one another but not necessarily interacting. Parallel Teaching happens when each educator in the pair takes a half of the class. This is a perfect option when co-teachers have two topics to cover or two views on the same topic to share, or when they simply need to reduce the student–teacher ratio. Where do the teachers take their groups? That depends not just on the available space, but also on the purpose of the division and the time planned for the activity or instruction.

For example, co-teachers may choose to divide the class in half so that one group can research the Federalists while the other one researches the Anti-Federalists. This task may involve quiet online exploration, in which case both groups might stay in the classroom (it may be better to have one "side" facing the front of the classroom with one co-teacher, while the other "side" is facing the back of the room with the other co-teacher). Alternately, one co-teacher might take their group to the library while the other co-teacher keeps their group in the classroom. When it is time to use the research to prepare for a debate, one co-teacher may take their group to the hallway or outside so that the noise level is not too high in the classroom. During the debate, both co-teachers would have their teams in the room, engaged with one another. On the other hand, if Parallel Teaching is used for a five-minute activity, students may stay in the same room, possibly standing up and walking to different areas to separate the two groups. Examples of such quick activities include brainstorming ideas for an essay or reviewing difficult math problems from homework.

Parallel Teaching can be used in three ways: same content/same way, same content/different way, and different content (Karten & Murawski, 2020; Murawski, 2010). Co-teachers who merely want to reduce the student–teacher ratio by dividing the class in two would choose the first version (**same content/same way**). Since both educators are engaging their students similarly and covering the same material, it is imperative that both feel confident about their knowledge of the content. For example, teachers may take respective halves of their Pre-K class to separate carpet areas in order to read aloud from the same book. Or fifth-grade teachers may divide the class in half to introduce students to the same social skills curriculum, using the smaller group size to help young people better engage with topics like bullying.

The second version of Parallel Teaching (**same content/different way**) is based on the idea that not only do students learn differently, but educators also have preferences in the way they teach! Thus, if co-teachers have different ways of introducing or reinforcing the same content, they do not need to compromise, negotiate, or cajole each other to do it "their way." Instead, both teachers can teach in their preferred style, and students can either choose their preferred group—which fits nicely with the philosophy of UDL—or be assigned to a group. In the second case, young people can later switch groups in order to get exposed to a different way to learn the material. Certainly, this second introduction to the same material will support their learning while also exposing students to different ways to learn content and demonstrating that it is acceptable to have different opinions (Karten & Murawski, 2020).

Finally, the third version of Parallel Teaching is **different content**. In this approach, the two co-teachers can engage in completely different tasks, thus making the maximum use of *flexible grouping* **[SE_HLP17]**. Co-teachers may select this strategy for a variety of reasons. For instance, this is a perfect choice if during co-planning it becomes apparent that there are two main tasks for a lesson (e.g., (1) Finish writing an essay and (2) Introduce new content) and that both might take a similar amount of time (e.g., 20 minutes). Parallel Teaching allows educators to "divide and conquer" it in such a way that students are not bored.

Co-teachers should be careful not to divide and conquer *all* activities and instruction, becoming essentially two teachers doing their own thing, as opposed to co-planning and merely dividing and conquering a few identified tasks (Strogilos et al., 2016). Rather than having the whole class work for 20 minutes on the writing task, followed by 20 minutes of all students receiving direct instruction by a teacher while the other co-teacher looks on, both educators can be engaged simultaneously, while students have the opportunity to move during class time. If, during co-planning, co-teachers identify two key aspects of the same lesson (e.g., Federalists/Anti-Federalists, mitosis/meiosis, antonyms/synonyms, multiplication/division), they may choose to break the class in half, teach one aspect of the lesson to each team, and then have students from different groups get together and teach one another. This use of Parallel Teaching is based on the ability of *both* educators to teach the content masterfully; if one of them does not know the content adequately, Parallel Teaching is not the best approach.

Applying CWPT to Parallel Teaching

Let's apply CWPT to Parallel Teaching. Co-teachers may decide that they want to introduce the two different roles in CWPT, tutors and students, through parallel instruction. One co-teacher may take half of the class to the back of the room to review the role of the tutor and appropriate/inappropriate tutoring feedback. Concurrently, the other instructor may work with the second half of the class at the front of the room, reviewing their roles as students. The co-teacher may describe how to get points for answering questions correctly and how to respond when a tutor provides feedback about a question not answered correctly. After both co-teachers spend 15 minutes with their respective groups, students are provided with a two-minute transition break to chat with one another as they move to the group in which they have not yet participated. For the following 15 minutes, co-teachers repeat their instruction, and at the end of 32 minutes, all students have been taught the roles of both a tutor and a student, ready to engage in CWPT as an evidence-based strategy for the rest of the school year.

Station Teaching

When teachers put students into small learning groups, with specific roles and tasks to be accomplished collaboratively, these are termed "cooperative learning groups" (Gillies, 2016). On the other hand, when small groups are created to have students rotate through each of the different tasks required at each center, or station, this is termed Station Teaching. Teachers may choose to create only three stations (e.g., Elimination station, Graphing station, and Substitution station when working with systems of equations in secondary math) or many stations (e.g., for metaphors, similes, personification, alliteration, onomatopoeia, allegories, allusions, hyperbole, symbolism, and so on when studying figurative language in English/language arts). Tasks at the stations can vary in length. For example, co-teachers may choose to have students answer five one-minute questions, rotating through stations as their "ticket out the door," or they may have students participate in three 10-minute stations in one class session, or they may choose to have students engage in one 30-minute station, different each day, for a week until the young people have experienced all the five stations. The options are endless.

Just as co-teachers can choose the subject of each station, the number of stations, and the length of tasks for each station, so too can they determine the level of teacher support at each station. For stations that require direct instruction or are more complex in nature, co-teachers may plan for one of them to stay at that station as students rotate through. The co-teaching partner who is not at that station may circulate among the other stations or sit at a different station the whole time. Stations can require students to work collaboratively as a group, or they can require students to work independently (e.g., on a worksheet, quiz review, homework). The stations not manned by a co-teacher might involve a small-group collaborative project, or show a captioned video, or require group problem solving, or may even be assisted by a paraprofessional if one is available.

Stations do not need to happen all in the same day, nor do they need to occur all in the same space. If empty rooms, a hallway, or an outdoor space is available, one or more of the stations may meet there, provided it does not take too long to transition to that space. If stations take place over the course of multiple days, a station may meet in the library or other venue. Students need to be taught how to transition respectfully between stations, be provided an appropriate amount of time to do so, and be reminded when the time is up by a stopwatch, bell, or other indicator. Many co-teachers choose to display the time left in each station on a screen using an online stopwatch, to help with class and time management for both teachers and students.

The benefits of Station Teaching are numerous. This approach helps to divide content, creating "chunks" that are easier for students to retain and for instructors to teach. Frequently, co-teachers who have less expertise in particular content can identify a specific aspect of the lesson that they would be able to teach confidently. If not new content, this may include mini-lessons in study or test-taking skills, a test review, going over homework or grades, assistance with organization, or even activities related to students' social emotional learning needs. In addition, the movement inherent to this approach helps to provide necessary brain and physical breaks to students. Differentiation needs are more easily identified, and differentiation strategies are more easily applied, with the smaller groups.

Applying CWPT to Station Teaching

Station Teaching and CWPT can be a strong match. Using this combination, co-teachers may choose to embed CWPT into their lessons on a regular basis. Once all students are familiar with the process and roles of both student and tutor, CWPT can become a regular station activity. As one co-teacher works with a station and provides direct instruction on new content related to the subject, the other co-teacher might work with a station reinforcing previously learned material, teaching new vocabulary, or offering strategies related to study or social skills. A third, independent station could be for CWPT. Already knowing how to engage in the process, students can pair up and use this evidence-based practice for the allotted time before transitioning to their next station. During their co-planning time, co-teachers may consider which students would make strong partners and pair them prior to the Station Teaching activity. Any additional scaffolds might be available to those who require them during the independent CWPT station. Making various scaffolds available to all students meets the philosophy of UDL.

Alternative Teaching

Despite the most engaging large-group instruction, the use of various small groups, and well-intentioned universally designed lessons, veteran teachers recognize that there will almost always be some students who "get it" more quickly than their peers and some who simply need more reinforcement. The Alternative Teaching approach recognizes this need and provides options to address it. Cook and Friend (1995) emphasize that this large-group/small-group approach was designed to allow for "reteaching, preteaching, and enrichment" (p. 8). In the many years since their original publication, this need has not changed. Alternative Teaching allows co-teachers to quickly identify and address the needs of the few, not relegating these young people to a "pull-out" class or waiting until they fail or are bored before their needs are met.

The ability to have one co-teacher work with a small group of students who need something different than most has an immediate draw. This has been the rationale supporting self-contained and resource classes of students with disabilities in the past. It has also led to these same students falling further behind their peers as they continue to be pulled out and miss critical instruction (Rodriguez & Murawski, 2021). Thus, a major component of *successful* Alternative Teaching is ensuring that, when this approach is employed, the larger group of students is not moving ahead in the content while the smaller group is missing out. Often during an instructional period, there are times when students are not learning new content, for example, warm-up, homework review, independent practice, watching videos, projects, peer work, and wrap-up activities. There are, of course, exceptions to this general rule. For example, if a small group of students is identified as having already mastered the content to be taught, that small group may work with one of the co-teachers on enrichment or extension activities while the large group is introduced to the new content. Please note that many experts in gifted education implore teachers to ensure that these activities are indeed enriching or extending and not merely "busy work" (e.g., Hughes & Murawski, 2001).

Like its regrouping counterparts Parallel and Station Teaching, Alternative Teaching also requires co-teachers to consider the groupings and use of space. This approach is frequently applied to support students who might be struggling and need reteaching or preteaching. Therefore, it is imperative that co-teachers work proactively to ensure that Alternative Teaching is not used solely for this purpose and that the same students are not always selected to meet with the same instructor. Otherwise, the result is a "class within a class" feel; the small group ends up working as a de facto pull-out special education group of students, leading to segregation, stigmatization, or embarrassment, which is the opposite of the intended inclusive results (Scruggs & Mastropieri, 2017).

Applying CWPT to Alternative Teaching

Time to apply Alternative Teaching to CWPT! Using this approach, co-teachers may recognize that, while CWPT is helpful to most of their learners, a handful may need additional Specially Designed Instruction prior to participating. In that case, as one co-teacher monitors the class participating in CWPT, the other might take a small group to work on their reading, fluency, comprehension, or even behavior skills that would enable them to participate later in CWPT activities. Conversely, co-teachers may recognize that additional sessions of CWPT would be helpful for some students, above and beyond what their peers do. In that case, while one co-teacher engages the large group in some review activities, a project, or even watching a video, the other instructor might have a small group of students (or even just one pair) engage in additional CWPT practice to reinforce specific skills.

Considerations for Regrouping Approaches (Parallel, Station, Alternative)

Parallel, Station, and Alternative Teaching are considered "regrouping" approaches because students are moved into smaller groups (Friend & Cook, 2021). In each of the different co-teaching approaches, educators need to pay attention to time, space, and noise. In addition, educator roles should be discussed proactively.

Time

Partners need to identify how long they will be spending in the small group so that both groups conclude their work at the same time. If one wraps up group work significantly earlier than the other, this can lead to issues with class management. Therefore, both teachers need to determine in advance how long they will be spending in the small group, *and* they also will need to be respectful by keeping to that time. Should additional time be required, a co-teacher can ask their partner (via text, instant message, verbal, or nonverbal cues) for extra time. However, this may derail the rest of the lesson, so adding time should be kept at a minimum. The longer co-teachers work together and use regrouping approaches, the better they will become at judging how long certain tasks will take. A good strategy for managing groups and time is that, if not all the desired content is covered with the first group, all remaining groups should only cover that same amount of the material. After a quick debrief with your co-teacher, you can determine when you will make up the remaining content with the whole group.

Space

Co-teachers who have large classrooms; have easy access to unused classrooms, small theaters, or empty gyms; or can frequently go outside will have fewer issues with space. For everyone else, space is an issue. Even co-teachers sharing small classrooms or working with classes of 40 students in a regular-sized classroom can use regrouping strategies. In fact, we'd argue that those students *need* the regrouping more than others! Simply moving chairs to face in another direction may be the only option for some, especially during the COVID-19 pandemic, when students were not allowed to leave their chairs; however, other instructors can have students physically get up and move to a different space. Most students not only like but *require* more regular movement than they are given in a typical school day. Even moving to stand in groups at the back of the room, or to be allowed to sit on a desk/carpet/yoga ball, can be more engaging (Frödj et al., 2023). Find out what spaces are available when you co-teach. Is there an available conference room or a classroom whose teacher has planning during that time? Do not let a lack of an alternative space deter you and your partner from breaking students into smaller groups!

Noise

One consideration that often stops co-teachers from using a regrouping approach is the potential for significant and distracting noise. While space is determined by the capacity of the school and the classroom itself, noise issues can be directly mitigated by teacher instruction and reinforcement. We personally err on the side of liking a bit of "managed chaos" and "student talk" when instructional topics remain the priority. However, like most educators, we also know that when all the students are talking at the same time, it can be a headache—not just to us as teachers, but also to some learners in the classroom, who will be extremely distracted. Thus, there needs to be a healthy balance of opportunities for student talk paired with clear expectations about the voice and activity levels at which young people are allowed to engage with each other.

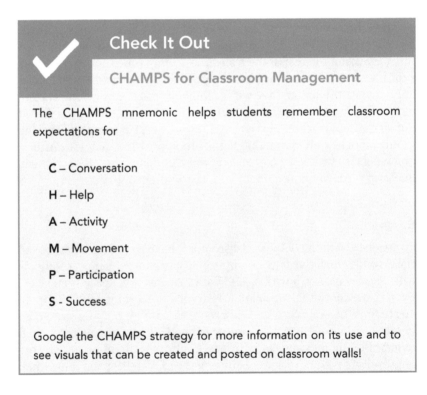

Check It Out

CHAMPS for Classroom Management

The CHAMPS mnemonic helps students remember classroom expectations for

C – Conversation

H – Help

A – Activity

M – Movement

P – Participation

S - Success

Google the CHAMPS strategy for more information on its use and to see visuals that can be created and posted on classroom walls!

Using strategies like CHAMPS (Sprick et al., 2021) can help students learn how loud they are allowed to get when transitioning between groups or when working in small teams. In addition, teaching students how to use whisper voices or bring their volume down is a worthwhile activity for the beginning of every semester. (You can reinforce this idea through a humorous exchange between loud or excited co-teachers). When working in small groups in the same class space, co-teachers need to practice projecting their voices only as far as the last student in their group.

Roles

Each one of the regrouping approaches requires co-teachers to take an instructional role. This is both a positive aspect, in that it helps to establish or support parity between teachers, and also an aspect that requires attention, since both teachers need to feel confident about their instructional roles. If both co-teachers are equally versed in the content, conversations about the regrouping approaches will focus only on the logistics. However, if one co-teacher is unsure about the content to be taught, which happens frequently at the secondary level with more complex curriculum (King-Sears et al., 2014), co-teachers may hesitate to regroup students, feeling safer in a large group where the content expert can answer difficult questions that may arise. We would like to emphasize the need to regroup students. First, smaller student–teacher ratios are better for students *in so many ways*; second, if teachers don't intend to regroup, what is the overall purpose of having two credentialed teachers? The following list offers suggestions for meaningful small-group activities for a co-teacher who feels ill-prepared to teach new content to a group.

Strategies for Small Groups Regardless of Content Expertise

- Go over the syllabus or group norms

- Teach a test-taking strategy

- Teach a study skills strategy like cover-copy-compare, summarizing, or self-monitoring comprehension

- Teach a social skills strategy like turn-taking, asking and answering questions, expressing an opinion/disagreeing with an opinion, or asking for help

- Teach a classroom management strategy like CHAMPS

- Oversee CWPT groups

- Introduce social emotional learning program components

- Do "check-ins" with students to gauge their energy or feelings

- Review homework and classwork grades

- Implement an organizational strategy

- Engage a group in a review game like Kahoot!

(Continued)

(Continued)

- Teach students how to use an app like Quizlet or Class DoJo

- Model journal writing

- Supervise a lab

- Take a group outside for an activity

- Encourage a discussion around a particular topic

- Share/discuss current events

- Read a story aloud

- Circulate multiple stations as students work independently on tasks

- Monitor small-group projects

- Walk a group to the library

Matching Personnel to the Approaches

By definition, true co-teaching requires co-planning, co-instructing, and co-assessing by professional educators. In the ideal world, all of those components should be in place. In the real world, co-teachers struggle to get the time they need to co-plan, the professional development they need to know how to effectively co-instruct, and the supports they need to co-assess in ways that respect varied neurodevelopmental profiles of their students. In addition, not all classes have two professional educators. What then happens in classes that have one or more paraprofessionals but no second credentialed teacher? What elements of these approaches can be used by teachers fortunate enough to have assistants or adult volunteers? How might other service delivery specialists, like speech-language pathologists, occupational and physical therapists, or behavior specialists engage in some of these approaches?

Other professional educators, such as specialists identified above and others like them, may be able to co-plan, co-instruct, and co-assess with a classroom teacher. These individuals bring their own areas of expertise to the shared inclusive classroom. As the classroom teacher learns some of their techniques to use with future groups of students, the specialist gains access to larger groups of students for their various interventions and strategies.

Paraprofessionals and adult volunteers fall into a different category. While their support and help are invaluable, they may not have the same level of experience or expertise. They cannot be expected to co-plan, as they are typically not provided either the time or the pay to do that; nor do they typically engage in co-assessment with a teacher. On the other hand, these individuals are wonderful additions to the classroom when it comes to co-instruction. Being able to have another adult in the room to run a station, monitor an independent group, play an instructional game, or circulate around the class answering questions and using proximity control to help with behavior is considered extremely useful by most educators. While these activities would not qualify as "co-teaching," educators can certainly still use the five co-instructional approaches as guides for ensuring that students are engaged and that any adults in the room are being utilized efficiently, effectively, and purposefully. With today's diverse classes, there is absolutely no excuse for having an adult simply standing at the side of the room, waiting to participate!

Aligning the Approach With the Need

"We're teaching middle school math. Which approach should we use?" "We have five students with learning disabilities and two students on the autism spectrum. Which approach is best?" These are questions we hear frequently from teachers. Unanimously, our response is: "Um . . . we don't know!" While that may not sound very helpful, given that we are the authors of this book, the reality is that the selection of the "right" approach (if there is such a thing) depends on a multitude of variables. The questions in the following list can help each team select the strategy that works for their situation.

Which Co-Teaching Approach Should We Use?

When selecting which co-teaching approach to use, consider the following variables:

- Content expertise of both co-teachers

- Ability to break the content into "chunks"

- Ability to have content taught out of sequence

- Time available to teach the content

- Other topics that need to be addressed and activities that need to occur during that lesson (e.g., test review, social skill lesson, taking attendance, reviewing homework)

- Space available for smaller groups (in the room, in the hallway, outdoors, in a nearby class, in the library, in an auditorium, etc.)

- Energy level of students (do they need to move and/or wake up?)

In addition to the variables on the previous page, there are questions that you and your partner might ask one another when co-planning (e.g., "Does the content *need* to be taught using a large-group model?"). Be careful here; push yourselves to use smaller groups whenever possible. Too many lessons are taught as whole-group when they could just as easily be taught in smaller groups with lower student–teacher ratios. If the lesson absolutely must be taught keeping the class together, use OTOS or Team Teaching. If co-teachers want to get students' attention by modeling or role-playing in front of them, they have selected Team Teaching. On the other hand, if it makes sense to use proximity control, circulating, and even collecting data while one teacher leads instruction, obviously OTOS is the best approach.

The three regrouping approaches (Parallel, Station, and Alternative) tend to be used less frequently than their whole-group counterparts (Team, OTOS). When asked, teachers often explain this phenomenon by reporting that they don't have sufficient time to plan, that the special educator doesn't know the content well enough to teach a group, or that they are simply more used to the whole-group approach (Friend et al., 2010). While a lack of time for co-planning can certainly be a significant deterrent, we strongly believe that co-teachers who truly want to meet students' needs should regularly use regrouping approaches; it is well established that students *need* differentiation, smaller group sizes, and strong connections with their teachers. The regrouping approaches address these needs far better than the whole-group approaches can. In addition, using small groups to enable special educators to check in on students' social emotional well-being, organizational and study needs, grades, behavioral skills, and progress on IEP objectives is a valuable use of these regrouping approaches. These strategies do not require special service providers to have the same level of content knowledge as their general education colleagues.

Consider the flowcharts in Figures 2.1 and 2.2 that depict how instructors might determine which co-teaching approach they would like to use. These examples show the thinking process that may occur during decision making.

FIGURE 2.1 Co-teaching Decision-Making Matrix

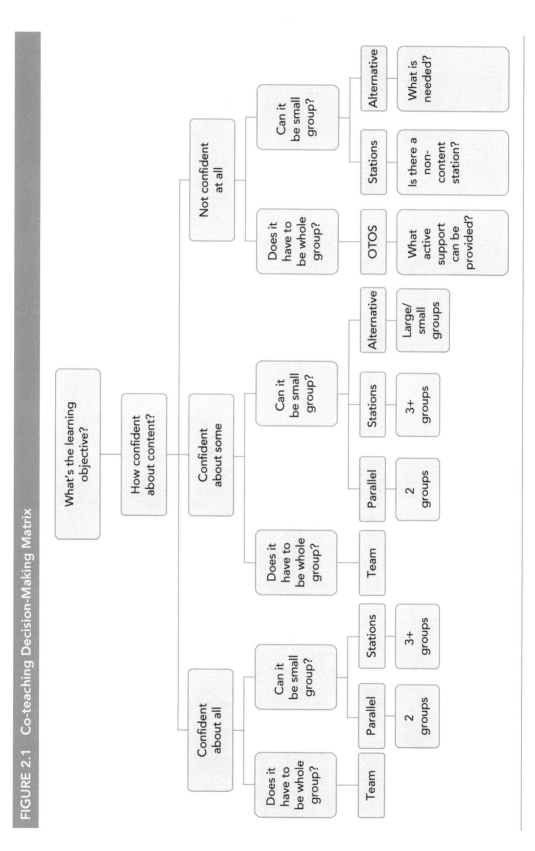

FIGURE 2.2 Choosing a Co-teaching Model

Learning objective: Students will be able to write a strong paragraph.

Co-teachers should ensure they both know the standard and essential question of the lesson.

Do both teachers feel confident about the content?

The general education teacher feels less confident, but the special education teacher feels very confident with all aspects of the lesson.

Do students need to stay in the whole group?

Definitely not. In fact, with writing, small groups are better. Thus, eliminate Team Teaching and OTOS.

Does the general education teacher need to do all the direct instruction?

No. The special education teacher feels that, after planning, they could also do the instruction.

Are the students all at the same level?

Absolutely not. Some are very low, and some are quite skilled already.

Should we use Alternative Teaching?

Perhaps. But that might be better after students are provided with direct instruction and are ready for practice. Otherwise, it may create tracks of students and start feeling like "pull-out."

Should we use Parallel Teaching (same content/same way)?

Perhaps. But there are many aspects to writing a paragraph. Maybe we could break up the various skills and introduce them in different ways to engage students more. Also, smaller groups may let us provide more feedback and differentiation.

What might Station Teaching look like with this objective?

The special education teacher could introduce a graphic organizer to teach students the various aspects of a paragraph. The general education teacher could teach a small station on writing a topic sentence, as that is frequently a difficult skill. An independent station could be set up for students to brainstorm and bullet a list of things they like and might be interested in writing a paragraph about. Another independent station might be a short YouTube video on writing interesting and engaging paragraphs or how to hook a reader.

We have our approach!

Summary

Co-teaching occurs between two licensed professionals who share responsibility for a group of learners when planning, instructing, and assessing. Five co-teaching models facilitate the use of ***flexible grouping*** **[SE_HLP17]**. Co-teachers may consider student needs, features of content, and their own skills or preferences when ***setting up and managing group work*** **[GE_HLP9]** with the co-teaching models.

Relationships, Roles, and Responsibilities

3

It is not easy to open one's classroom to another colleague, as happens in co-teaching situations, or to share information and be willing to listen to potentially differing opinions, such as during IEP and other collaborative team meetings. In each of these situations, participants need to have a measure of trust—in the situation, in the process, and in the other individuals involved. Being able to find one's place within a team, recognize others' strengths, and truly consider collaborative actions that will positively impact students in an inclusive environment requires mutual trust and respect (Suter et al., 2009). As Egeci and Gençöz (2006) put it, "believing that one can trust and depend on another person guides his or her selection of particular behaviors in security-threatening situations and these attitudes also affect relationship satisfaction" (p. 389).

Building Relationships: The Role of Trust and Psychological Safety

How can collaborative teaming or co-teaching be considered a "security-threatening situation"? Hackett and colleagues (2021) addressed this in research on co-teaching teams. In this study, co-teachers acknowledged that having another adult enter "their classroom" can be anxiety-producing. Without proactive communication and a culture of trust, one educator entering another educator's room to co-teach might be seen as evaluative, which can be destabilizing to the relationship. Another possibly threatening situation is when the special educator is perceived as merely a visitor, which is a relatively common dynamic, leaving both partners viewing the room, content, and lesson plan as the general educator's domain. For co-teachers to develop a truly collaborative partnership, they need to be able to give one another constructive feedback, ask questions, and take risks. It is this comfort with risk-taking that requires partners to feel what Hackett and colleagues (2021) call **psychological safety**.

While trust has often been identified as important for collaboration, the concept of psychological safety has only recently been added as an equally crucial component. Hackett et al. (2021) write that "trust relates to *giving the other person* the benefit of the doubt while psychological safety captures the extent to which one believes that the *other will give you* the benefit of the doubt when taking risks" (p. 107). When you feel able to voice an opinion, disagree with a colleague, ask a question, or offer a new idea, without worry that someone will make fun of you or otherwise humiliate you, a level of psychological safety is present. On the other hand, if you stay quiet during a team meeting because you are afraid that you will be embarrassed if you say the wrong thing, psychological safety is missing.

The literature often points out that family members tend to avoid true collaboration with schools due to a lack of trust (Kelty & Wakabayashi, 2020). It is possible that some of this dynamic is instead due to a lack of psychological safety. The same holds true with co-teaching partners; special educators voice concern about not knowing the content sufficiently and being embarrassed, while general educators worry that they will be evaluated by their special education peers. Because high psychological safety has been correlated with improved task performance, lower task conflict, increased information sharing, and interpersonal feedback, school administrators and team participants should proactively look for ways in which collaborating parties can feel safe when communicating, such as those offered in Table 3.1.

To **build a respectful relationship** [GE_HLP10] requires participants to trust one another and feel psychologically safe. If colleagues are able to take risks, share ideas, and make mistakes without fear of negative repercussions, true collaboration is possible and relationships can develop. Think about someone you trust. If that person unintentionally offended you, your relationship would likely cause you to reach out and talk to them, share why you were offended, and seek to understand what happened. You would likely use strong communication skills to work it out, and you would forgive that person (we hope) as they learn from their mistakes. This is the goal of establishing respectful, trusting, and psychologically safe collaborative relationships. According to Hackett et al. (2021),

> educational organizations that want staff to engage in team learning need to provide a culture that recognizes that experimentation involves success and failure, where concern for accountability is balanced by recognition of support needed for new practices, and where constructive conflict and speaking up about difficult topics are accepted as necessary for learning to occur. (p. 125)

TABLE 3.1	Strategies for Enhancing Psychological Safety
With co-teachers	Complete the SHARE worksheet (Murawski & Dieker, 2013; see **bit.ly/3xpe50d**). Proactively come to a consensus about how to run the class collaboratively and what to do if one co-teacher inadvertently embarrasses the other.
With team members	Discuss the concept of psychological safety and collaboratively identify ways to share difficult topics or ask hard questions. Look into how to create "safe and brave" spaces by bringing in an expert to share techniques for collaborative teams.
With administrators	If an administrator participates in a team activity, they should remind team members at the beginning that they are an equal member, with no more power (in this situation) than anyone else. The administrator should acknowledge that what is shared in the group stays with the group (yes, just like in Las Vegas!) so that members feel comfortable and safe sharing ideas, concerns, and struggles.
With specialists	Start collaborative endeavors by actively acknowledging that each of you has different skills and knowledge. Recognize that you may not do things perfectly the first time and that this is a learning experience.
With paraeducators	Meet with paraprofessionals at the beginning of the school year and come up with communication strategies that value the support the para provides, while also ensuring the teacher feels secure that the para is not sharing private information with others.
With families	Create a table tent that says, "We are all learning," and mention it at the beginning of meetings. Discuss the fact that this is a "no-judgment zone" and that you recognize cultural, learning, teaching, and child-rearing differences.

Building Relationships: The Role of Strong Communication Skills

Building trust and psychological safety when working toward collaborative relationships requires strong communication skills. TeachingWorks (2019) emphasizes that ***communicating with families*** is one of the essential high-leverage practices **[GE_HLP11]**, though communication in general is regularly identified as an integral aspect of successful collaboration (Wang et al., 2019). Collaborative communication has been defined as "the act of sharing information and expressing ideas while working together to achieve a common goal" (Bojic, 2022, para. 4). More than merely sharing information, collaborative communication involves continual feedback, problem solving, listening, empathy, and creative conflict resolution. All these skills need to be layered with multicultural awareness and respect for differences (Richards-Tutor et al., 2016), an ability and willingness to communicate via a variety of channels and platforms (McLeskey et al., 2017), and a true desire to reach a consensus that prioritizes students and their outcomes over our own needs, desires, and insecurities.

Miscommunication happens all the time. Why is it so difficult to get a group of well-meaning adults to come to an agreement? Simply put, we do not all communicate in the same way; our different communication styles, paired with our diverse frames of reference, result in frequent misunderstandings and, unfortunately, conflict. When communicating for collaborative purposes, we need to *share* information and we need to *take in* information. Sharing information can be done verbally (orally or in writing) and nonverbally. It can be done in a unidirectional manner (e.g., emails, texts, phone messages, webinars, announcements) or in a more interactive or inclusive approach (e.g., meetings, conversations). It can involve asking different types of questions (i.e., open or closed) or making different types of statements (e.g., descriptive, evaluative, advising). Taking in or receiving information might include active listening, using silence, providing minimal encouragement (e.g., "I see"), or even offering nonverbal signals (e.g., looking at watch, eye roll).

At the onset of any collaborative teamwork, it would benefit members to spend at least a few minutes talking about the need for collaborative communication, trust, and psychological safety. If teams are working together for a significant period of time, the first meeting may even be about defining what communication will look like and recognizing how diversity in gender, generation, culture, and experiences will add to the collaborative outcomes (and how it may also challenge or even strain communication efforts). While diversity in team makeup is almost always heralded as a positive characteristic and one resulting in more innovation and creativity, Wang et al. (2019) investigated how surface-level diversity versus deep-level diversity might impact collaboration and communication on a team. Recognizing multifaceted layers of culture (e.g., team culture, organizational culture, national culture), Wang and colleagues connected surface-level diversity to readily detectable demographic attributes (e.g., nationality, racial ethnicity), whereas deep-level diversity was associated with unobservable attributes (e.g., personalities, attitudes, values). Interestingly, it was the deep-level attributes that were found to make the most impact on creativity and innovation on interdependent tasks. Thus, teams are encouraged to recognize and discuss diversity beyond merely that which is easily observable.

Sharing one's values, attitudes, and preferences—especially when they may differ from the majority's—can be difficult at best. It requires a team, be it a pair of co-teachers or a larger group of individuals, willing to be transparent and brave in their communication. Transparency in communication, wherein both "good and bad" information is shared openly with all team members, can strengthen collaboration and innovation as well as support psychological safety (Hutchison, 2020).

"Brave spaces" were originally conceptualized by Arao and Clemens (2013) as settings in which individuals acknowledge the discomfort of discussing certain topics and establish norms for having those important conversations. Brave spaces were designed to lay ground rules for coping with discomfort, while productively and respectfully challenging others with diverse experiences, beliefs, or opinions. Brave spaces were specifically created with students in mind, and typically are introduced when identifying common areas of bias (e.g., racism, homophobia) and issues related to social justice. However, collaborative teams who will be working together frequently may also want to recognize that there will be times of disagreement; they should determine collaboratively if they would like to bravely address issues openly and transparently or choose instead to negotiate, compromise, or otherwise find a quicker, possibly less powerful, solution. Both options are available, but the choice needs to be made collaboratively and proactively.

Much has been written about communication skills, styles, preferences, and needs. We cannot do this topic justice with one section of one chapter; we can only emphasize the importance of using strong communication skills to build relationships. However, given the recent move to increased communication online following the COVID-19 pandemic, one more caution should be added to this section. Just as text messages will lead to more miscommunication than a phone call, so too can virtual communication (e.g., Zoom, FaceTime, Google Meet) increase the possibility of misunderstandings compared to face-to-face communication. While the use of online meeting tools may actually improve participation by families and individuals often excluded due to issues of time, transportation, childcare, and similar barriers, educators should recognize that these tools may also have negative ramifications. Virtual communication may result in *decreased* opportunity to read body language, chances for participants to bond and form deeper relationships, motivation to participate, and communication levels, while *increasing* the feeling of isolation, likelihood of team members multitasking during the meeting, and opportunities for miscommunication (Alawamleh et al., 2022). Consider the use of both in-person and virtual platforms for team meetings to get the best of all worlds and offer options to participants. Table 3.2 offers additional strategies for communicating in teams.

TABLE 3.2   Strategies to Improve Communication

Take a breath! Learn to actively listen by stopping your own talking.
Take notes. Show your interest and keep your attention focused by writing ideas down. Let your colleagues know you are taking notes so they aren't offended when you look down often.
Take time. Stop trying to multitask and grade papers or read emails during collaborative meetings. Be present. Don't look at your phone or watch. Use the time wisely.

(Continued)

(Continued)

Determine what is relevant. Avoid information overload. No one likes irrelevant information, especially when time is of the essence. Be thoughtful about what—and how much—you share.
Determine strengths. Delegate and respect differences. Don't try to do it all or say it all.
Determine a schedule and agenda. How often do you really have to meet and how can you use that time most efficiently? Could some work be done in advance or online?
Show trust. Cultivating trust is difficult but starts with showing trust to others. Teams that trust each other are more willing to take risks, be vulnerable, and compromise.
Show gratitude. Recognize individual and group efforts. Communicate appreciation in a variety of ways, recognizing that some people like showy thanks while others would prefer a personal note.
Show follow-through. If others recognize that you are following through on an action identified during a team meeting, they will know you listened and cared.
Share your resources. Communicate what you have to offer to the team, be it a physical resource or your personal expertise. Be open about your own needs as well.
Share your personality. Be personable. Have fun. The more collaborative and cohesive a team feels, the more likely they will work through potential issues or conflicts. Make your team meeting an enjoyable place to be.
Share snacks. While this does not technically come under communication skills, we feel that the sharing of snacks always seems to make it easier to communicate with others!

Identifying Roles on Collaborative Teams

Roles and responsibilities are often used interchangeably when discussing teams. However, they are actually different, and we are treating them here as such. **Roles** are a broader concept than responsibilities. One's role on a collaborative team refers to one's position on the team or to what part one is playing on that team. For example, are you there because you are a school administrator and bring knowledge of the district's resources to the table? Are you there as someone with a lot of expertise in Positive Behavioral Interventions and Supports (also known as PBIS) and in classroom management? Do you offer a different frame of reference based on your education, title, culture, languages, identity, or relationship to the student? Each of these questions helps determine our role on a team. On the other hand, when multiple people seem to fill a similar role, there can be a feeling of redundancy. It is important for each individual on a collaborative team to recognize that they play a significant role and that they bring something unique to the dynamic. **Responsibilities** are the actual tasks the team needs to accomplish that may be divided randomly or may be role-specific.

In this section, we discuss how to determine roles, how parity plays a significant factor when determining roles on co-teaching teams, and how roles may change over time. We also look at how roles on educational teams can encompass more than merely an academic focus, specifically exploring the role that social behaviors play in student success.

Determining Roles

As mentioned, each member of a team—no matter how small or large the team may be—needs to feel essential. As Wang and colleagues' (2019) research highlighted, the diversity on a team may be surface-level or deep, and it may encompass anything from observable demographic differences to differences in philosophy, attitude, or values. Some teams will be created with pre-identified roles. For example, based on the IDEA (2004), IEP teams include individuals with specific titles who have a relationship to the student with disabilities (e.g., administrator, school psychologist, general education teacher, special education case manager, family member, student). In this instance, it is easier to identify roles because they tend to come with the individual's title.

Other teams, however, may be composed of all members of a particular group (e.g., all math department teachers, all fourth-grade teachers). In these situations, it may be a bit more difficult to determine discrete roles. When all members share the same title, it is helpful to consider what the purpose of the team is and what roles might be identified to help the team meet that purpose. For example, if your role is to ensure the team stays focused during planning meetings, you can help identify responsibilities or tasks that will help accomplish this goal. Even if you end up delegating some of those tasks, you will continue to play the role of "focus master"!

Sometimes roles overlap, are not clear, or multiple roles need to be met by fewer people, which may occur between co-teachers. While certain roles are stereotypically determined by teachers' titles (e.g., general education teachers are typically considered content experts, while special education teachers are often described as experts in differentiation strategies), each co-teaching team needs to decide on its own preferred roles. Murawski and Dieker's (2004) SHARE worksheet, linked in Table 3.1, allows potential co-teachers to not only consider their personal expectations, attitudes, and hopes regarding a collaborative relationship, but also document their preferences in areas like noise level, materials management, student behaviors, and lesson planning in order to share with their prospective partners. While some of these will result in specific responsibilities, others will help educators identify the roles they want to have in their co-teaching situation. Thinking about these topics proactively, writing them down, and then sharing them with a potential co-teacher will allow both of you to discuss these areas and come to a consensus before entering the shared classroom.

Ensuring Parity

In Chapter 1, we introduced the importance of parity, of having members of a collaborative team recognize and value the input and diverse expertise and experiences of each participant. We also identified issues that may arise around the notion of parity when collaborating with different members, to include families, general educators, related service providers, and paraprofessionals. We waited to discuss the dynamic created, established, and sometimes even destroyed between co-teachers for this chapter on roles, responsibilities, and relationships because of the unique application of parity to co-teaching situations.

Blackley (2019) notes:

> When [the concept of parity] is applied to a co-teaching model, it refers to the equality between the two teachers delivering instruction to the same class. Believe it or not, parity may just make or break your co-teaching dynamic *regardless* of the quality of your instruction. (para 8)

Friend and Barron (2016) clarify that the concept of parity "implies equal value but not equality" (p. 3). Each individual should feel like an integral part of the collaborative relationship, despite having significantly different contributions to the work. In fact, while this is a key factor of strong collaborative outcomes in all collaborative teams, when there are only two individuals working together—such as in co-teaching—that need for purpose, respect, trust, and a sense of equality truly comes to the forefront.

One of the most frequently cited barriers to co-teaching is when one partner, most often the special education teacher, takes a secondary role in the classroom, being treated as a paraprofessional as opposed to an equal educational partner (Friend & Barron, 2016; King-Sears & Jenkins, 2020). A lack of parity between co-teachers may happen because one teacher does not know the content as well as the other, because of differences in personality or work ethic, or because of a lack of professional development around how to share and maximize a co-teaching classroom (Karten & Murawski, 2020). Parity in the co-taught classroom requires both parties to recognize and value their distinct areas of expertise and to make space for one another to take those roles. In 2019, Rytivaara and colleagues examined teams of co-teachers and had them share their stories. The teams in their research described the process of determining co-teaching roles and how they found commitment, engagement, and negotiation important components of the process. Participants in the study were able to co-construct a frame for their collaboration, which resulted in teams finding ways to integrate their pedagogical thinking and classroom practices to benefit *all* learners, not just those receiving special education services. The following list offers strategies to enhance parity in co-teaching relationships.

Strategies to Enhance
Parity on Co-teaching Teams

- Put both names on the door and inside the room. Even if co-teachers are only together for an hour a day, it makes an impact on students to see both names as they enter the room.

- Make sure both teachers have keys to the room and to locked cabinets. When one teacher has to wait with students for the other one to arrive and unlock the door or to give access to materials, there is an obvious lack of parity.

- Ensure that both teachers' names are on syllabi, report cards, letters home to families, and learning management systems.

- Provide both teachers access to the gradebook, ensuring that both can input grades.

- At the elementary level, make sure both instructors are listed as the teachers for class pictures (as opposed to one being the teacher and the other one unlisted or listed as a paraprofessional). This will require letting the photography studio know so they can set up for two equal teachers.

- Send both teachers to professional development on the topics they co-teach. Too often, the general educator is provided professional development on content and special educators are provided professional development on differentiation or co-teaching, when both teachers need both.

Changing Roles Over Time

Though team members may identify roles early on, those roles may change over time. Participants may find that a quieter member actually has strong leadership skills and eventually becomes the leader. Additional roles may be identified that were not required or realized early on. Roles are also impacted by relationships. Depending on the purpose of the collaborative team, these relationships may take minutes, months, or years to develop; in some cases, unfortunately, they don't develop at all. Consider the myriad teams in a school district. Some, like a district-level administrative team, may stay the same for a decade, while others, like an IEP team, may meet only once a year and involve different people each time. Despite these differences, teams that meet regularly—even when roles are replaced by different individuals (e.g., a new president of the Parent–Teacher Organization)—can build trust and relationships that continue even as the individuals change. Team development over time is often characterized as "forming, storming, norming, and performing" (Egolf & Chester, 2013, p. 142). To get through these stages, teams need to recognize and embrace the need to have roles, develop relationships, and allow for the flexibility needed over time.

Pratt's (2014) research identified a three-phase model for the development of successful co-teaching relationships and roles. In phase one, co-teaching teams are identified, either voluntarily or put together in an arrangement by an administrator. In phase two, which she calls the "symbiosis spin" (p. 7), team members begin to develop their partnership, learning from one another, reflecting on lessons together, complementing one another's skills, and determining their own unique roles relative to this partnership. Phase three involves team members continuing to build their complementary skills, becoming more interdependent and seamless. Naturally, not all teams successfully negotiate the three phases. Those who do manage the three phases seem to have a commitment to collaboration and are willing to share their professional knowledge and develop joint co-teaching practices. The need for time to develop roles and relationships and to negotiate how a team will work together is one of the reasons Murawski and Dieker (2013) admonish school leaders to leave strong teams together over time, letting their skills build, as opposed to separating them to create new partnerships.

Determining Areas of Focus

Another aspect needed for identifying roles on a collaborative team focused on inclusive practices is determining the area of focus. Though the first area that may come to mind when considering student success in schools is almost always academic, students' behavioral and social outcomes and needs must also be respected. Team members might want to formulate specific roles to ensure that these needs are being actively identified and strategies are being created to bring about positive social and behavioral outcomes.

Modeling appropriate communicative and collaborative behaviors has been identified as a potential benefit of co-teaching for years (Jackson et al., 2017). Students who do not see strong communication skills used at home with family members can watch the adults in their classroom discuss topics, negotiate differences of opinion, problem solve, manage conflicts, and celebrate agreements. The modeling of these social behaviors provides all students with examples to learn from for their own collaboration.

Not all students will be able to pick up cues from mere modeling, however. Some young people, especially those who struggle with social skill deficits, may need additional Specially Designed Instruction and practice on communication, collaboration, and social behaviors. Being able to embed lessons that address social emotional learning, positive behavior supports and interventions, and communication skills can be difficult for a general education teacher. By collaborating with specialists like speech-language pathologists, occupational and physical therapists, school counselors and psychologists, behavior intervention coaches, and special educators, classroom teachers can learn to connect their content instruction with other areas of student need. Specialists can share ways to include these topics and strategies in grade-level curriculum, and lessons can even be co-taught so that small groups can focus on differentiated needs or levels of need. Friend (2016) noted that the purpose of co-teaching is not to provide students with two adults with similar backgrounds, but to ensure that Specially Designed Instruction is available in the inclusive classroom to those who need it. Thus, **using and teaching social behaviors [SE_HLP9]** is a key high-leverage practice.

Connecting to Practice

Focusing on Social Behaviors in a Collaborative Team

Mr. Ramón, the general education English teacher, finishes a mini-lecture on the upcoming research paper that the students will be expected to complete soon. Ms. Weichel, the special education teacher, raises her hand while walking around the room. Mr. Ramón acknowledges her: "Yes, Ms. Weichel? I love how you raised your hand." Ms. Weichel smiles and says: "I have a question, Mr. R. You said the students will be completing these research papers by the end of the semester, but we haven't shared an actual deadline. Is now a good time to do that?" Mr. Ramón responds: "Oh right! Yes. They'll be due November 29." Ms. Weichel then responds: "OK. Now we have a date, but I know I personally struggle with long-term projects. Can we talk about strategies students might use to help make sure everyone is able to do this on time?" As the co-teachers begin to discuss ways to ensure everyone completes each aspect of the long-term assignment (e.g., checklists, small groups, peer reviews, model papers), students are brought into the conversation. In this way, Ms. Weichel is an active participant even when in the support role and even if she does not feel like a content expert. In sharing a similar example, King (2022) calls Ms. Weichel's subtle questions "amending" and suggests that "her 'mock student' approach to gaining the floor is not insignificant" (p. 8). Not only does raising her hand and waiting to be nominated by Mr. R implicitly model expected turn-taking behavior to the students, but it also enables her to seamlessly interject in a helpful yet nonintrusive way at a moment when Mr. R is leading the lesson. Thus, co-teachers have taken on roles that allow them to model social behaviors to students while also serving to develop a positive and respectful environment between co-teachers themselves.

Establishing Responsibilities on Collaborative Teams

While roles may be title-specific, self-identified, group-created, or developed and changed over time, responsibilities relate to *tasks* the collaborative team needs to accomplish in order to achieve their goals. As with any situation requiring teamwork, collaborating with other adults with the goal of improving inclusive practices in education can be absolutely wonderful and worth it, but it requires a lot of work. Some relationships with others will come naturally and be relatively easy to establish, while developing other relationships will take time, communication, and a strategic application of many different skills. The identification of key roles and responsibilities, and the subsequent delineation of who will take on these responsibilities, can help manage the workload.

Identifying Tasks

One of the first necessary actions is to identify tasks required to accomplish team goals. These tasks will vary based on the situation. Table 3.3 provides examples of common tasks that may be identified in advance. Team members can determine who is doing each job, so that (a) available assignments are all taken and (b) everyone feels involved. Provided that each person accomplishes their identified tasks, having responsibilities delineated and distributed can make collaboration feel less onerous than working alone! Naturally, if one collaborator does not follow through with their tasks, trust can be derailed between partners, making the collaboration more difficult and less beneficial. In that case, it is essential that colleagues feel empowered to use their communication skills to address problems with the follow-through and to determine how these problems impact the activity and, even more importantly, the interaction and trust between partners.

TABLE 3.3   Identifying Responsibilities on Collaborative Teams

IEP TEAMS	GRADE-LEVEL/ DEPARTMENTAL TEAMS	CO-TEACHING TEAMS
☐ Communicate with family to secure dates	☐ Email DoodlePoll to group to determine date for meeting	☐ Take roll daily
☐ Remind team members to have reports/assessments one week prior to meeting	☐ Send reminder the day before with what everyone is meant to bring/do	☐ Have warm-up prepared daily
☐ Create name tags for meeting	☐ Bring snacks/drinks	☐ Update class website

IEP TEAMS	GRADE-LEVEL/ DEPARTMENTAL TEAMS	CO-TEACHING TEAMS
☐ Welcome family members and do introductions	☐ Be in charge of tech	☐ Be in charge of tech
☐ Ensure water/snacks are available and offered	☐ Take minutes/notes at meeting	☐ Photocopy materials
☐ Be "jargon catcher" at meeting to catch acronyms	☐ Consider impact of decisions on English learners	☐ Make weekly positive calls to families
☐ Be time-keeper	☐ Be time-keeper	☐ Be time-keeper for stations and small groups
☐ Have technology ready to project onto screen	☐ Consider impact of decisions on gifted learners	☐ Update IEP progress monitoring data sheets
☐ Make copies of notes/ reports	☐ Consider impact of decisions on students with disabilities	☐ Take lead on identifying accessibility of lessons (captioned videos, etc.)
☐ Follow up with families after meeting	☐ Follow up with reminders to group	☐ Update calendar with pacing plan

Delegating Responsibilities

How does one determine who does what? After first identifying tasks to be accomplished, collaborators can begin to discuss their personal strengths and preferences. The goal is not to divide up tasks equally, but to have colleagues select jobs that they prefer to do and have skills to do. Ultimately, all collaborators should feel that the division of labor is equitable, rather than exactly equal. If everyone feels valued and believes that their unique skills are being used and respected as important to the task, it is more likely that follow-through will occur.

A common misperception in co-teaching is that both teachers must divide all work equally. If that were the case, both co-teachers would plan everything together, teach similarly, and then grade half of all assignments. Given the common marriage analogy often applied to co-teaching situations (e.g., Murawski, 2010), this would be like a married couple each taking a side of a trash bag as they carry it to the curb or each person washing half of a dish. Not only would that take an exorbitant amount of time, but it does not make sense; it also does not consider the reason co-teaching is selected in the first place. As first posed by Murawski and Spencer in 2011, the essential question for co-teaching is, "How is what co-teachers are doing together substantively different and better for students than what one teacher would do alone?" (p. 96).

A co-taught class should *not* be like a typical general education class but with two teachers. Instead, the special educator or specialist should be adding their unique element—focusing on ensuring accessibility, differentiation, engagement strategies, and Specially Designed Instruction (Friend, 2016; King-Sears & Jenkins, 2020). In addition, special education teachers have the extra tasks of assessing students for special education eligibility, writing IEP goals and objectives, and collecting data for annual and triennial meetings. Thus, while co-teachers should feel that their load is equal, the actual work might differ significantly. "Dividing and conquering" is a frequent refrain among strong co-teachers. The goal, however, is that parity is achieved as partners use their strengths to adapt their shared class in a way that meets their students' diverse academic, behavioral, and social needs.

One caution should be made when team members are determining their varying responsibilities. While taking the "divide and conquer" stance helps with time management and role identification, the goal is not to divide those responsibilities or roles so much that collaboration is no longer occurring at all. Communication and collaboration between colleagues are still required to share tasks or determine who will take lead on what; all team members should be aware of what the others are doing and why. Strogilos et al. (2016) identified teams wherein the resulting efforts looked more like "I'll do my work and you do yours," as opposed to a collaborative effort based on a discussion of what needed to be done and who would be the best to do it. The goal for co-teachers is to still co-plan how to engage and teach their shared students, not to create a class within a class. The goal for larger collaborative teams is still to ensure they are benefitting from the diversity of expertise and skills of their team members as they pursue the goal of having more inclusive environments.

Consider responsibilities that fall solidly within the wheelhouse of a particular role, as opposed to those that might be shared among participants. For example, assessing expressive language skills is clearly the responsibility of the speech-language pathologist. However, if teams are using a transdisciplinary approach, the speech-language pathologist may train others to collect formative assessment data related to expressive language skills. Additional responsibilities that are less role- or expertise-specific may include welcoming family members to meetings, managing materials, de-escalating potential conflict situations, ensuring that suggested strategies are culturally sensitive and relevant, and so on. Identifying these responsibilities is important, but who takes them on can vary based on strengths, interests, skills, or even the context of place and time.

Table 3.4 depicts an example of a form that may be used by co-teaching partners. By identifying typical responsibilities required in any classroom, teams can then determine who will take on what responsibilities each week. Some roles may become the regular task of one teacher, while another instructor takes on a different regular role, but the open-ended structure of the form allows roles and responsibilities to shift as needed. For example, if one co-teacher is about to have an unusually busy week due to a high number of triennial IEP assessments due, their partner may offer to take on more of the shared roles that week. Some responsibilities may not be needed one week, while others may come up monthly, and yet others may need to be added for a special activity. This type of form can be printed, laminated, and used to leave notes on with dry erase as co-teachers plan together weekly. Alternatively, it can be made available as a Google Doc or similar online document.

TABLE 3.4 Co-teaching Responsibilities Chart

Our Roles and Responsibilities

Week of: _____ Class: _____

TASK	MR. X	MS. Y	DATE DUE
Submit attendance daily	X		M–F
Create warm-up activities for this week (5–10 min each)	X		M–F
Create exit activities for this week (5–10 min each)		X	M–F
Make five positive parent calls home this week	X		M–F
Sign Javier's Check-In, Check-Out card daily		X	M–F
Collect frequency data on Sally's out-of-seat behavior	X		M–F
Talk to school IT about tech issues with algebra software	X		by Tues
Find a captioned version of *A Beautiful Mind* movie		X	by Thurs
Other:			
Other:			
Other:			

Implementing Norms and Routines

Just as norms and routines are beneficial for PK–12 students, collaborators too should develop and ***implement shared norms and routines for discourse and work*** **[GE_HLP5]**. Once roles have been determined and responsibilities identified, these responsibilities can be connected to regular activities that become routine. Routines help provide structure and consistency; norms offer shared understanding of how these routines will play out.

Create time at the beginning of a collaborative activity, be it a team meeting or co-teaching situation, to discuss various norms and to come to a consensus about them. Routines for discourse might include morning text messages to check in, weekly co-planning meetings, bimonthly overviews of curriculum and pacing, and even codes for how to tell your partner that you need to have a difficult conversation with them. Routines for work might include a school psychologist or counselor coming into a general education class every Monday to conduct the morning meeting around social emotional topics, a special education teacher sending out academic and behavioral questionnaires to teachers and families before IEP meetings, a check-in between a family and a teacher daily, or a physical education and adaptive physical education teacher prioritizing the co-planning of a shared activity weekly with their respective students. In each of these cases, identifying and implementing shared norms and routines helps collaboration occur more smoothly between participants.

A lack of time is one of the most commonly identified barriers to collaboration and communication by educators (Casserly & Padden, 2018; Mofield, 2020). Once teams establish routines and norms, agreeing on a structure within which flexibility can occur, collaboration will actually take less time (Karten & Murawski, 2020). For example, a co-teaching team may determine that they will always meet to plan on Tuesdays and Thursdays from 3 p.m. to 4 p.m. (routine), that they will take turns bringing snacks (routine), and that the special educator will always plan the week's warm-up activities, while the general educator will plan the exit activities (routine). They may also decide that each participant will follow through with any agreements made in the last planning session (norms), will come prepared with the warm-up and exit ideas for the week (norms), and will respectfully listen to one another's ideas for upcoming lessons without negating or interrupting (norms). Proactively identifying routines saves time for partners who have to make those decisions regularly, while having norms ensures that collaborative meetings are indeed collaborative.

Reflection on Relationships, Roles, and Responsibilities

As noted in Chapter 2, the definition for co-teaching has evolved to add "co-reflection" to Murawski's (2003) original definition of "co-plan, co-instruct, and co-assess."

Chapter Connections

Learn more about collaborative reflection in Chapter 12.

The addition of this term emphasizes the importance that educators place on reflection and the impact of reflection on educational practices. Preservice educators are often asked to reflect on their practices by master teachers or university supervisors; once in the classroom, teachers are expected to continue their reflective practices as a method of continuous improvement (Murawski & Lochner, 2018). This type of reflection should also become a regular aspect of teams working to build inclusive practices, as collaborators use reflection to analyze interactions and behaviors and make improvements.

When considering relationships, roles, and responsibilities, reflection is the fourth "R" that could be easily attached as another crucial element. At the team level, participants might use reflection to determine if the right members are present or even if the team would benefit by adding an additional member with diverse expertise (Suter et al., 2009). They might reflect on the relationships created on the team and consider if they would characterize the team as collaborative, competitive, effective, ineffective, or even antagonistic. Do team members feel supported and interconnected, or do they resent or even try to avoid meetings? If relationships are stable and responsive, take time to reflect on roles. As noted previously, roles might need to change over time, as might the specific responsibilities assigned to each member. Encourage regular reflection on relationships, roles, and responsibilities. The following list offers some team reflection questions that may facilitate this process.

Team Reflection Questions

- How do we want to reflect on our relationships, roles, and responsibilities? Would we feel more comfortable sharing through anonymous feedback notes or through oral dialogue?

- How often do we want to reflect on our processes and relationships? Can we create a routine for reflection?

- How can we build in norms to ensure that we can give and receive feedback to one another respectfully?

- What will we do as a team if relationships appear to be difficult or uncollaborative?

- How can we ensure that all team members feel valued and heard?

- What norms can we establish for managing conflict collaboratively?

- Do we want to create certain roles to help us communicate more effectively (e.g., facilitator, consultant, time manager, jargon catcher, reflection reminder, cheerleader)?

Collaborative reflection is an important action for collaborative teams who are working toward more inclusive practices. Teams need to build in a structure of some kind for regular review of what is working and not working, why, and what can be done for improvement. You may even want "reflect" to be one of your task responsibilities or "reflection reminder" to be one of your team roles!

Summary

Meaningful collaboration occurs when team members establish ***respectful relationships*** **[GE_HLP10]** by communicating in ways that promote psychological trust and parity. Efficient collaboration occurs when teams build on those relationships to clearly define roles and responsibilities. As collaborative teams and co-teachers ***communicate with each other and with families*** **[GE_HLP11]** and ***establish norms and routine for their work*** **[GE_HLP5]**, they ***teach social behaviors*** **[SE_HLP9]** to students through modeling.

Collaborating for Academic Success

Introduction to Section II

Collaborating for Academic Success

//

In 1947, Martin Luther King Jr. published an article in the Morehouse College literary journal in which he described the purpose of education. He wrote: "The function of education . . . is to teach one to think intensively and to think critically" (p. 124). King defined thinking intensively and critically as intelligence. However, he asserted that there was more to education than the intelligence derived through academic pursuits. He continued: "We must remember that intelligence is not enough. Intelligence plus character—that is the goal of true education" (p. 124). The dual purposes King described for education are those supported by the high-leverage practices and aligned with the goals laid out in this book. On one hand, we recognize the vital role of traditional academic skills—reading, writing, calculating, speaking, listening, etc.—with a focus on critical thinking and applications. On the other hand, there is no doubt that a meaningful education must also address social emotional learning, developing the character traits that allow students to have positive interpersonal relationships in the classroom and beyond.

The general and special education high-leverage practices are designed to give educators the skills to address these dual purposes. Our text is designed to show how collaboration forms a network in which the general and special education high-leverage practices and the myriad of frameworks for instruction in academic and social emotional skills are interconnected. In this section of the text, we focus on exploring the invaluable role of collaboration in promoting academic growth for all learners. The third section provides a more comprehensive focus on collaborative strategies for social, emotional, and behavioral growth.

Academic Success for All

The Every Student Succeeds Act, signed in 2015, was intended to codify the principles of equitable education for the purpose of preparing *every student* for college and career opportunities (U.S. Department of Education [USDOE], 2016b). *Every* student! That's a big expectation.

"Every student" includes learners with disabilities, giftedness, diverse cultural backgrounds, and linguistic differences. It includes students from urban, suburban, and rural communities, those with nearly limitless resources and those whose families strive to make ends meet each day. Ensuring that every student succeeds is a lofty goal that educators work toward each day. It is, without a doubt, challenging and worthwhile.

In all our encounters with educators, we see a deep commitment to ensuring that all students are academically successful. We also know, from our own experiences and from research, that ensuring success for all students requires teamwork (Maras et al., 2015). Even the most highly qualified and experienced teachers will, at times, find that their "teacher tool kits" are insufficient to fully meet the needs of a learner or group of learners. This is the nature of providing equitable instruction for all. No single educator has all the answers. Collaboration is a necessity.

A number of frameworks exist in which educators, family members, students, and community members collaborate to ensure academic success. These frameworks include Multi-Tiered Systems of Support, Response to Intervention, and UDL, which we defined in the introduction to the first section. In Table SII.1, we add two important frameworks that will facilitate our discussion about academic growth.

TABLE SII.1   Principal Concepts Related to Academic Growth

RESEARCH-BASED PRACTICE	DEFINITION
Differentiated Instruction	Differentiated Instruction describes individualized teaching methods used to meet the unique needs of a student. Teachers may differentiate content, process, product, or environment to meet learners' needs. Differentiation of content involves changes to what the student learns. Differentiation of process changes how the student learns. Differentiation of product describes adjustments to the way in which the student demonstrates knowledge. Differentiation of the environment involves changes to the physical space in which learning occurs. While UDL and Differentiated Instruction have some common areas of focus, UDL is proactive and universal, while Differentiated Instruction is responsive and targeted to individual students.
Specially Designed Instruction	Specially Designed Instruction is highly individualized and intensive instruction that is provided to learners with disabilities for the purpose of addressing needs that stem from a disability. Specially Designed Instruction is documented in a student's IEP. Specially Designed Instruction is primarily provided by special education teachers. IDEA specifies that Specially Designed Instruction must include research-based methods.

Differentiated Instruction and Specially Designed Instruction are deeply interconnected with Multi-Tiered Systems of Support, Response to Intervention, and UDL, though they are often discussed separately. As we move through the chapters in the second section of this book, we show the relationships between each of these frameworks and the role that collaboration plays in bringing them to the classroom to promote academic growth for all learners. In Chapter 4, we discuss co-assessment to understand academic needs of learners in inclusive settings. Chapter 5 addresses co-instruction, with an emphasis on co-teaching to meet academic needs of all learners. In Chapter 6, we shift the focus to collaborative strategies for intensive academic intervention. Finally, we close the second section with a discussion about collaborative academic assessment and progress reporting in Chapter 7. In each chapter, we show how collaboration in a variety of forms, paired with the high-leverage practices, promotes academic growth.

Assessment of Group and Individual Academic Needs

4

Each year, in the weeks leading up to the first day of school, teachers eagerly await rosters that list names of their students. These rosters trigger a flurry of activity, as teachers begin to prepare learning spaces and materials. Before school even begins, and certainly during its first days and weeks, instructors seek information that will help them teach every student on their rosters. The process of gathering information about students for the purpose of making educational decisions is called **assessment** (Overton, 2015). For most people outside the field of education, this term is likely associated with tests and quizzes. Some of us envision multiple-choice bubble sheets or "blue books" for essay exams. Others may think about computer-based adaptive tests, presentations, or projects. These are all assessments that serve the purpose of measuring learning outcomes. Assessment, however, is not just intended to measure what learners have achieved. Assessment is also used to guide instructional planning and delivery.

The two purposes of assessment are sometimes categorized as assessment *of* learning and assessment *for* learning. In the former case, which we discuss in Chapter 7, assessments tell us how effective our instruction has been.

Chapter Connections

Find out more about the assessment *of* learning in Chapter 7.

This is also called **summative** assessment. In this chapter, we address assessment *for* learning, which is generally called **formative** assessment. Formative assessment is conducted using formal and informal sources of information to evaluate learning in progress and to make decisions about teaching. Educators conduct formative assessment when they ask questions during group instruction, listen to student discussions, review student responses on exit tickets, or observe young people working through problems. Formative assessment is focused on the process of student learning and on how educators can know if students are on track for success *before* summative assessments occur. We address formative assessment later in this chapter.

We propose that there is another type of assessment *for* learning that begins in the earliest days of the school year, sometimes right after teachers receive rosters. This assessment involves the collection and analysis of information needed to provide **Differentiated Instruction**. Differentiated Instruction occurs when educators make modifications to curricula, materials, and methods to address specific needs of individual students or groups of students (Tomlinson et al., 2003). Differentiated Instruction requires knowledge of individual students' strengths, needs, and interests as the foundation of instructional planning. It is not formative because it is not about monitoring student learning, but it is foundational to ensuring academic success for every student in a classroom.

Collecting and interpreting information to prepare for Differentiated Instruction and to make instructional decisions that ensure the success of every student is a daunting task. The rich diversity of students in U.S. public schools means there is a lot to consider. Evaluating and then meeting the needs of these learners requires collaboration. **Co-assessment** describes a process in which two or more individuals collaboratively gather and interpret information in ways that help them reach a deeper understanding compared to what either educator could understand alone (Conderman & Hedin, 2012). Co-assessment deepens educators' understanding of what students need in order to experience academic success.

Co-assessment *for* student learning is at the heart of the special education high-leverage practices that advise educators to *use multiple sources of information to develop a comprehensive understanding of student strengths and needs* **[SE_HLP4]** and to *interpret and communicate assessment information to stakeholders to collaboratively design and implement education programs* **[SE_HLP5]**. In co-assessing to prepare for Differentiated Instruction, collaborating educators will want to answer the following questions: Who are our learners? What do they need to be successful? What preferences and interests do they have? What academic skills do they have that set the stage for our learning goals? The high-leverage practices from general education offer some strategies for answering these questions. They suggest that educators **lead a group discussion [GE_HLP1]** and **elicit and interpret student thinking [GE_HLP3].** We address these strategies and others in this chapter.

As the school year goes on, educators continue to engage in co-assessment *for* student learning, transitioning to formative assessment. The same assessment high-leverage practices are relevant. However, the focus shifts to answer the question: Is our instruction effectively meeting the needs of *all* learners? Through these early and ongoing collaborative assessment practices, educators continuously work to ensure that all learners experience academic success.

Co-assessment to Prepare for Differentiated Instruction

It is a common practice to give students a few weeks to shake the cobwebs of summer break from their brains before administering any formal academic assessments at the beginning of the school year. That timeframe, however, is perfect to learn about students through review of existing documentation, collaboration with special service providers, and informal assessments. There is a lot to learn before academic instruction truly commences. Educators engaged in co-assessment to prepare for Differentiated Instruction will want to gather information about individual students' strengths, needs, and preferences. A combination of existing data sources mixed with some informal assessments should lay a strong foundation for instructional planning early in the school year. More formal assessments can be added later. Because educators are seeking information about diverse learners as they prepare for Differentiated Instruction, collaboration with specialists and families can be helpful to locate, interpret, and understand how to apply information.

Co-assessment With Educational Specialists

The diversity of students in public-school classrooms and our national commitment to serve all students means that multiple young people in each classroom likely receive one or more special services, such as special education, English for speakers of other languages (ESOL), gifted education, and school health services. These services are often provided by trained specialists in coordination (ideally, in collaboration) with classroom teachers. Table 4.1 offers information about the percentage of students in several special service categories as well as possible sources of written documentation about students and school-based specialists who may be helpful collaborators.

TABLE 4.1   Special Student Populations and Resources for Collaboration

STUDENT GROUP	PERCENTAGE OF THE SCHOOL-AGE POPULATION	SOURCES OF WRITTEN DOCUMENTATION	SCHOOL-BASED SPECIALISTS
Students with chronic health conditions requiring medical management (e.g., asthma, diabetes, seizure disorders, food allergies)	40% of school-age population in 2017–2018 (CDC, 2021)	Student Health Plan, Seizure Action Plan, Diabetes Medical Management Plan, Section 504 Plan	School Nurse
Students with disabilities *not* requiring specialized instruction	3% of public-school students in 2017–2018 (Civil Rights Data Collection, 2018)	Section 504 Plan	Section 504 Coordinator, Section 504 Case Manager, School Nurse
Students with disabilities requiring special education	15% of school-age population in 2020–2021 (National Center for Education Statistics, 2022)	Individualized Education Program	Special Education Teacher, Related Service Providers
English learners	10% of K–12 public-school students in 2018–2019 (USDOE, Office of English Language Acquisition, 2021)	Home Language Survey, Language Proficiency Assessments	ESOL/ESL Teacher, Interpreter
Students with gifts and talents	3% of public-school students in 2017–2018 (Civil Rights Data Collection, 2018)	Some states and school divisions use Written Education Plans	Gifted Education Teacher

The information in Table 4.1 paints a clear picture. Each year, classroom teachers will serve students with unique learning characteristics and have the responsibility to *use multiple sources of information to understand student strengths and needs* **[SE_HLP4]**, then use assessment information *to collaboratively design and implement education programs* **[SE_HLP5]**. The level of collaboration between classroom teachers and specialists can vary. At the most basic level, classroom teachers and specialists work together to know what services students receive and to develop schedules. Although this doesn't truly meet the definition of co-assessment, it is a necessary first step for meeting student needs. Classroom teachers and specialists who share students must work together to ensure that young people receive the services they require. Services documented in an IEP specify the settings (general education or special education) and amounts of service time that must be provided. There is no flexibility in meeting IEP service requirements, therefore it is important that teachers and specialists work together to understand those requirements and then implement them consistently. Other service plans may also specify the frequency, duration, or timing of services. In some cases, there will be more flexibility than that associated with IEP services. In other cases, for example, medication management, there may be very little flexibility.

Coordination of service delivery is an important collaborative action. While this is a low level of collaboration, that doesn't mean it is easy. Classroom teachers may have multiple service providers pulling students from their classrooms or pushing in to provide service. As a result, classroom teachers may want to protect instructional time for their content requirements. At the same time, specialists often serve students in multiple grade levels, or even multiple schools, and must work around academic content instruction, lunch schedules, and so forth. For many specialists, building a schedule is like assembling a puzzle that is upside down and backwards while the pieces are moving. Once the specialist's schedule is established, it is important that classroom teachers try to avoid making changes that could prevent a student from receiving scheduled services.

Classroom teachers may find it helpful to develop a tracking sheet to document the services that students receive and the times that those services are scheduled. The tracking sheet could include students' names, the types of special services they receive, and the dates/times of those services. While this information is protected under the Family Educational Rights and Privacy Act, the law states that school employees, contractors, and volunteers who have a legitimate educational interest may have access (USDOE, 2021a). Therefore, the information should be shared with teachers, paraprofessionals, and substitute teachers to ensure that the necessary services are provided.

Another level of collaboration that allows educators to develop knowledge of student learning needs is **consultation**. Consultation occurs when one educator, usually the classroom teacher, holds primary responsibility for directly providing services to the student but acquires information from other specialists to support student learning (IRIS Center, 2022). Consultation may occur between any two education professionals in support of any instructional needs and may also include family members. For example, Mr. Kyle, a physical education teacher, has a student, Eva, with type 1 diabetes. According to Eva's Diabetes Medical Management Plan, her blood sugar level could be impacted by strenuous exercise. Mr. Kyle engages in a consultative co-assessment with the school nurse and Eva's family, reviewing common activities in the physical education curriculum and Eva's specific health care needs to determine when accommodations or special monitoring is needed.

Deeper co-assessment practices occur through interdisciplinary collaboration and transdisciplinary collaboration (Dillon et al., 2021). **Interdisciplinary collaboration** takes place when classroom teachers and specialists mutually engage each other in ongoing shared decision making. They co-plan assessments, collaboratively interpret findings, develop shared goals based on those findings, share knowledge about practices, and coordinate services to meet student needs. Educators engaged in interdisciplinary collaboration often provide services separately but with coordinated intentions (Dillon et al., 2021). Check out the example in the Connecting to Practice box.

Connecting to Practice

Interdisciplinary Collaboration in Action

Mrs. Khazmo, a special education teacher, and Ms. Peyton, a general education teacher, engage in interdisciplinary collaboration to teach Alina, a student who uses an Assistive and Augmentative Communication (AAC) device **[SE_HLP19]**. In preparation to include Alina in a co-taught social studies class, the two teachers collaborate with Mrs. Land, a speech-language pathologist, to assess what vocabulary is already accessible on Alina's device and determine what needs to be added to support her participation in the curriculum. The educators work together to identify a list of key vocabulary that will be relevant across the school year. Mrs. Land teaches Mrs. Khazmo and Ms. Peyton how to add, mask, and unmask vocabulary on Alina's AAC device. Mrs. Land also plans to work on key social studies vocabulary with Alina during their sessions in the speech room to supplement the work that Mrs. Khazmo and Ms. Peyton do in the classroom. Through these collaborative actions, all of the educators deepen their understanding of Alina's needs and how to meet them. Though Mrs. Land tends to work with Alina outside of the social studies class, her work contributes to academic goals shared by the three educators.

Transdisciplinary collaboration takes interdisciplinary collaboration to a higher level.

When engaged in transdisciplinary collaboration, "professionals from different disciplines collaborate together across all phases of their work" (Dillon et al., 2021, p. 37). They co-assess and co-plan for shared goals, as is the case with interdisciplinary collaboration. However, they also co-instruct for the purpose of achieving those goals. Co-teaching, as we've defined it in this text, is transdisciplinary collaboration. Expanding on the interdisciplinary collaboration that occurred with Alina in the Connecting to Practice box, transdisciplinary collaboration would occur if Mrs. Land occasionally co-taught with Mrs. Khazmo and Ms. Peyton during Alina's social studies block. The three educators could use Station Teaching, with

Mrs. Land leading a station on vocabulary development, projecting a version of Alina's AAC on the interactive whiteboard so that all students could use the multisensory tool to communicate ideas about the vocabulary words.

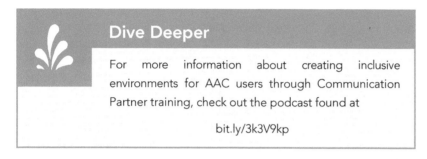

Dive Deeper

For more information about creating inclusive environments for AAC users through Communication Partner training, check out the podcast found at

bit.ly/3k3V9kp

This would also assist Alina's classmates in becoming strong communication partners with her. (You can learn more about Communication Partner training through the link in the Dive Deeper box.) Alternatively, the educators might determine that it is more important for Mrs. Land to work individually with Alina in the classroom, modeling strategies for Mrs. Khazmo and Ms. Peyton to use when the speech teacher is not there. This might take the form of the OTOS model.

As with interdisciplinary collaboration and consultation, transdisciplinary collaboration can occur with educators and specialists across disciplines to meet a variety of student learning needs. Transdisciplinary collaboration can be difficult due to the scheduling and staffing challenges. However, when specialists and classroom teachers collaborate in this manner, each one of them can deepen their knowledge about individual students as well as their own skill sets. A major aspect of transdisciplinary collaboration is the willingness of all parties to teach aspects of their areas of expertise to their partners, ultimately resulting in role release and enhancing everybody's skills.

Co-assessment of Medical, Physical, and Communication Needs

Regardless of the level of collaboration that educational professionals employ as they seek to co-assess student needs, there is some essential information that classroom teachers must acquire very early in the school year. Medical, physical, and communication needs are a top priority. Specialists, such as school nurses, physical therapists, assistive technology specialists, speech-language pathologists, and ESOL teachers, may be responsible for direct provision of services to students at specifically designated times. However, student needs often carry over into other times in the school day, making teachers and/or paraprofessionals responsible for ensuring that students are safe and ready to learn. For example, a school nurse might hold primary responsibility for ensuring that a student with seizure disorder receives daily medication at school, but the student's teachers and paraprofessionals must know how to respond to keep the student safe when a seizure occurs. The teachers and paraprofessionals would collaborate with the school nurse, the student's family, and the student to understand what the student's seizures may look like and what interventions are necessary.

Students may also have physical needs for mobility or positioning that are linked to medical conditions. As classroom teachers prepare for Differentiated Instruction, they need to proactively co-assess the ways in which students navigate the educational environment and physically access learning materials. For example, a student with complex physical disabilities may need to use a variety of specialized positioning equipment (a form of **assistive technology [SE_HLP19]**) for physical comfort or to manipulate learning materials. In this case, classroom teachers, physical therapists, and occupational therapists could engage in co-assessment of student needs using information about the student's physical characteristics and the routines of the classroom to select equipment and develop a schedule for its use. Student input is important here as well. Students can describe what works well for them, what they are physically comfortable with, and what is acceptable to them in settings with their peers. Once equipment is selected, the therapists would provide training to the classroom teachers to ensure that it is used safely and correctly. By collaborating and communicating about the goals of the inclusive classroom, the specialists can aid teachers in determining how to ensure that the student is physically included in group activities and that various learning configurations take all unique needs or equipment into account.

While communication needs may seem less critical than medical needs, we believe that functional communication is a basic human right. Therefore, educators working with students who communicate with assistive technology or in languages other than spoken English must develop understanding of those communication systems and come up with strategies to support communication as quickly as possible.

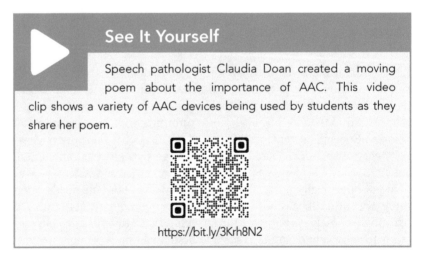

See It Yourself

Speech pathologist Claudia Doan created a moving poem about the importance of AAC. This video clip shows a variety of AAC devices being used by students as they share her poem.

https://bit.ly/3Krh8N2

Communication systems may include signed communication, AAC, use of interpreters, and combinations of these systems. Co-assessment of student communication needs and consultation with specialists, such as speech-language pathologists, assistive technology specialists, Deaf education teachers, or ESOL teachers, is an important first step in developing the skills that support students in communicating across settings and purposes.

The assessment processes we have described here do not fall under the traditional view of co-assessment. These processes do, however, show how *multiple sources of information come together to elucidate student strengths and needs* [SE_HLP4]. In this case, the derived information is essential for ensuring student safety and access to academic learning opportunities. When engaging in co-assessment at the beginning of the school year, educators should make it their priority to actively seek information about students' medical, physical, and communication needs.

Key questions for identifying needs include: What medical, physical, or communication needs does the student have? What supports need to be provided in the classroom? When are those supports needed? How are the supports implemented? Once these questions are answered, plans for Differentiated Instruction also need to specify who will provide the supports. It is important that plans include backup service providers when student health and safety needs are involved. Therefore, the supports should be documented and shared in a way that allows all classroom teachers, paraprofessionals, substitute teachers, and others who work with a student to keep them safely engaged in the learning environment. The form found in Table 4.2 is an example of a tool that can be used to track these needs as well as other accommodations and modifications that students require.

TABLE 4.2   Tracking Tool for Student Supports

STUDENT NAME	MEDICAL/PHYSICAL SUPPORTS	COMMUNICATION SUPPORTS NEEDED	INSTRUCTIONAL ACCOMMODATIONS AND MODIFICATIONS
Eva	Monitor blood sugar levels using a Continuous Glucose Monitor linked to a tablet during Physical Education. Responsible Educator: Mr. Kyle or Mrs. Abbott Send Eva to nurse for medication prior to lunch. Responsible Educator: Mrs. Jennings or substitute Respond to alerts about low blood sugar by contacting nurse and providing glucose tabs or orange juice. Responsible Educators: All teachers	N/A	Provide additional time for classwork or reduce assignment length when Eva is out of class for health needs. Responsible Educators: All teachers

(Continued)

(Continued)

STUDENT NAME	MEDICAL/PHYSICAL SUPPORTS	COMMUNICATION SUPPORTS NEEDED	INSTRUCTIONAL ACCOMMODATIONS AND MODIFICATIONS
Alina	N/A	Keep AAC device within Alina's reach at all times. <u>Responsible Educators</u>: All teachers Plug AAC device in for charging each afternoon. <u>Responsible Educator</u>: Mrs. Khazmo or Mrs. Land Add or unmask new vocabulary. <u>Responsible Educator</u>: Mrs. Khazmo or Ms. Peyton	Allow additional processing time for language production with AAC device. <u>Responsible Educators</u>: All teachers Reduce language complexity on written or spoken assessments. Accept terms/concepts available on AAC device. <u>Responsible Educators</u>: All teachers

Co-assessment of Instructional Needs for Differentiated Instruction

As they conduct early co-assessment (and continuously, as the year progresses), educators need to learn about accommodations and modifications that students require. Accommodations and modifications are individualized supports provided to students to meet their unique needs. Chapter 6 offers detailed information about the differences between these two types of support.

Accommodations and modifications are consistently documented on IEPs and 504 plans for students with disabilities. These supports may also be documented in Multi-Tiered Systems of Support intervention plans or in plans for English learners. In some states, accommodations for students receiving gifted education are documented on Written Education Plans (e.g., Ohio Department of Education, 2018). For example, a gifted student may need tools to support their organizational skills to fully achieve educational goals. It is important for *all* educators to understand that they are legally responsible for providing any documented accommodations and modifications. Because the supports are highly individualized, classroom teachers may want to collaborate with specialists and students to ensure that the accommodations or modifications are fully understood. Educators may also want to describe accommodations and modifications in a tracking document such as the one provided in Table 4.2. As with medical, physical, and communication needs, it is important to document who will be responsible for providing accommodations and modifications and to establish plans to ensure that the supports are provided even when the primary classroom teacher or special educator is absent.

Co-assessment of Group Needs

In addition to assessing the unique needs of individual students in preparation for Differentiated Instruction, educators will want to co-assess academic skills, interests, and preferences of all the students in their classes early in the school year. This co-assessment facilitates formation of instructional groupings and the selection of methods or materials. Co-assessment to understand group needs can occur through review of existing data sources and the administration of new assessments. Collaboration between co-teachers, or among members of grade-level or content-area teams, can make the assessment process more meaningful. It may occur informally or through formal structures, such as professional learning communities. Because many sources of information are available, it is important for team members to define co-assessment responsibilities to increase efficiency.

Co-assessment With Existing Data

Whether working with a co-teacher, a professional learning community, a grade-level team, or some other collaborative arrangement, educators may want to review existing data sources early in the year to co-assess students' academic strengths and needs. Standardized test data from prior years can provide important information about the foundational knowledge that students have as they arrive at school. Collaborating teachers will want to examine group data for trends related to overall strengths and needs. In many cases, standardized test data can be disaggregated by learning objective. Collaborating educators can identify skills that need to be targeted in preparation for future instruction.

In addition to standardized test data, data from literacy screenings are often available for elementary students. Data from the last assessment of the prior school year can provide information about student reading levels and support the formation of instructional groupings. In many cases, literacy screening data are available for group and individual analysis. For example, collaborating educators may be able to determine that 85% of students in fourth grade were reading at grade level, 5% were reading below grade level, and 10% were reading above grade level. With this information, the teachers could plan for remediation and extension opportunities. They may also seek to identify patterns related to specific skills, such as overall student success with literal versus inferential comprehension questions, to guide instructional pacing. More time would be dedicated to teaching skills that the students collectively struggled with, and less time dedicated to skills that were consistently demonstrated as strengths. Individual student scores can also be pulled for more detailed analysis when students are performing above or below grade level, facilitating Differentiated Instruction. Engaging specialists in discussions about individual student data is a great way to plan for equitable instruction.

Collaboratively Administering Screening Assessments

Screenings, such as the literacy ones conducted in most elementary schools, are often administered to all students as part of Multi-Tiered Systems of Support. In the elementary grades, screenings are typically administered three times a year (fall, winter, and spring) using brief assessment tools that compare student performance to expected benchmarks. The data from screening assessments allow school teams to identify young people who may need additional support. Collaborating teachers generally do not have input on the administered screeners. They can engage in co-assessment by planning who will conduct the screenings and by identifying responsive practices for any student who needs support to fully demonstrate their knowledge.

It is important that collaborating educators and family members discuss the use of accommodations as they relate to screenings. In some cases, an accommodation invalidates the results of a screening assessment. For example, some screening measures have a timed element. Removing the time limitation may be a necessary accommodation for some students with disabilities or those learning English. However, the score derived from an untimed test administration cannot be compared to the benchmark scores that were established with time-limited administration. Collaborative teams need to determine if the assessment should be conducted with or without the accommodations and consider how to interpret resulting scores. In all cases, when assessing a student with disabilities or linguistic differences, teams need to look at the results considering the student's known characteristics (J. E. Brown & Sanford, 2011). Teams should ask: "Does this score reflect the student's knowledge of this content, or is it a result of a known factor related to language learning or processing?"

At the secondary level, universal academic screening generally occurs by evaluating existing data sources. Data regarding student grades, attendance, and behavioral referrals are strong predictors of high school completion and are among the most common screening sources (USDOE, 2016a).

Dive Deeper

Want to learn more about early warning systems? The *Forum Guide to Early Warning Systems* published by the National Forum on Education Statistics is available here:

bit.ly/3Ke9BAZ

State and federal guidelines have established threshold scores for each of these data points, often called "Early Warning System Indicators," which serve to identify students in need of intervention. School or division teams may also choose to establish their own threshold scores based on the population of students they serve. This requires co-assessment with education professionals who are knowledgeable about the indicators and versed in the statistical analysis that distinguishes concerning data points from nonconcerning data points.

Co-assessing Students' Interests and Preferences

The frameworks of UDL and Differentiated Instruction both acknowledge the value of incorporating student interests and preferences into instruction. According to the UDL guidelines proposed by CAST (2018), using options to activate students' interest promotes engagement and persistence, and develops learners who are purposeful and motivated. In a literature review of Differentiated Instruction for academically diverse classrooms, researchers came to similar conclusions related to developing tasks in alignment with individual students' interests (Tomlinson et al., 2003). According to Tomlinson and colleagues (2003), a key question for assessment in preparation for learning is, "What motivates this particular student and how do I design work that is responsive to these motivations?" (p. 129).

One way for educators to assess student interests and preference is to use interest inventories. These informal paper- or computer-based assessments ask students questions about their interests outside of school, such as favorite sports, movies, music, television shows, and games. They also often ask about students' preferences in school, such as favorite or least favorite subjects, personal goals, and the ways they like to learn. A wide variety of interest inventories and surveys can be found through a web search. Educators engaged in co-assessment can work together to identify or create interest inventories that are developmentally appropriate for the students with whom they work. Consider language complexity, incorporation of visual supports, and response mode as important factors when designing or adapting an interest inventory to be accessible and meaningful. Once inventories are completed, educators can co-analyze the responses to identify common topics that will capture the interest of multiple learners when incorporated into learning activities. They can also document information about individual students to support differentiation. Interest inventories are one example of assessment to *elicit and interpret student thinking* **[GE_HLP3]**.

Engaging students in *discussion* **[GE_HLP1]** about interests and preferences is another way to elicit their thinking. The ultimate intent of this high-leverage practice is to use student discourse as a strategy for knowledge sharing (TeachingWorks, 2019). One crucial factor for effective group discussions is whether students know how to respectfully engage each other even when they have different ideas or opinions. The second crucial factor is that educators lead discussions in ways that ensure *all* voices are heard, including those that need to be heard through alternative means such as AAC or signed communication. Group discussions around student interests can provide a low-stakes opportunity for young people to share their ideas and learn about each other while collaborating teachers model and prompt respectful listening and speaking.

When whole-group discussions are used as assessments by co-teachers, the OTOS and Team Teaching models can be particularly useful. With OTOS, one teacher can lead the discussion encouraging and supporting participation by all group members, while the other takes notes documenting student interests and preferences. When using Team Teaching, educators can model respectful disagreement, role-taking, and the sharing of diverse interests. Small-group discussions are also helpful and can be organized by using Station, Parallel, or Alternative regrouping approaches to co-instruction. Restorative circles, such as those discussed in Chapter 9, also provide a good structure for collaborative group discussions.

Collaborative Formative Assessment

You may recall that we defined formative assessment as the use of information to evaluate learning in progress and to make decisions about teaching. It is the most traditional form of assessment *for* learning. Formative assessment can occur through formal and informal means. Informal formative assessment is embedded into the day-to-day act of teaching. It occurs when teachers elicit written or verbal responses from students, interpret those responses, provide feedback, and make any necessary instructional adjustments as instruction is occurring. We propose that informal formative assessment should occur in every lesson. Formative assessments provide information about student learning "not once a year or every few weeks, but *continuously* while the learning is happening" (Stiggins & DuFour, 2009, p. 641). Informal doesn't mean that the formative assessment is entirely unplanned. Teachers will want to strategically plan opportunities to ***elicit and interpret student thinking*** [GE_HLP3] through ongoing and varied assessment techniques.

Discussions based on "know, want to know, and learned" (KWL) charts provide an example of an informal formative assessment activity. By engaging students in a ***group discussion*** [GE_HLP1] about what they *know* and *want to know* about a topic before instruction begins, teachers simultaneously assess prior knowledge and recruit interest in the topic.

Chapter Connections

Find out more about the assessment of learning in Chapter 7.

After instruction is provided, student discussion centers around what students have *learned*, providing formative assessment of the knowledge acquired. Although informal formative assessment occurs during solo-taught instruction, co-teachers can collect more nuanced information and respond with varied instructional groupings.

Formal formative assessment describes the use of more intentional and focused prompts to elicit information about student understanding. The assessments themselves, and the analysis that occurs after they have been administered, allow educators to identify different levels of student performance and understanding. While informal formative assessment may just identify whether students are understanding content or not, formal formative assessments allow educators to identify degrees of understanding (Westbroek et al., 2020). Formal formative assessments often result in tangible products that can be examined after the assessment is administered, potentially allowing multiple educators to be involved in co-analysis of the learning outcome. Formal formative assessments do not have to be complicated. Exit tickets, quizzes, and student conferences using a check sheet of target skills are all examples of formal formative assessment.

Common formative assessments are a unique type of formal formative assessment often used for co-assessing group learning needs. Sometimes called "benchmark assessments," these school-level measures are designed to track progress toward year-end achievement goals. The assessments are called "common formative" because identical measures are used by all teachers with the purpose of assessing progress toward goals common to all students within the grade or subject area. These assessments are collaboratively developed by teacher teams, education leaders, and curriculum specialists to provide periodic evidence of progress (Stiggins & DuFour, 2009). However, once developed they are often used for multiple years without modification. Therefore, the more frequent collaborative engagement occurs when administering the assessments, interpreting, and acting on the results, rather than in the development phase.

When administering the assessments, collaborating educators need to make plans to ensure that the assessments are accessible to all learners. This means that legally required accommodations and modifications must be implemented. Once the tests are administered and scored, collaborative teams meet to analyze outcomes at the school level, classroom level, and individual student level. Within the larger analysis, teams seek to determine if the group of students is making progress toward the end-of-year goal. Guidelines associated with Multi-Tiered Systems of Support are often used for decision making. Teams examine the assessment data to determine if the universal instruction is effective, which happens when at least 80% of students are performing at the expected level.

The data may be broken down to evaluate the progress of student subgroups in alignment with state and federal accountability indicators (the subgroups can include students in different race/ethnicity groups, English learners, students with disabilities, and students from economically disadvantaged backgrounds). This information paints a picture of how well the school is meeting the needs of all learners. Similar analysis may be done at the classroom level, with the goal of ensuring that each teacher is providing effective Tier 1 instruction. If common formative assessment data reveal that teams or individual teachers are not effectively meeting the needs of most learners, administrators can arrange for professional development to guide teachers in improving Tier 1 instruction. More commonly, educators use common formative assessment data to identify specific learning objectives that need additional attention or reteaching to ensure student success in the long-term outcomes. Additionally, once Tier 1 instruction has been demonstrated to be effective, the data from common formative assessments can help instructors to identify students who need Tier 2 supports. Collaboration is key to understanding and acting upon common formative assessment data to benefit students.

Curriculum-based measurement is another type of formal formative assessment that can be used to monitor the progress of groups of learners or individual learners. This measurement is an evidence-based assessment practice in which brief, but highly sensitive, measures are repeatedly used to evaluate progress toward an end-of-year goal (Overton, 2015). Because each curriculum-based measurement contains questions representing the full range of expected learning for the school year, they are excellent for documenting student progress over time. Curriculum-based measurements are available to address a broad range of foundational academic skills, generally in reading, writing, and mathematics, although vocabulary matching measurements are appropriate for any subject area.

Most curriculum-based measurements are administered for one to five minutes to a group of learners, and many are available for free! Special educators often receive training in how to select, administer, and score these measurements as part of their educator preparation programs. Therefore, they can be great collaboration partners in using this assessment technique. Like common formative assessments, data from curriculum-based measurements can be used to determine if Tier 1 instruction is effective for most students when used as a classwide assessment. Many published curriculum-based measurements have established benchmark scores for different times of the school year, especially for the elementary grades. Curriculum-based measurements can also be used to identify students in need of Tier 2 services and to monitor progress when students receive Tier 2 or Tier 3 intervention.

Check It Out

Curriculum-Based Measurement Resources

Intervention Central provides an overview of curriculum-based measurement as well as free access to several measures and scoring norms.

bit.ly/3IuOBET

The National Center on Intensive Intervention has a free and very informative module describing the use of curriculum-based measurement for reading assessment.

bit.ly/3ItMzEV

Summary

Teachers, specialists, students, and family members all make valuable contributions to co-assessment *for* student learning. By engaging in **group discussions [GE_HLP1]**, analyzing existing data sources, and conducting new formative assessments, collaborative teams deepen their **understanding of student thinking [GE_HLP3]**. The **comprehensive understanding of student strengths and needs [SE_HLP4]** that develops from co-assessment allows educators to **design equitable educational programs [SE_HLP5]** that lead to academic success for all learners.

Co-instruction to Meet All Learners' Academic Needs

5

The purpose of collaboration and co-teaching is not merely to work together; colleagues must have a shared goal in mind. That goal is often focused on student success. Success, like our students, comes in many forms: academic, behavioral, social, and emotional. In this chapter, we focus on how educational professionals can collaborate most effectively in the shared classroom to meet learners' diverse academic needs. Merely having more adults in the room is insufficient and does not constitute co-teaching (Karten & Murawski, 2020), just like having students with and without disabilities in the same room and simply breathing the same air does not constitute inclusion (Moore, 2018).

Adults need to know how to communicate and interact as they co-instruct so that all students can benefit academically, even when they enter a class with significantly different academic abilities, backgrounds, skills, and interests. This requires a knowledge of the co-instructional approaches offered previously, as well as an understanding of how to implement UDL, Differentiated Instruction, and Specially Designed Instruction. Differentiated Instruction and Specially Designed Instruction will be the focus of Chapter 6 with an eye to more individualized supports for students with disabilities, so this chapter concentrates on strategies that apply to all students. We address UDL in depth.

Reflect on Chapter 2, where we emphasized that co-teaching requires co-planning, co-instructing, and co-assessing. We also clarified that individuals who are not certified professionals in their craft, such as paraeducators and parent volunteers, do not actually co-teach, since they are not actively and equally engaged in co-planning and co-assessing. They may, however, co-instruct if they are led by professional educators. In that case, though, they are not officially co-teaching a class; they are an active and supportive part of the instructional team. Co-instruction is what we do with students when they are in classes with us. How do we meet their needs, embed their interests, engage their minds and bodies, build their skills, and ensure rigor and progress no matter where they currently are in the content?

Making Adaptations for Students

Before we jump into a deeper examination of how co-instruction can, and should, include UDL, Differentiated Instruction, and Specially Designed Instruction, it may help to review how teachers typically address students' diverse academic needs. As classes become more inclusive, academic diversity has increased at all grade levels. ***Providing scaffolded supports* [SE_HLP15]** to help with this range of ability is an expectation that can be challenging but necessary. Teachers may find themselves with students operating at two to four grade levels above or below the one being taught. While some students may be working on an alternative curriculum or on IEP goals instead of the grade-level content, the goal for all students is to work toward various presentations of college- or career-ready skills. Indeed, even those students who may be working on functional skills still need to be challenged academically (Browder et al., 2014). The most common approach to addressing these diverse needs has been to provide different ***academic adaptations to achieve specific learning goals* [SE_HLP13]**. These adaptations fall into the categories of modifications and accommodations.

In a nutshell, **modifications** are those adaptations that significantly change expectations, so the student is no longer working on the grade-level standard. **Accommodations** are changes that work around barriers but do not significantly change the standard or lower academic expectations. The easiest explanation of the difference between the two is to consider a math worksheet that has 20 problems on it, arranged from very simple at the beginning to more complex at the end.

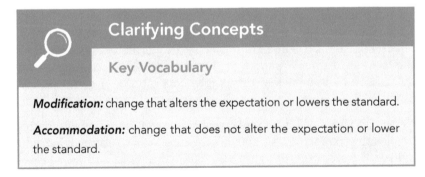

Clarifying Concepts

Key Vocabulary

Modification: change that alters the expectation or lowers the standard.

Accommodation: change that does not alter the expectation or lower the standard.

The grade-level standard is to be able to solve all levels of the problems on the page. A modification would be if the student were allowed to complete only the first five problems; this would mean that they did not demonstrate competency of the more complex, grade-level math. An accommodation would be if the student was allowed to complete only the last five problems. In this case, though only five problems were completed, the student would have met the grade-level standard.

While modifications are not as frequently offered for most students in general education classes, accommodations are very common. Typical accommodations include offering extra time, allowing for technological supports (e.g., voice-to-text, calculators) or organizational supports (e.g., graphic organizers, timers, reminders), reducing barriers (e.g., fewer choices, less text on page, easier reading levels), and allowing for additional choice in how the student demonstrates mastery of the material (e.g., verbally, visually, kinesthetically).

Though teachers are legally required to implement accommodations, they sometimes have concerns about their validity or ease of use (Mathes et al., 2020). These concerns can lead to disagreements between special and general educators, or between teachers and families, or even between teachers and students. In an article about how COVID-19 leveled the playing field for one student with dyslexia, 16-year-old Grace wrote about the accommodations she was entitled to on her 504 Plan (Lochner, 2021). Prior to moving to a virtual world due to the pandemic, Grace shared that her teachers would say they couldn't provide her with extra time; they didn't have the capacity to allow "do-overs" or different ways of responding to material, despite the fact these accommodations were legally required per her plan. They were not willing to have her use speech-to-text software and expected her to follow along with long lectures and extensive reading materials. Moving to a new and virtual world required her teachers to do things differently—for everyone.

Because of COVID-19, assignments were due at midnight instead of when class ended (allowing Grace extra time). Technology wasn't only allowed, it was encouraged. In addition, "all of the sudden, there were do-overs allowed because teachers assumed everyone was struggling so they went above and beyond to make sure we would understand the content by providing private sessions or videos" (Lochner, 2021, p. 12). Grace was happy to report that some teachers recognized they were competing with TikTok and Snapchat and so found ways to incorporate them academically; instructors found ways to have students work on collaborative projects rather than on mundane lengthy tests. One of Grace's final reflections was, "When teachers say they don't have time or they have too many students to be able to provide my accommodations, it's just not true. When they had to figure it out for the pandemic, they did" (Lochner, 2021, p. 12).

As a student, Grace likely did not realize the incredible amount of collaboration and communication that was occurring as teachers tried to navigate the changes brought by the pandemic. While the outcomes may have been a boon for students like Grace, who were able to access adaptations needed, the pandemic required a massive learning curve and incredible amounts of flexibility as teachers pivoted almost overnight. Those who could reach out and collaborate with others were able to benefit from those supports. As we move into the discussion of UDL, consider how many of the accommodations formerly offered to just one student with a disability might easily be offered to an entire class, thereby also reducing work for teachers.

Universal Design for Learning

One of the major frameworks that can positively impact instruction in an inclusive classroom is UDL. UDL is an education framework grounded in neuroscience and supported by several federal policies and statutes, including the Every Student Succeeds Act (U.S. Department of Education [USDOE], 2016b). UDL is considered the best practice for teaching all students in an inclusive learning environment (CAST, 2018). It is a way to envision educational settings, instruction, and materials as adaptable, rather than rigid. Since it is well established that students learn differently, why not proactively plan for those differences? This aspect of proactive planning is the foundation of UDL (Murawski & Scott, 2019).

Universal design has its origins in architecture, where contractors recognized that it made more sense to build in accessibility features (like ramps, elevators, and larger bathrooms) than to add them later. David Rose, the godfather of UDL, recognized that accessibility features, such as assistive technology, could and should be applied to education for all. Dr. Rose, Dr. Ann Meyer, and researchers from the Harvard Graduate School of Education formed CAST to share research, technology, ideas, and resources related to UDL. The connection between architectural design and education is simple: Why do we create lessons for the "average learner" only to then have to make myriad adaptations for learners who are not "average"?

In fact, Todd Rose debunked the whole concept of the "average" learner in a viral TEDx Talk, "The Myth of Average." Todd shared anecdotes and research emphasizing how there is no truly average student.

See It Yourself

"The Myth of Average" by Todd Rose, TedX Sonoma County

https://bit.ly/3xLT8N4

Instead, learners vary according to multiple characteristics. For example, one "average" student may be strong in math, weaker in reading, excellent in writing creativity but struggle with grammatical structure; love dogs, interact well with adults, and have a phobia of spiders. Another "average" student may be strong in math calculation but weaker in conceptual application, love to read fiction, spell perfectly but hate to write; prefer cats, be shy, and play soccer. Yet another student may be viewed as gifted by one teacher and as having a disability by another. So many factors come into play daily, and UDL emphasizes the need to expect and celebrate learner variability! In fact, a major aspect of a UDL framework is to teach "to the margins" instead of to the middle.

What does this look like? By expecting and planning for differences, which makes a whole lot of sense in an inclusive classroom, collaborating educators can be proactive in identifying materials, offering choice to maximize engagement and accessibility, and thinking about the best ways to provide instruction to match students' neurodevelopmental pathways. Knowing the various areas where students frequently struggle, teachers can **build scaffolded supports [SE_HLP15]** into their **systematically designed lessons [GE_HLP14, SE_HLP12]** so that any learner can use them as needed. In the recent past, teachers would create a lesson geared to meet the "typical" grade-level student's need, then make various adaptations for students who were gifted, or had learning disabilities, or needed other supports. Collaborating teachers with a UDL mindset, however, would ask themselves questions such as those in the following list *while* they are crafting their lessons, not afterward.

Questions to Ask When Planning a Universally Designed Lesson

Is this lesson accessible to a student who . . .

- struggles with reading (ability or interest)?
- has a sensory impairment (hearing/sight/touch)?
- already knows the material (gifted/twice-exceptional)?
- has a physical disability (can't walk/can't raise hand)?
- lacks interest or motivation related to this topic?
- struggles with attention or behavior?
- has difficulty with social skills?
- is significantly behind in grade-level content?
- struggles with organization or following directions?

If not, what can we do to proactively build in supports that will help this student but also be of potential use to all students?

CAST emphasizes that UDL requires teachers to embrace multiple means of **representation** (how the material is offered to students), **engagement** (how the students make meaning of the information), and **action and expression** (how the students demonstrate their attainment of competencies). Student choice and student voice are also major components of a UDL-focused classroom. Adults working collaboratively in a class to co-instruct can build on their different teaching styles and preferences to enhance their instruction. For example, providing multiple means of representation, one educator may teach long division using graph paper, while the other may use manipulatives. Students can choose which teacher to work with when practicing their division skills.

Teachers may also utilize differing *strategies to promote active engagement* **[SE_HLP18]**. An example of this may be when a teacher allows students to choose if they'd like to work alone, with a partner, with a small group, or with adult support. A collaborating paraprofessional may sit with any students who prefer adult support, allowing the classroom teacher to circulate and help the rest of the learners. Finally, "multiple means of action and expression" relates to allowing students various ways to demonstrate their knowledge. If teachers wait until the end of a lesson to see who retained and comprehended the content, it may be too late. A high-leverage practice related to action and expression emphasizes the need for teachers to *use student assessment data, analyze instruction, and make adjustments* **[SE_HLP6]**. Varied forms of action and expression allow teachers to make adjustments. In an inclusive classroom, this could mean that co-teachers frequently ask leveled questions, play academic games like Kahoot!, encourage students to share their understanding in different formats, and give young people a choice in how they demonstrate that they have learned the material.

Why is UDL such an important concept in the chapter focused on co-instruction? If all the adults in a classroom have the same inclusive mindset and willingness to recognize, respect, and plan for differences, they can work collaboratively to address those differences. Co-planning and co-instructing with UDL reduce tendencies to single out differences, to consider differences as "more work," or even to inadvertently engage in ableism. A class or school setting that truly embraces the philosophy of UDL simply expects individuals to have their own pathways, interests, abilities, needs, and personalities manifesting in a variety of ways. Co-instruction facilitates this philosophy because collaborating educators bring varied strategies and experiences into the classroom. Consider the following vignette that depicts a collaborative team incorporating UDL into co-instruction.

Connecting to Practice

Vignette 1: UDL and Co-teaching

Collaborators: Mrs. H, 10th-grade English co-teacher

Mr. L, special education co-teacher

Instructional Objectives: Students will demonstrate understanding of figurative language, word relationships, and nuances in word meanings.

Co-instructional Approach: Parallel Teaching

Recognizing the academic differences in their students, Mrs. H and Mr. L decide to use Parallel Teaching to address their objective. They know that breaking the students into two groups will provide a smaller student–teacher ratio, so students will feel more comfortable asking questions and teachers can better check comprehension. Keeping their mini-lectures to 20 minutes will help keep student attention, as will the smaller group size. Switching groups after 20 minutes will provide students with a brain break and kinesthetic movement, which many will need. Mrs. H will introduce figurative language and have a graphic organizer ready for those who want to use it. Though her goal is to have all students demonstrate understanding of at least three forms of figurative language (simile, metaphor, personification), she is prepared to have Will (a student with an intellectual disability) focus on simile. She has materials ready to introduce hyperbole, allusion, symbolism, idioms, and puns for students who appear ready for more challenges. In his group, Mr. L recognizes that identifying nuances in word meanings can be very challenging for some learners. Thus, he is prepared to offer a variety of examples through multiple means of representation. He has different shades of green in a piece of fabric, different textures of a piece of wood, two different versions of the same song, and multiple examples of nuances in different levels and forms of literature. Through discussion, hands-on examples, and visual cues, he will engage all learners and ensure they are prepared to demonstrate understanding of nuances in word meaning.

Differentiated Instruction

While UDL is about educators being proactive in utilizing a variety of materials, curricula, and pedagogical strategies in recognition of diverse learners in a class, differentiation is about being responsive to specific students' needs. UDL is about teaching "to the margins" in an effort to cover as many different learning needs as possible without actually knowing what those needs may be. Differentiation is about **_designing lessons_ [GE_HLP14, SE_HLP12]** and environments to meet the needs of a particular student.

Let's use Jimmy as an example. Knowing that Jimmy can't stand for someone to walk behind his desk, teachers can ensure his desk is at the back of the room or that a screen is placed behind him. Knowing that Jimmy struggles with transition and requires structure, teachers can provide a visual schedule for the whole class (which is more UDL) but be sure to individually review it daily with Jimmy to explain any nuances that may not be clear. Knowing that Jimmy loves *Star Wars*, the teachers use *Star Wars* examples when possible and allow Jimmy to connect content instruction with *Star Wars* references. In fact, they've been shocked by how easily Jimmy can link English, math, science, and even social studies and art with *Star Wars*! These are all examples of how Differentiated Instruction helps to meet Jimmy's unique instructional needs.

Table 5.1 depicts the similarities and differences between UDL and differentiation, giving credit to the anonymous individual on the internet who first crafted this comparison. Note that while a key component of UDL is its proactive nature, Differentiated Instruction is considered responsive. To universally design a classroom or lesson, teachers are not required to know their students; conversely, to differentiate, one must know one's students—and know them well!

Just because teachers may recognize that students will vary in their reading ability when they enter a language arts class does not mean that teachers can always proactively prepare for the specific variation. For example, having a variety of reading levels or types of reading materials is UDL. But what happens when Zahir, a student with a visual impairment, enters the class and there are no books in Braille? Or when Hannah only communicates using assistive technology and will need vocabulary about the reading unit loaded into her Dynavox? Or when Beatty informs you that they have already read everything you have available and would prefer something nonfiction and at the college level? In each of these instances, educators need to be prepared to differentiate and may want to collaborate to do so!

Differentiating instruction requires evaluation and communication. In most instances, much of the information should be available in a student's IEP or other formal documentation.

Chapter Connections

Trying to decide how to group? Review the co-teaching decision-making flowcharts on pages 43 and 44 of Chapter 2.

However, knowing that a student needs Braille, or assistive technology, or additional enrichment can be intimidating to the typical teacher. What is most important is to know that, with each challenge presented, there is an individual out there with expertise in that area. This is where collaboration comes into play! Instructional coaches, special education teachers, and even specialists at the district level can be invited to not just provide consultation but actually join the class and co-instruct, modeling techniques and strategies to help the students with disabilities access the curriculum to the fullest extent possible.

TABLE 5.1 UDL and Differentiation Comparison	
UNIVERSAL DESIGN FOR LEARNING	**DIFFERENTIATION**
Proactive	Responsive
Design of instruction prior to arrival of students	Retrofit instruction for students
Removes barriers to learning	Works around barriers
Evaluates environment, classroom, culture of learning	Evaluates the student
Focuses on variability among students	Focuses on individual disability
Teaches to the margins	Modifies for the individual on the margins
Intentional	Cause/effect

Although there are clear differences, there are also many similarities between UDL and differentiation. For example, Tomlinson and colleagues (2003), some of the world's leading experts on differentiation, have written that a teacher's proactive response to learner needs is shaped by the following general principles: (1) the environment should encourage and support learning, (2) the curriculum should be of quality, (3) assessments should inform teaching and learning, (4) instruction should respond to student variance, and (5) educators should lead students and manage routines. Obviously, each of these principles also applies to UDL. Both UDL and differentiation strategies may occur through content, process, product, or environment. While UDL is proactive and generally applied so any student might benefit as needed, Differentiated Instruction is typically based more specifically on a student's readiness, interests, and learning profile (Tomlinson et al., 2003). Once again, this is where collaboration for academic co-instruction occurs. In the following Connecting to Practice vignette, we demonstrate the interactions of UDL, Differentiated Instruction, and various forms of co-instruction as applied in an elementary setting.

Connecting to Practice

Vignette 2: Elementary Co-instruction Example With UDL and Differentiated Instruction

Collaborators: Ms. A, 1st-grade general education co-teacher

Ms. B, 1st-grade special education co-teacher

Instructional Objectives: Students will write informative/explanatory texts in which they name a topic, supply some facts about the topic, and provide some sense of closure.

Co-Instructional Approach: One Teach–One Support/Team Teaching/Alternative Teaching

Ms. A welcomed students to the front carpet, where she let them know they would be writing about their favorite topics. She asked students to raise their hand and share their favorite topics, which she wrote on the whiteboard paired with her best drawings. As Ms. A frontloaded ideas with the majority of the class (UDL), allowing them to voice what they might write about (UDL), Ms. B pulled Sami and Cady to a small table in the back (Alternative Teaching). Ms. B told Sami and Cady that she and Ms. A have been impressed with how kind the students have been to Li; the teachers were wondering if the two girls would work at a table with Li during writing. Li often got distracted and frequently called out for help. The teachers believed that Sami and Cady could help her by using the "focus pointers" (sticks with pointer fingers on them) when Li was distracted. Both girls eagerly agreed, and Ms. B thanked them as they returned to the large group. Having peer models and attention support was necessary for Li (Differentiated Instruction). Ms. B joined Ms. A at the front of the room and together they modeled coming up with facts about a shared topic (UDL/Team Teaching). They let students choose where to sit and with whom as they began to work on their writing (UDL); Sami and Cady asked Li to join them, and she was thrilled to do so. The co-teachers provided a graphic organizer template for all students to help guide their thought process (UDL). Knowing Li's favorite interests (horses and dogs), Ms. B squatted next to Li and asked which she would like to write about. Providing Li with limited choices helped Li focus (Differentiated Instruction). As Ms. A circulated around the room, Ms. B provided Li with a small handheld recorder and a timer (Differentiated Instruction). She asked Li to say everything she knew about dogs (her choice) into the recorder for two minutes; the teacher promised to return when the timer rang. At that time, Ms. B would take Li to a small table and help her identify the facts she recorded and then Li could put them on paper using inventive spelling (Alternative Teaching).

Formative Assessment
Strategies During Co-instruction

While Chapter 4 addressed the co-assessment of individual and group academic needs and Chapter 7 will address co-assessment in terms of evaluating and reporting academic progress, instruction and assessment are integrally linked. ***Checking student understanding during and at the conclusion of lessons* [GE_HLP15]** is a high-leverage practice designed to ensure that teachers are spending their time efficiently and productively. How do we know what to teach if we haven't assessed prior knowledge? How will we know how to differentiate if we haven't assessed students' readiness, interests, and learner profiles? Clearly, as teachers and collaborating professionals are engaged in co-instruction, they need to embed formative assessment techniques into their regular instructional activities. Black and Wiliam (2009) describe the purpose of formative assessment as eliciting, interpreting, and using information about student achievement to make decisions that are better informed than they would be without the assessment data. Collaboration among educators and students adds to the value of formative assessment.

Educators must be open to feedback from students to gauge what they know, do not know, and what will motivate them to learn. Research has demonstrated that there is a direct correlation between the time interval between eliciting information from students and using that information to improve instruction. The shorter the time interval, the greater the chance of impact on learning (Wiliam & Leahy, 2015). Warm-up and anticipatory activities, homework reviews, one-minute check-ins, quick writes, exit tickets, tickets in the door, Flipgrid videos, and Socratic seminars are activities that can inform academic instructional decision making. Managing these activities and then making sense of the data is a key benefit of having more than one adult academically engaged with a class.

Sometimes it can be difficult to separate co-instruction from co-planning and co-assessing! They exist in a loop, each informing the other. Three areas that can support formative assessment during co-instruction are recognizing Funds of Knowledge, increasing opportunities to respond, and efficiently utilizing technology, including assistive technology.

Funds of Knowledge

Students do not start school as a blank slate. They arrive each day with a plethora of skills and knowledge that has been culturally and historically passed down and developed for them to function in their culture (Esteban-Guitart & Moll, 2014). That culture may be from another country, or it could be a culture of homelessness, or of a literacy-rich environment, or of abuse, love, or racism. Funds of Knowledge could include knowing everything about the Manchester United football club and its history, how to fix a broken engine, how to paint tennis shoes with beautiful flowers, how to avoid questions about one's living arrangements, or how to speak multiple languages. Using Funds of Knowledge in the classroom helps to make it more culturally relevant and motivating to students. It acknowledges and celebrates diversity so that students can relate culturally to the class content.

When educators learn about students' Funds of Knowledge, they can leverage those strengths to offset young people's academic deficits, building the curriculum with themes that align with the observed strengths or patterns (Esteban-Guitart & Moll, 2014). Knowing the assets that students bring to the inclusive classroom can help co-teachers find ways to tap into those interests and connect them with learning objectives. Asking questions, providing interest inventories, offering questionnaires that seek to gather more information about students' diverse areas of expertise, and inviting families to come and share their cultural backgrounds are all ways to collect data that can be embedded into formative assessments. Notice how awareness of Funds of Knowledge influences the co-teaching in the following vignette.

Connecting to Practice

Applying Funds of Knowledge to the Co-taught Classroom

With a large population of English learners, Ms. Hernandez and Mr. Smyth wanted to be sure they were always recognizing the varying Funds of Knowledge their students brought with them to school. For the introduction to the new novel, *The House on Mango Street* by Sandra Cisneros, they broke the class into six small groups and used Station Teaching to encourage students to share their experiences and knowledge with their peers around the following topics: Identity, Dreams, Homes, Society/Class, Gender, and the Power of Words.

Opportunities to Respond

Asking students questions is a strong pedagogical technique for learning more about them and engaging them in learning, not to mention a strong way to incorporate formative assessment. However, question asking needs to be purposeful and strategic, not just random. One evidence-based strategy is to increase students' opportunities to respond (Common et al., 2020). When using opportunities to respond, teachers increase their use of questions or prompts that elicit student responses. Collaborative planning can focus on identifying questions, embedding questions into instructional materials, and identifying varied ways in which students can respond.

Teachers can use increased opportunities to respond in inclusive classrooms to identify and address diverse academic needs. One strategy involves response cards (e.g., mini-whiteboards, Plickers, or colored index cards). Frödj and colleagues (2023) document the vast body of research demonstrating positive effects of response cards on academic growth and on reducing behaviors of concern. Increasing opportunities to respond is effective in inclusive classrooms, because it is engaging for students with and without disabilities. A key benefit of response cards is that collaborating teachers can immediately recognize students who are experiencing success and those who aren't, allowing educators to **make adjustments to improve student outcomes [SE_HLP6]**. As one teacher is asking a question, the other can be monitoring responses and gathering data. These data can be used to help create groups, determine who needs reteaching or enrichment, and determine if the class as a whole is ready to "move on." When using opportunities to respond, co-teachers should reinforce correct responses and provide corrective feedback when errors are observed. Ms. Hernandez and Mr. Smyth connect opportunities to respond and co-teaching in the following vignette.

Connecting to Practice

Applying Opportunities to Respond to the Co-taught Classroom

Ms. Hernandez and Mr. Smyth want their students to engage and respond regularly, but they have noticed that some of the students who struggle with language tend to sit quietly while others take over and answer most questions. To provide more opportunities to respond, the co-teachers divide the class in half using Parallel Teaching. Both ask similar questions designed to elicit student feedback, but they do it with smaller numbers and give five seconds of thinking time before requesting answers. This adds processing time and allows more students to respond.

Instructional Technology and Assistive Technology

A chapter on co-instruction would not be complete without attention to the use of **instructional technology and assistive technology [SE_HLP19]**. Both instructional technology and assistive technology can be low- or high-tech. Instructional technology refers to tools used in any phase of teaching or assessment for all students. Assistive technology is "any item, piece of equipment, or product . . . that is used to increase, maintain, or improve the functional capabilities of a child with a disability" (IDEA, 2004, section 300.5). COVID-19 required many educators to increase their use of various technology-based instructional and assessment methodologies to meet the needs of all learners, demonstrating the value of instructional technology as a feature of UDL.

The potential applications of instructional technology within UDL were recognized before the pandemic as well.

The National Education Technology Plan (USDOE, 2017) addressed the need for educators to incorporate modern technology into instruction to create engaging and meaningful learning experiences that prepare students for their futures. This challenge continues for educators at all grades, subjects, and areas of expertise. Co-teachers working in the same inclusive environment need to find ways to use instructional and assistive technology to learn more about their students, identify ongoing needs and challenges through formative assessment, and provide the most effective instruction possible. Some strategies using instructional and assistive technology described by Israel et al. (2014) include text-to-speech and speech-to-text, digital pens, interactive whiteboards, mobile learning devices, graphic organizers with e-presentation software, video games, virtual dictionaries, animated tutorials, content acquisition podcasts, and much more. The Innovation Configuration offered by the CEEDAR Center on supporting content learning through technology for K–12 students with disabilities (Israel et al., 2014) also reviews various suggestions for selecting technology, including assistive technology, to specifically meet students' needs and Specially Designed Instruction. Let's connect instructional and assistive technology to co-teaching practices.

Connecting to Practice

Applying the Use of Instructional and Assistive Technology to the Co-taught Classroom

After the worst part of the COVID-19 pandemic, Mr. Smyth and Ms. Hernandez were thrilled to be back in the classroom, but their students frequently mentioned a preference for working with technology. As they continued their focus on *The House on Mango Street*, the co-teachers incorporated instructional technology as much as possible. As the educators started the writing unit, they used Team Teaching to introduce various graphic organizers by projecting the websites on their SMART Board and modeling how to use them. Then, they formed two heterogenous groups for Parallel Teaching. Mr. Smyth discussed style with his group, offering various types of writing styles in hard copy and online and having students identify them. Students could use erasable highlighters or online highlighters. In Ms. Hernandez's group, the students discussed identity—their own and that of the characters in the book. Ms. Hernandez added specific words to Juan's AAC device so he could participate in the discussion with his peers, a great example of using assistive technology. The instruction eventually led to a writing activity on identity. Students were allowed to use speech-to-text, online graphic organizers, and other technological supports.

Flexible Grouping

Flexible grouping **[SE_HLP17]** allows students to work alone or with their peers. Grouping patterns should change often depending on lesson goals and objectives. Students can work independently or individually with a teacher, work in pairs, work in small groups of same or mixed ability, or stay as a large group for the whole-class instruction. Teachers may work with a small group, helping students with the required instructional task, or may circulate as students work independently or with their peers. Teachers who have a strong ability to use flexible grouping can *dynamically coordinate and adjust instruction during a lesson* **[GE_HLP6]**. As they see students' attention wane or questions increase, they can break students into smaller groups to help differentiate and support individualized learning needs. This also provides an opportunity for increased use of instructional and assistive technology.

Flexible grouping requires teachers to consider specific activities and purposes, as well as student learning needs, as they intentionally create and dissolve student groups. Though students are clustered in classes by grade and subject, assuming that they are at about the same academic rate and level is a mistake. Teachers now recognize that most classes include a wide array of abilities and interests. Being able to formally or informally group and regroup students in a variety of ways throughout the day can help students and teachers be more productive. Grouping arrangements are used flexibly to accommodate learning differences, promote in-depth academic discussions, and facilitate collaborative student interactions. Students can be grouped according to the specific goal of the task, the activity itself, the level of support needed, the outcomes required, the interest of the students, Funds of Knowledge, context, and social readiness. Groups can be based on formative assessment data, or they can be heterogeneous and completely random. Collaborating educators may make flexible grouping decisions when co-planning, co-instructing, or analyzing outcomes from co-assessments.

Collaborating educators will want to proactively determine the goals of small groups when forming flexible groups. For example, if a speech-language pathologist were to come into an inclusive classroom during station time, students might be grouped by their speech or language needs. They might rotate through two content instruction stations before getting to a station focused primarily on enhancing their speech and language skills.

A behavior coach might collaborate with a general education classroom teacher to suggest that students work in partners, with purposeful partnerships created to support students' behavioral or social skill development. Cooperative learning groups could be created to provide students with the opportunity to take on specific tasks, such as facilitator, recorder, reporter, or encourager (Klingner et al., 2012). Co-teachers could select one of the three regrouping approaches (Alternative, Parallel, and Station

Teaching), depending on the goal of the activity, the strengths of the teachers, and the learning needs of the students.

When creating flexible groups, teachers need to establish norms for those groups. Having a discussion with students about how the groups will be created and managed is a strong pedagogical choice. Teachers can describe how the classroom will be configured in various ways throughout the typical school week. Murawski (2010) suggests making this a game with students that she calls the Configuration Olympics. She describes having students work against a stopwatch to create different configurations within the classroom, to include the whole group; partners; small groups of three, four, or five stations; and two large groups for Parallel Teaching. Give each configuration a unique name (A/B/C or 1/2/3 can work, but Pancake, Unicorn, and Honey will do, too) and put a visual depiction of each configuration on the wall to help with students' memory. Through this fun activity, students learn to shift groups quickly and efficiently. In addition to knowing how to form the groups, teachers must also have a conversation with students about the allowed noise level, the procedure for transitioning between groups, and behaviors within the small groups. Students who struggle with social skills, attention, or behavior may need additional teaching regarding their roles.

Summary

While co-teaching occurs between two certified educators, co-instruction is a valuable practice in which teachers, related service providers, paraprofessionals, and even volunteers can make meaningful contributions to student learning. Effective co-instruction requires *systematically designed instruction* [SE_HLP12] and *lesson planning focused on learning outcomes* [GE_HLP14]. Co-instruction allows for more *flexible grouping* options [SE_HLP17]. Through intentionally planned groupings, co-instructors can *provide scaffolded supports* [SE_HLP15], *promote active engagement* [SE_HLP18], and increase the frequency at which they *check student understanding* [GE_HLP15]. Through this collaborative engagement, educators can more effectively *adjust instruction* [GE_HLP6] and *adapt learning activities and materials* [SE_HLP13] to meet the needs of all learners.

Providing Specially Designed Instruction in Inclusive Settings

6

Connecting to Practice

Mrs. Park and Mr. James
Collaborate for Inclusion

Mrs. Park is an elementary special education teacher. She supports students in grades K–3 representing a broad range of special education eligibility categories. Her students are working toward the standards of the general education curriculum. Traditionally, most students in the special education program have received a portion of their language arts instruction in the general education class and a portion in the special education class. The time spent in the general education classroom is intended to give students access to the grade-level standards, while the time in the special education classroom is focused on intensive intervention aligned with the student's IEP goals. Mrs. Park has found that her third graders consistently make good progress toward their IEP goals, but they are not as successful as she would expect on the state's end-of-year reading assessment. She believes that her students need more exposure to, and support with, the general education reading curriculum. Mr. James, a third-grade teacher, has agreed to co-teach language arts with Mrs. Park. Mrs. Park is excited about the opportunity for her third graders to participate in Mr. James's engaging literacy instruction, but she is also uncertain about how to provide the intensive and individualized instruction aligned with each of her students' IEPs through co-teaching.

Mrs. Park's concern is not uncommon. Educators have the responsibility to meet two core requirements of IDEA. They must ensure that students with disabilities have access to the general education curriculum as well as to Specially Designed Instruction that addresses individualized learning needs. As reflected in Mrs. Park's story, effectively addressing both requirements can be challenging. Co-taught classrooms involving a special educator and general educator have long been proposed as a solution to the challenge. This suggestion is based on the belief that these teaching teams can form deep connections between the general education curriculum and individualized intervention for students with disabilities (Weiss & Rodgers, 2019). Unfortunately, this has not always worked out well. There is evidence that co-teaching teams have made progress in providing general education instruction, but Specially Designed Instruction is often lacking in co-taught classrooms (Solis et al., 2012; Weiss & Rodgers, 2019). There is also evidence that teachers, like Mrs. Park, are seeking strategies to connect high-quality general education and Specially Designed Instruction.

Providing Specially Designed Instruction in Inclusive Settings

The most inclusive and successful co-taught classrooms feature two types of instruction: high-quality, accessible general education and Specially Designed Instruction (Friend, 2016). In these classrooms, general educators, special educators, and other members of the collaborative team bring forth their specific areas of expertise to benefit students. The content knowledge most typically held by general education teachers is the foundation of high-quality general education instruction. General education teachers often have deep knowledge of the grade-level or content-area standards and good understanding of students' typical developmental progression toward meeting those standards. Skilled general education teachers also understand how to implement the general education high-leverage practices to create effective Tier 1 instruction (TeachingWorks, 2019). Special educators often bring expertise in accessibility and intervention to the co-taught classroom. When special educators and general educators work together, integrating UDL and high-leverage practices for general education and special education, the general education content becomes more meaningful and accessible to all students.

In contrast to the shared responsibility for high-quality, accessible general education, the delivery of Specially Designed Instruction has been the domain of special educators (Rodgers et al., 2021). In fact, many consider Specially Designed Instruction to be the core distinction between special education and general education (Barrio et al., 2021).

Clarifying Concepts

Although special educators are the experts in delivering Specially Designed Instruction, other collaborative team members are critically important for establishing goals of this highly individualized instruction.

As described in Mrs. Park's story in the opening vignette, Specially Designed Instruction has often been delivered in separate special education classrooms. Transitioning this instruction to more inclusive settings has remained a challenge. Part of the challenge is that, although Specially Designed Instruction is a legal requirement, it is not consistently defined for practitioners. In fact, the legal definition in IDEA is intentionally broad to provide IEP teams flexibility in planning services that meet the varied needs of students with disabilities (Rodgers et al., 2021). This flexibility has led to a variety of practices being described as Specially Designed Instruction, ranging from accommodations and board games to one-on-one discrete-trial intervention. Not all of these practices meet the intention of the law.

IDEA (2004) defines Specially Designed Instruction as adaptations to content, methodology, or delivery of instruction to meet the unique needs of a student with a disability. Specially Designed Instruction is intended to give students with disabilities access to the general education curriculum and assist in achieving educational standards. In interpreting this definition, practitioners and education researchers have questioned what teaching actions constitute Specially Designed Instruction, where it can be provided, and who can deliver it.

Specially Designed Instruction in Action

Specially Designed Instruction is an individualized and intensive approach that is fully customized to meet the specific needs that result from a learner's disability. Specially Designed Instruction must be distinct from whole-class instruction. Let's emphasize that again: this instructional strategy is *not* simply really good whole-class instruction, no matter how good it is! Specially Designed Instruction may address foundational skills that promote access to the general education curriculum and the educational environment. These skills are often documented in IEP goals. Specially Designed Instruction may also address grade-level concepts when taught using highly individualized materials or methods that increase intensity, explicitness, and feedback (Shepherd et al., 2016). Specially Designed Instruction can be delivered in any setting.

Although this type of instruction is primarily provided by special educators, including related service providers (e.g., speech-language pathologists, occupational therapists, adapted physical education teachers, and other licensed specialists), general education teachers and paraprofessionals can deliver Specially Designed Instruction as well, provided they have been trained in what to do and how to do it. It is important to note that state and local regulations differ in describing the circumstances under which individuals other than special educators can provide Specially Designed Instruction. For example, some school divisions specify that the special educator must be physically present when the general education teacher or paraprofessional is delivering Specially Designed Instruction, while others require only that the special educator co-plan the instruction with the other professionals. It's a good idea to check with your administration if you are uncertain about what is allowed in your school division.

Although accommodations may be important elements of a student's instructional plan, accommodations alone are not Specially Designed Instruction. For example, using a calculator as an accommodation in math class is not it. On the other hand, systematically *teaching* a student when, where, and how to use their calculator accommodation is, indeed, Specially Designed Instruction. In delivering it, teachers are working toward individualized goals for each student and are using practices that have already been supported by research (i.e., high-leverage and evidence-based practices).

Writing IEP Goals to Support Specially Designed Instruction in Inclusive Settings

The value of goal setting in education is evident in the fact that it is identified as a high-leverage practice for both general and special education. Both indicate that goals should reference curriculum standards, be carefully sequenced, and be based on student assessment data (McLeskey et al., 2017; TeachingWorks, 2019). The general education high-leverage practice establishes **goal setting** as an explicit process designed to elicit purposeful and equitable instruction [**GE_HLP13**]. The special education high-leverage practice elaborates that goal setting should promote progress in general education and other "contextually relevant curricula" (McLeskey et al., 2017, p. 1), allowing for **goals to focus on academic standards or functional skills** [**SE_HLP11**]. Beyond the value as a practice steeped in research, goal setting is a legal requirement in special education. IEP teams are required to create measurable annual goals that address academic and other educational needs associated with a student's disability. These IEP goals are deeply relevant to the discussion of Specially Designed Instruction.

IEP goals must be based on the individual strengths and needs of a student as documented in the present levels of performance section of the IEP. When goals are written with grade-level standards in mind, there may be increased opportunities to provide Specially Designed Instruction in inclusive settings (F. Brown et al., 2020). IEP goals that are closely aligned with grade-level standards are generally called **standards-based goals**, though they are sometimes called **standards-referenced goals.** The key difference in these two types of goals is that the process for developing standards-based goals begins with an instructional standard, while the process for standards-referenced goals begins with a high-priority skill selected to improve a student's quality of life (Hunt et al., 2012). Standards-referenced goals are less common than standards-based goals and may be used for students who require significant adaptations to the general education curriculum. We will focus on standards-based goals here, though you can find more information about standards-referenced goals in the Dive Deeper feature.

Dive Deeper

Want to learn more about the process for writing **standards-referenced goals** for students requiring significant adaptations to the general education curriculum? Dr. Pam Hunt provides step-by-step guidance in a presentation that can be found at

bit.ly/3XENd6Z

In either case, collaborative teams sharing knowledge of curriculum and student characteristics can successfully develop goals to address the unique learning needs of a student with a disability and ensure their access to the grade-level curriculum. The general educator can help the team understand expectations of the grade level. The special educator and other specialists can help the team interpret assessment and progress data as well as understand learning patterns that are prevalent with certain disability characteristics. The student and family members can share information about preferences, priorities, and prior learning experiences. These factors become useful in developing standards-based IEP goals, which then increase opportunities for Specially Designed Instruction in inclusive settings. In addition, as team members collaborate to share their expertise, they can concurrently not only determine which standards-based IEP goals are appropriate, but begin to brainstorm how they may be implemented in inclusive settings!

Writing Standards-Based IEP Goals

When writing standards-based goals, the IEP team begins with a grade-level standard and makes adjustments to address the student's individual learning characteristics (Caruana, 2015). The short Connecting to Practice vignette about Sophia, a student in Mrs. Park and Mr. James's co-taught class, provides context for the five steps of writing standards-based goals. A summary of the steps and examples of how Mrs. Park and Mr. James collaborated with the IEP team to develop standards-based goals in reading and self-advocacy for Sophia can be found in Table 6.1.

Connecting to Practice

Sophia

Sophia is a student in Mrs. Park and Mr. James's third-grade co-taught class. She has a learning disability in reading. She also has speech-language impairments in expressive and receptive language. Sophia independently reads at an early first-grade level. She will need decoding and reading comprehension goals. In addition to her reading difficulties, Sophia's academic performance is impacted by her concern about seeking assistance in class. Sophia desperately wants to fit in with her peers and is afraid to ask questions that will make her stand out. When she doesn't understand something, she often puts her head down or asks to go to the restroom.

Step 1: Identify a High-Priority Grade-Level Standard. A standard is considered high priority in the general education curriculum when there is an expectation that it will be mastered by all students in a grade level (F. Brown et al., 2020). Standards that are applicable across multiple content areas and those that are relevant to students in life beyond the classroom can also be considered to have high priority. General education teachers are often well versed in identifying the high-priority standards for a grade level. However, the student and family are important members of the team determining the relevance of a standard to the student's life beyond school. Knowledge of student preferences and aspirations plays a crucial role in prioritizing goals.

Step 2: Conduct a Task Analysis of the Grade-Level Standard. Task analysis is an evidence-based practice that involves breaking complex tasks into single steps or skills that can be explicitly and systematically taught one at a time (Browder et al., 2014). Many special education teachers have experience conducting task analysis and will bring that skill as a strength to the collaborative team. General educators may be less familiar with the term, but are likely familiar with a similar, though less intensive, practice sometimes described as "unpacking the standard" (Wiggins & McTighe, 2012). In collaborating to develop a standards-based goal, the general educator may take the lead on identifying the subskills contained within the standard, while the special educator and other specialists may work to identify foundational and functional skills that are necessary for performing the standard, but not necessarily included in it. The student and family members can help the team recognize steps of the task analysis that the student is already performing, and those for which the student will need intervention. When these individuals come together with their own areas of expertise and frames of reference, the task analysis process becomes much more manageable.

Step 3: Select Elements of the Standard That Are Logical Next Steps. Once the team has broken the grade-level standard into discrete tasks, they select elements of the task analysis that the student would be expected to achieve within one year. The IEP team should use assessment data and knowledge of the student's learning characteristics to determine which elements of the task analysis are likely to be learned through general education instruction (with UDL and accommodations) and which elements will be appropriate for Specially Designed Instruction. The latter ones may directly lead to the creation of IEP goals.

Step 4: Customize Presentation and Response Formats. Grade-level standards are sometimes very specific in stating how material will be presented to a student (e.g., printed text, graph) and how the student will demonstrate knowledge (e.g., write a paragraph). IEP teams have the flexibility to customize presentation and response formats to align with student needs (Caruana, 2015). For example, a team may write a standards-based IEP goal for a student with dyslexia specifying that the student uses audio formats of grade-level passages and composes paragraphs using speech-to-text applications. The teachers, specialists, student, and parents can all contribute to information about the young person's needs related to accessing and responding to information.

Step 5: Write the IEP Goal. In completing steps 1 through 4, the collaborative team will have the groundwork for a goal that actively engages the student in the general education curriculum while building on individual strengths and targeting needs. The final step in the process is to write a measurable and objective goal in the format required by the school division. In this step, special educators are likely the experts in goal format, but general educators and other team members can offer meaningful insights into how the goal can be measured and what the criteria for mastery will be.

The incorporation of standards-based goals into the IEP increases access to the general education curriculum and opportunities for students with disabilities to receive Specially Designed Instruction in inclusive settings. The student's individual learning goals, whether traditionally academic or more functional, are already linked to learning activities that will occur in the general education classroom. You don't have to be worried that you won't know how to implement Specially Designed Instruction activities in the inclusive setting. As IEP team members collaborate to determine when and where services will be provided to meet the IEP goals, they can also work together to discuss how to make it happen. Table 6.1 shows how it was done for Sophia.

TABLE 6.1   Writing Standards-Based IEP Goals

	VIGNETTE APPLICATION: SOPHIA	
STEPS FOR WRITING STANDARDS-BASED IEP GOALS	**ACADEMIC GOALS**	**FUNCTIONAL GOALS**
1. Identify a high-priority grade-level standard.	Mr. James, the general education teacher, shares that comparing and contrasting are important skills in third-grade. The skills are addressed in the Common Core Standard for literature and informational text. In this grade, students are also expected to compare and contrast ideas in science and social studies.	After hearing about Sophia's concern related to seeking assistance in class, Mr. James shares that third graders work toward the Common Core language standard that involves asking questions to check understanding. This standard is addressed in all areas of the curriculum.
2. Conduct a task analysis of the grade-level standard.	Mr. James identifies the two Common Core Standards related to comparing and contrasting. The standard for literature reads: "Compare and contrast the themes, settings, and plots of stories written by the same author about the same or similar characters (e.g., in books from a series)" (Common Core State Standards Initiative [CCSSI], 2010, p. 12). Mr. James "unpacks" this standard, explaining that students must be able to understand the concepts of theme, setting, and plot before they are asked to compare and contrast these story elements. The standard for informational text reads: "Compare and contrast the most important points and key details presented in two texts on the same topic" (CCSSI, 2010, p. 14). Mr. James shares that this standard requires students to distinguish main ideas and details in text. Mrs. Park, Sophia's special education teacher, and Ms. Martinez, the speech pathologist, recognize that there is a lot of complex vocabulary and conceptual knowledge for Sophia to process in relation to this standard. Sophia will need to link the terms "compare" and "contrast" to her existing understanding of "same" and "different." She will need to identify relationships between text elements and use a variety of phrases to compare and contrast in spoken and written formats.	The standard requires students to "ask questions to check understanding of information presented, stay on topic, and link their comments to the remarks of others" (CCSSI, 2010, p. 12). Mr. James states that third graders are taught to generate questions after previewing text to aid in their comprehension when reading. Students are also invited to ask questions periodically throughout lessons. Mrs. Park explains that she and Mr. James use the phrase "What questions do you have?" to encourage students to feel comfortable asking questions during instruction. In conducting a task analysis of this standard, Sophia's team recognizes that students must self-evaluate their understanding of information, know how to form questions, and determine if their questions or comments are considered to be on topic.

VIGNETTE APPLICATION: SOPHIA		
STEPS FOR WRITING STANDARDS-BASED IEP GOALS	**ACADEMIC GOALS**	**FUNCTIONAL GOALS**
3. Select the elements of the standard that are logical next steps for the student.	Sophia's mother notes that Sophia uses terms like "bigger," "smaller," "better," and "faster" when comparing familiar objects or activities. Mrs. Park agrees that Sophia can make comparisons when discussing concrete concepts such as physical characteristics of objects. She has a limited range of adjectives and adverbs for making the comparisons. Sophia is not familiar with some abstract concepts in the standard, such as *theme* and *plot*. The team determines that Sophia is ready to work toward comparing and contrasting fairly concrete concepts such as settings, characters, and problems (an element of plot) in literature, as well as concrete facts in informational texts. They would like to increase her use of descriptive vocabulary to support comparing and contrasting.	Ms. Martinez and Mrs. Park report that Sophia knows how to form questions related to familiar and literal concepts (e.g., "When is recess?"). Sophia's questions are generally on topic, but she sometimes struggles with finding words for new concepts, making it difficult for her to convey what she is uncertain about. Sophia's mother shares that Sophia is nervous about asking questions that will make her seem less capable than her peers. The team is uncertain about Sophia's ability to consistently self-evaluate her understanding during group discussions. The team determines that a logical next step will be for Sophia to recognize that she doesn't understand something and seek assistance in a subtle way that does not draw the attention of her peers.
4. Customize presentation and response formats to meet student needs.	The team identifies the following presentation and response customizations: Sophia will need text at a reduced readability level for independent work. She will be able to process specific aspects of grade-level passages that are read aloud. Sophia will need a graphic organizer, such as a Venn diagram, to assist in comparing and contrasting. In the early phases of instruction, Sophia will benefit from a word bank of descriptive vocabulary to support comparing and contrasting.	The standard specifically states that students will ask questions. In practice, this usually means verbally asking questions in all types of instructional groupings (whole group, small group, one on one). In recognition of Sophia's concern, the IEP team determines that it would be appropriate for her to use a nonverbal signal to indicate that she needs assistance, then ask her question privately until her confidence improves.
5. Write a measurable and objective IEP goal using the school-division format.	Sophia's team develops the following goal: Given two related passages at her independent reading level and a graphic organizer, Sophia will compare and contrast a teacher-specified text element (e.g., characters, settings, problems, facts) using grammatically and semantically accurate sentences in four out of five assessments by May 21, 2024.	Sophia's team considers the following goals for inclusion in the IEP: Given a classwide prompt to self-evaluate understanding, Sophia will select and display a nonverbal signal that portrays her level of understanding in 80% of measured opportunities by May 21, 2024. Given an individualized opportunity to ask questions to check understanding of presented information, Sophia will ask at least one on-topic question in four out of five measured opportunities by May 21, 2024.

Delivering Specially Designed Instruction in Inclusive Settings

Developing standards-based IEP goals is a positive step toward providing Specially Designed Instruction in inclusive co-taught settings. Two major points must be taken into consideration by the collaborative team when taking next steps and making decisions regarding Specially Designed Instruction. First, even those with the most inclusive philosophies must recognize that it is not always appropriate to deliver Specially Designed Instruction in general education settings. Privacy matters must be taken into consideration. For example, self-care skills often need to be taught in privacy. Another example is when students with significant delays in academic skills need to practice foundational skills far below grade level. They may not want to practice those skills in front of their same-age peers, and educators need to be considerate of these feelings.

Second, some research-based interventions simply require too much time to be delivered within the general education instructional block, while also allowing the student to participate in the general education instruction. For example, some highly structured math and reading interventions require an alternative setting due to the time requirement (e.g., 60 minutes at least three times per week) and delivery method (e.g., small group or one on one). Some schools have managed this by having students with intensive intervention needs take an extra block of reading or math as a learning lab or resource class. Alternately, some schools schedule flexible intervention/enrichment periods into the school day for all students. Given those two major considerations, the next steps for the collaborative team include (a) identifying evidence-based and high-leverage practices to be used as the Specially Designed Instruction and (b) finding time in the instructional block to provide the Specially Designed Instruction.

High-Leverage Practices for Specially Designed Instruction

The high-leverage practices for special education specify evidence-based instructional practices that should be incorporated into Specially Designed Instruction, regardless of the setting in which it is provided. These practices include *using explicit instruction* **[SE_HLP16]**, *providing intensive instruction* **[SE_HLP20]**, *teaching cognitive and metacognitive strategies* **[SE_HLP14]**, and *teaching students to maintain and generalize new learning* **[SE_HLP21]**. These practices are highly interrelated features of *systematic instructional design* **[SE_HLP12]** and can be integrated with other evidence-based or research-based practices. While some of these may appear self-explanatory, let's quickly review them.

Explicit instruction is an elaboration of **GE_HLP2**: *explain and model content, practices, and strategies*. Explicit instruction is a methodology in which the teacher overtly demonstrates the skills to be learned, then systematically fades support until the student can perform the task independently.

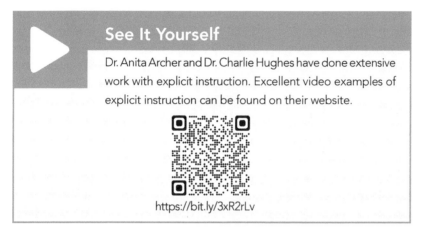

> ## See It Yourself
>
> Dr. Anita Archer and Dr. Charlie Hughes have done extensive work with explicit instruction. Excellent video examples of explicit instruction can be found on their website.
>
> https://bit.ly/3xR2rLv

This is a lot like what parents do for their children on a regular basis; think about how we teach our children to drive, for example. We model the techniques, guide our children through practice (often while pumping the imaginary brake on the passenger side of the car), then release them to drive independently once we are reasonably confident in their skills. Explicit instruction can be used to provide high-quality, accessible general education instruction; however, it is also an essential element of Specially Designed Instruction. All explicit instruction lessons employ gradual release with the teacher or co-teachers initially modeling the skill or concept, then transitioning to a phase of guided practice before releasing the students to do independent practice. Explicit instruction also includes high rates of active student responding and teacher feedback.

In addition to being explicit, Specially Designed Instruction also needs to be intensive. **Intensive instruction** is provided to small groups of students with similar instructional needs. It uses frequent, sensitive assessment to monitor student progress and guide instructional decisions (McLeskey et al., 2017). You've probably heard of "data-based decision making," right? Well, intensive instruction is driven by data. When data indicate that students need more support, intensity can be adjusted by changing the frequency or duration of instructional sessions, reducing the group size, or adding additional supports. Intensive instruction is also relevant to Response to Intervention. When implementing Response to Intervention teams use data to track how the student responds to particular interventions, how intensive those interventions were, and the fidelity with which the interventions were provided. Fidelity describes the degree to which an intervention was delivered as designed. When an intervention is not provided with fidelity, collaborative teams will be unable to determine if lack of progress is attributable to student need or the educators' failure to consistently implement the intervention. When providing Specially Designed Instruction in inclusive settings, co-teachers need to establish consistent routines to ensure that it is delivered as designed and at the level of intensity needed for student progress.

Cognitive and metacognitive strategies are effective elements of Specially Designed Instruction and can be layered to increase the intensity of intervention. Researchers have found that students with disabilities have fewer cognitive and metacognitive strategies, and they are less efficient at using them than their peers who do not have disabilities (Botsas, 2017). Therefore, cognitive and metacognitive strategy instruction is a valuable element of Specially Designed Instruction. **Cognitive strategies** refer to techniques that students can use to support memory, solve problems, and develop organizational skills. We can sometimes tell students that these are their "thinking tools." There are many types of cognitive strategies that can be applied across academic and social emotional skills. Mnemonics are a familiar cognitive strategy that can be particularly effective in helping students remember lists or sequences. For example, the acronym mnemonic "HOMES" is used by many to remember the names of the Great Lakes: Huron, Ontario, Michigan, Erie, and Superior. Checklists, visual supports, summarizing, and outlining are also examples of cognitive strategies.

In order to use cognitive strategies effectively, students need to know when to apply them. This requires **metacognition**, the ability to make judgments about one's own learning. **Metacognitive strategies** describe techniques used to intentionally self-monitor and self-regulate learning (Botsas, 2017). Students with disabilities can benefit from developing metacognitive strategies for academic and social emotional skills (McLeskey et al., 2017).

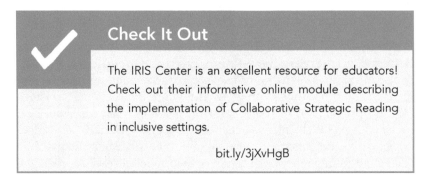

Check It Out

The IRIS Center is an excellent resource for educators! Check out their informative online module describing the implementation of Collaborative Strategic Reading in inclusive settings.

bit.ly/3jXvHgB

One metacognitive strategy that can be used to support reading comprehension is called the "Click & Clunk" strategy. This strategy is one element of Collaborative Strategic Reading (Klingner et al., 2012), a research-based reading intervention that incorporates both cognitive and metacognitive strategies. When using the Click & Clunk strategy, students are taught to pause at predetermined points in a reading to consider if they fully understand what they have read. When the content is well understood, students describe it as "clicking." Words or phrases that cause comprehension challenges are called "clunks." Once students have learned to identify "clunks" in their reading, they are taught to apply cognitive strategies such as breaking an unfamiliar word into syllables to determine meaning.

Merely learning a skill isn't enough, however. Inconsistent learning, memory, application, and retention of skills are common challenges for many individuals with disabilities. Thus, Specially Designed Instruction also needs to include instruction to support maintenance and generalization of skills. Students have achieved **maintenance** of a skill when they can use the skill after ongoing instruction has ended. Co-teachers can facilitate maintenance by using systematic prompting. A **prompt** is an additional support added to a question or request with the intention of helping a student provide the correct response. Educators need to adjust the types and frequency of prompts used during instruction to promote skill mastery and maintenance and ensure that students do not become dependent upon adult support to complete a task (King-Sears & Jenkins, 2020). Again, think back to our driving example. A parent's prompt might be to yell, "Slow down!" but we certainly can't continue to be there every time our child takes the car out, so we transition over time to simply saying "Remember to drive slowly!" as they leave the house. Teachers can also promote skill maintenance by scheduling review sessions at regular intervals throughout the school year.

Generalization is the ability to use a previously learned skill in a new setting, with new materials, or with new people. Generalization can be difficult for some students with disabilities. Therefore, plans for generalization need to be systematically incorporated into Specially Designed Instruction. Co-teaching provides a natural opportunity for generalization because students practice learned skills with multiple educators. For example, if Sophia learns the Click & Clunk strategy for monitoring her reading comprehension in a small-group activity with Mrs. Park, then practices the skill in a whole-group science lesson led by Mr. James and during her speech-language sessions with Ms. Martinez, she will have practiced with multiple teachers in varied activities. This increases the likelihood that Sophia will use the Click & Clunk strategy across settings, materials, and people in the future.

Using Co-teaching Models to Deliver Specially Designed Instruction

Because Specially Designed Instruction must be intensive, individualized, and distinct from the whole-class instruction used to provide high-quality, accessible general education instruction, it can only be provided using the co-teaching models that allow for small groups of students with similar learning needs to work together. Station Teaching and Alternative Teaching both provide this option.

Chapter Connections

Need a quick refresher on the co-teaching models? Go back to Chapter 2 for more details!

Station Teaching, sometimes called "centers," involves dividing students into groups that then rotate through various learning stations, some of which can be teacher-directed (Karten & Murawski, 2020). When employing Station Teaching to provide Specially Designed Instruction, co-teachers can use data and IEP documentation to form groups of learners with similar instructional needs. Co-teachers provide Specially Designed Instruction when students with IEPs and their peers with related learning needs rotate into their station. For example, Mrs. Park and Mr. James might choose to use Station Teaching during their introductory lessons on comparing and contrasting informational texts. After a brief whole-class mini-lesson reviewing the use of Venn diagrams, students would be divided into groups for rotations. Students who need additional explicit instruction for vocabulary development, like Sophia, might be placed in one group that would work with the special education teacher during the first rotation. During this rotation, Mrs. Park would teach foundational vocabulary needed to compare and contrast animal habitats in preparation for the independent activity to be completed at another station. Sophia and the other members of her group would leave the first station with a word bank to support their future work.

In subsequent rotations at the vocabulary station, Mrs. Park could work with other student groups to expand their compare and contrast vocabulary or revise vocabulary used at the independent station. When participating in the station led by Mr. James, Sophia's group might receive additional support in selecting facts from leveled reading passages about animal habitats and placing those facts in a Venn diagram. Finally, Sophia's group could use the word bank and completed Venn diagram to write sentences comparing and contrasting animal habitats at the independent station. Stations can be flexible as well. For example, if necessary, Sophia might even stay at Mrs. Park's station for another round, providing her with extra time for practice, and simply not go to the final station of independent practice.

To avoid stigmatizing any group, these more homogeneously created groups would not be used every time stations are conducted. There will be many times that Sophia can easily be included in a heterogeneously created group as well. It all depends on the goals of the stations and the strengths and needs of the students.

Alternative Teaching uses a large-group/small-group approach, in which the small group often receives teacher-directed intervention or enrichment, while the large group proceeds with a grade-level activity with guidance or oversight from the second teacher (Karten & Murawski, 2020, p. 11). In order to use Alternative Teaching for Specially Designed Instruction, co-teachers need to identify times when students who require intervention can be excused from whole-class learning activities without missing new grade-level content. Mr. James and Mrs. Park could utilize Alternative Teaching to explicitly preteach the elements of a plot diagram in preparation for a whole-class activity.

Sophia and a small group of other students who need intensive instruction might work with Mrs. Park while students in the large group journal about a problem and solution that they've experienced as Mr. James circulates. In the small group, Mrs. Park would describe the purpose of a plot diagram (using explicit instruction, an evidence-based practice), model its application via think-alouds (another evidence-based practice), then guide students in creating the diagram to document a brief, familiar story with a clear problem and solution. In this way, Sophia and her group members would become familiar with the process of using the plot diagram and have an opportunity to review the concept of problem and solution before participating in the whole-group activity.

Summary

Educators have a legal obligation to ensure that students with disabilities have access to the general education curriculum *and* receive Specially Designed Instruction that allows them to make progress toward their individualized learning goals. Specially Designed Instruction requires that educators *systematically design lessons aligned with those goals* **[SE_HLP12, GE_HLP13]**. Within those well-planned lessons, educators use *explicit* and *intensive instruction* **[SE_HLP16, SE_HLP20]** to *explain and model content* **[GE_HLP2]**. They also teach *cognitive and metacognitive strategies* **[SE_HLP14]** and teach skills across settings and people to *promote generalization* **[SE_HLP21]**. Collaboration between general and special educators as well as the development of standards-based IEP goals are important steps toward providing Specially Designed Instruction in inclusive settings.

Co-assessment: Evaluating and Reporting Academic Progress

7

When Alice asked the Cheshire Cat which path she should take, his answer was fitting not only for Alice, but also for those of us planning and delivering equitable instruction. It "depends a good deal on where you want to get to" (Carroll, 1865/1986, p. 62). In order to choose the best path for academic learning, we must know where we want to go and have defined methods for determining if we have arrived.

Up to this point, we have discussed co-assessment *for* learning as the collaborative work that educators do to understand student learning profiles in preparation for instruction, as well as ongoing formative assessment used to evaluate the effectiveness of instruction that is in progress. Here, we shift to focus on co-assessment *of* learning, also known as **summative assessment**. Summative assessments are broader in scope than formative assessments, evaluating student knowledge of multiple related concepts at the end of a unit, course, or school year. They answer the question, "Did our students achieve the learning outcomes we established?"

Chapter Connections

See Chapter 4 for collaborative strategies related to assessment *for* learning prior to instruction. See Chapter 5 for a discussion about collaborative formative assessment during instruction.

Making determinations about student achievement of learning outcomes requires that educators **use multiple sources of information [SE_HLP4]**. If concepts are truly important, we want to assess if our students know them and can use them when it matters. A single point-in-time measurement is unlikely to provide this information. To conduct assessment *of* learning effectively, educators must **select and design assessments [GE_HLP16]** that are well aligned with learning objectives in terms of the skills measured and the complexity of the performance requirements. Once assessments are administered, educators need to **interpret student work [GE_HLP17]** and **provide positive and constructive feedback to students [GE_HLP18]** in ways that **guide their future learning [SE_HLP22]**. Although summative assessments are designed to measure a learning outcome after the instruction toward that objective is completed, the information from those assessments should contribute to future teaching and learning.

Developing, administering, and interpreting summative assessments to address the broad array of learning objectives and diverse learner characteristics in inclusive settings is not easy. **Collaborating with professionals** increases the value and validity of the assessments **[SE_HLP1]**. Collaboration for co-assessment may occur between co-teachers, within grade or content-area teams, or between classroom teachers and specialists such as ESOL or special education teachers. Community partners may also contribute to the development of meaningful assessments. Through co-assessment, teams design, implement, and interpret assessments to provide an accurate picture of learning for all students.

Beginning With a Responsive Mindset

As with every other decision made in a classroom, educators' decisions about assessment are influenced by their own backgrounds. Decisions about the format and timing of assessments, the ways in which students are expected to demonstrate knowledge, and the wording of assessment questions are all influenced by teachers' values, beliefs, and experiences. In some cases, those factors align well with the needs of students. In other cases, various degrees of mismatch are present, potentially leading to inequitable practices for learners with disabilities and those from culturally or linguistically diverse backgrounds (Montenegro & Jankowski, 2020).

Equity-minded assessment is built around the premise that educators consider, as they plan and deliver assessments, the characteristics of *all* learners and the contexts in which learning will happen (Montenegro & Jankowski, 2020). It is a crucial practice for inclusive classrooms. Equity-minded assessment requires that educators identify and set aside assessment practices preventing diverse learners from demonstrating the full extent of their knowledge. It requires educators to consider how assessments can be meaningful, motivating, and accessible (Evans, 2021). The principles of equity-minded assessment are infused in UDL. Remember that UDL is about addressing the needs of diverse learners from the onset of planning. UDL applies to every aspect of instruction, including assessment.

The questions and considerations posed in Figure 7.1 can be useful for engaging stakeholders with diverse expertise in developing meaningful and equitable assessments. General education teachers often bring strong understanding of the skills that need to be assessed and traditional formats for conducting those assessments to the discussion. Specialists such as ESOL teachers, special education teachers, and related service providers tend to have extensive experience working with varied means of engagement, representation, action, and expression. Community members may offer insight into real-world applications of skills that help to make assessments authentic and meaningful.

FIGURE 7.1   Connecting UDL and Equity-Minded Assessment

Engagement How do assessment items promote student motivation?	**Representation** How are assessment items presented to students?	**Action & Expression** How do students respond to assessment items?
Consider ways to make assessments applicable to real-world experiences. Consider allowing student choice of topic or format. Consider level of rigor. Provide "just right challenges"—neither too easy nor too hard.	Consider options for physically accessing the test items (e.g., text, audio, images). Consider language complexity and vocabulary. Consider cultural references. Do they allow students to build on their experiences, or do they limit opportunities to demonstrate knowledge?	Consider response modalities that maximize accessibility (e.g., speak, write, draw, build, create). Consider offering students choices for responding. Consider when independent work or collaboration might be valuable assessment features.

Although UDL is an important starting point for equity-minded assessment, it is not enough. There will always be students who need individualized support for instruction and assessment. Equity-minded co-assessment requires educators to work together to ensure that *every* student with documented accommodations or modifications receives those supports consistently and without potentially stigmatizing attention. Accommodations need to be planned and implemented efficiently so there is no perception that the supports are a burden or that the learners receiving them are somehow inferior to other students. General education teachers, specialists, paraprofessionals, and even substitute teachers need to be aware of required accommodations or modifications for assessments. The Tracking Tool for Student Supports, shared on page 79 in Chapter 4, can be a useful tool for planning equity-minded assessment.

Developing or Selecting Summative Assessments

Summative assessments traditionally include tests, projects, and papers given at the end of instructional units. The high-stakes assessments required for federal accountability measures are also summative assessments. Fortunately (or unfortunately, depending on your perspective), classroom teachers generally are not responsible for developing the high-stakes end-of-course measures. Teachers have little control of those assessments, other than to teach the required skills and ensure that students' accommodations are provided. Therefore, our discussion of collaboration for summative assessment is focused on teacher-selected or teacher-developed assessments.

Selecting an assessment means that collaborating educators identify existing assessments that align with the learning outcomes. Educators may select assessments that were developed by textbook publishers or division-level curriculum specialists, those available on websites, or those used in prior years. Conversely, when collaborating educators **develop an assessment**, they may start from the learning objective and design every element from scratch. Alternatively, they may integrate elements from multiple existing assessment sources into a new measure that is distinct from any of the contributing sources.

In both cases, educators need to evaluate the assessments carefully to ensure they provide equitable opportunities for all learners to demonstrate competencies. In some cases, educators revise existing assessments to promote accessibility for individual students or small groups. It is a common practice for special education teachers and ESOL teachers to adapt assessments to ensure that required accommodations or modifications are provided. As an alternative to supports added after assessment development, proactive collaboration to integrate UDL features while assessments are being developed may improve accessibility for many students. Schools seeking to be proactive about equity-minded assessment should consider including specialists, such as ESOL and special education teachers, on grade-level or schoolwide curriculum teams so they can contribute to the development of inclusive assessments from the start.

Matching Learning Objectives to Assessment

An important element of equity-minded assessment is that all parties understand the learning outcomes to be measured (Montenegro & Jankowski, 2020). Educators need to understand the objectives as they develop the assessment and instruction. Students need to understand the objectives as they participate in learning and assessment. Family members need to understand what was taught and assessed to know what grades mean in the context of applied skills. That seems easy enough, right? Start with learning objectives, develop a test for these objectives, and teach students with the objectives and assessments in mind. It turns out that it is not so easy. Aligned assessments match not only the skills listed in an objective, but also the level of rigor and contextual applications. The complexity of standards, IEP goals, and other sources of learning objectives explains why rigor and context are not consistently captured in summative assessments (Ryoo & Linn, 2015). However, when educators collaboratively apply their varied knowledge related to learning objectives and assessment formats, they may find a better alignment.

Collaborating to Develop Aligned Assessments

A psychologist named George Miller (1990) developed a framework for considering rigor and context when assessing medical students' clinical knowledge. Miller described learning as a progression from factual knowledge to procedural knowledge, then to various levels of application. Miller's Pyramid lists four terms to describe depth of knowledge: Knows, Knows How, Shows, and Does. Miller asserted that accurate assessment of each level of knowledge requires careful attention to assessment format. Specifically, Miller recognized that certain question types are limited to eliciting factual knowledge, while others are more appropriate for assessing higher-order thinking and applications.

Miller's ideas about depth of knowledge and assessment alignment are applicable to all learning and assessment. We have adapted Miller's Pyramid to describe depth of knowledge and assessment formats aligned with each of these levels in Figure 7.2. The figure can be used by collaborative teams to analyze the level of rigor required by a learning objective and evaluate assessment items for alignment.

FIGURE 7.2 Connecting Miller's Depth of Knowledge With Assessment Formats

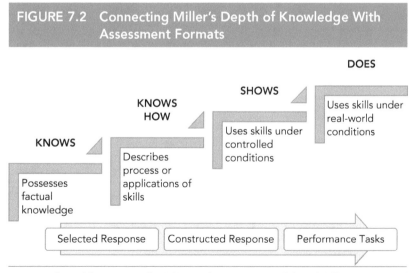

Source: Adapted from G. E. Miller (1990). "The assessment of clinical skills/competence/performance," *Academic Medicine, 65*(9), p S63-7) https://journals.lww.com/academicmedicine/Abstract/1990/09000/The_assessment_of_clinical.45.aspx

Through Miller's (1990) work, we can understand that certain types of test formats and response items are more suited than others to assessing application of knowledge. **Response items** are the prompts that elicit student responses. Informally, we would call them "test questions," though they may not actually have the grammatical structure of a question or be on a traditional test. Response item format is directly linked to rigor and should be one of the first considerations for collaborating educators evaluating or designing an assessment. Response item formats include selected response, constructed response, and performance tasks, as depicted along the arrow in Figure 7.2.

Selected response refers to assessment items where answer choices are provided to students. Multiple choice, true/false, and matching are examples of selected response items. They allow students to demonstrate knowledge of facts and would be in the "Knows" range of Miller's Pyramid. **Constructed responses** require students to generate answers on their own. Short-answer questions and essay questions are examples of constructed response items. The wording of the item determines the depth of knowledge that the student must demonstrate. Constructed responses can elicit factual knowledge (e.g., "list the planets in order by distance from the sun") or procedural knowledge (e.g., "describe the actions needed to conduct an experiment using scientific design"). In these instances, the items would assess depth of knowledge in the "Knows" and "Knows How" ranges of Miller's Pyramid. When selected for the right purpose and written well, constructed response items can move into the "Shows" level of assessment. For example, if a standard requires students to compare and contrast the point of view of two characters, a well-written essay question could provide the opportunity to demonstrate that knowledge.

The most effective manner for assessing knowledge in the "Shows" and "Does" ranges is to use performance tasks. **Performance tasks** require students to apply what they've learned to authentic contexts. The degree to which the assessment scenario is controlled determines if the assessment aligns with Miller's concept of "Shows" or "Does." Assessments must include the messiness of real-world experiences to evaluate depth of knowledge at the "Does" level.

We mentioned earlier that developing aligned assessments is challenging. Educators must consider the interaction of knowledge and application when selecting or designing assessment items. Consider the following Common Core Standard for literacy in science and technical subjects meant for ninth- and tenth-grade students. The students will "follow precisely a complex multistep procedure when carrying out experiments, taking measurements, or performing technical tasks, attending to special cases or exceptions defined in the text" (Common Core State Standards Initiative, 2010, p. 62). In preparing to select or develop assessments aligned with this objective, collaborating educators could use Figure 7.1 to think about the depth of knowledge that is required by the standard. In this case, assessment needs to be minimally at the "Shows" level and could certainly be at

Connecting to Practice

Miller's Pyramid and Co-teaching

Students aren't the only ones who need to demonstrate competency! In *Beyond Co-teaching Basics: A No-Fail, Data-Driven Model for Continuous Improvement*, Murawski and Lochner (2018) described and adapted Miller's Pyramid to apply it to co-teaching. Educators just learning about co-teaching might be able to identify or describe the co-teaching competencies (Knows), while other educators may be able to explain what those competencies would look like in action (Knows How). The goal of moving co-teaching from theory to practice, though, requires teams to demonstrate the core competencies through actually engaging in co-teaching (Shows). When the co-teaching competencies are embedded in the co-teachers' daily practice, then we know that they have truly mastered the competencies and are at the top of the pyramid, in the "Does" category.

the "Does" level. This standard requires hands-on application, so it would not be appropriate to assess it with a multiple-choice test or an essay. Further, the standard specifies assessment contexts—conducting experiments, measurement, or technical tasks—that need to be included in the assessment. It also adds layers of rigor, stating that the procedure is multistep and includes special cases or exceptions defined in text.

The wording of this standard provides evidence of the need for ***multiple sources of information*** **[SE_HLP4]**. A single assessment task would not be likely to capture all the contexts. This is the case for many standards. By co-analyzing learning objectives, educators can plan for assessments that fully address context and depth of knowledge. This ***collaboration among professionals increases opportunity for student success*** **[SE_HLP1]** in the classroom and beyond.

Assessment Formats

Assessment format is guided by a number of factors. In an ideal world, educators would have the time to develop assessments based on the context of learning objectives and the accessibility needs of students. Realistically, educators use what is familiar and readily available. When working with a collaborative team for co-assessment, educators may have the opportunity to try different formats that provide more meaningful and valid assessment for all learners. Here, we highlight benefits and challenges of different assessment formats.

Traditional Assessment Formats

Traditionally, assessments have been delivered through paper-based formats as soon as students are able to read and write. These formats are very familiar to most educators. Paper-based assessments have the benefit of being easy to produce (assuming that paper is available and the copy machine is not jammed). However, they may be associated with accessibility issues. For example, students with language or literacy difficulties may struggle to read or understand the response prompts; in this case an adult will be required to read the prompts aloud. Students with vision impairments may also require someone to read aloud; alternatively, they may need enlarged print or Braille versions of assessments. Students with fine motor difficulties may have difficulty manually writing responses and require scribes or alternative writing tools. While these adjustments are necessary to ensure equitable assessment, the provision of accommodations on paper-based assessments often makes the students who receive them noticeably different from their peers.

Over time, computer-based formats have become increasingly popular. Their use requires that all students have access to computers, something that is not feasible in all schools. When computers and internet access are available, a variety of universal supports become more readily accessible (UDL). For example, screen readers have become widely available, allowing individual students to have texts read (and re-read) to them at their preferred pace. It is also easy to adjust print size on a digital assessment. Computers have a variety of input options, such as touchscreens, mouse manipulation, typing, speech-to-text, and even eye-gaze control. Because many of these features are integrated into technology that is widely available in schools, they can be offered to all students. Therefore, computer-based assessments can increase equity in inclusive settings.

Check It Out

Information about accessibility tools that are readily available can be found for various platforms:

GOOGLE	MICROSOFT	OTHER
http://bit.ly/3xlr8tR	http://bit.ly/3XVbXrQ	http://bit.ly/3ZeAvwV

Educators who want to explore universal supports and accessibility options for assessment may benefit from exploring the resources provided in the Check It Out text box. However, technology integration also poses a great opportunity for collaboration. Teachers may collaborate with instructional or assistive technology specialists to learn how to integrate these options into assessment.

One concern about traditional assessments, whether they are paper- or computer-based, is that they tend to include response items that evaluate facts or procedures and provide fewer opportunities to measure deeper levels of knowledge acquisition (Villarroel et al., 2020). Think back to Miller's Pyramid: traditional assessments are often limited to the Knows and Knows How levels. Authentic assessments and portfolios provide more opportunities for evaluating deeper levels of knowledge (i.e., Shows and Does).

Authentic Assessment

Authentic assessments are sometimes called "performance assessments" or "performance-based assessments." Authentic assessments require students to demonstrate their knowledge through complex activities that approximate (or actually occur in) real-world situations. These assessments include a series of interrelated performance tasks to address open-ended problems for which there is more than one correct response (Maier et al., 2020). Authentic assessments are often cross-curricular, integrating content-specific learning objectives with research, literacy, technology, arts, or communication. Authentic assessments can result in products such as a story, model, or piece of art. They can also result in a performance, such as a lab demonstration, speech, presentation, play, or debate (Dixon & Worrell, 2016).

Authentic assessments have been shown to elicit positive educational outcomes such as deeper learning, college and career readiness, social emotional development, and positive teacher–student relationships (Maier et al., 2020). They also facilitate UDL practices. Opportunities for student choice and multiple-response options are easily embedded into authentic assessments. The adaptability of authentic assessments is both a benefit and a challenge. Because there is no single correct response to an authentic assessment, students need clear expectations about the requirements before they begin working on the project. Collaborating educators also need clear guidelines for evaluating the products or performances that result from authentic assessments. (See our discussion of rubrics later in this chapter to help address this concern.)

Timing and time management are also challenges associated with authentic assessment. Authentic assessments are completed over time, not as a "one and done" test. Collaborating educators will want to plan timelines to ensure that students are taught assessed elements in developmentally appropriate increments. Students, especially younger ones or those with executive function needs, may require scaffolded supports for time management and organization. It is also important to communicate what will be completed in class and what must be done outside of class.

Check It Out

GRASPS for Authentic Assessment (McTighe & Wiggins, 2004)

Goal–Establish a real-world goal to address or problem to solve.

Role–Assign an engaging role to the students (e.g., detective, journalist, scientist, a book character, a historical figure).

Audience–Define a real or simulated audience who will see or use the outcome of the assessment.

Situation–Create the situation or scenario that gives context to the goal or problem.

Products or **Performances**–Ensure that the assessment outcome is a *student-generated* product or performance. (Scaffolded support is allowed, but the final outcome must represent the students' knowledge.)

Standards–Be clear about the evaluation criteria for assessing the final outcome.

A final concern is that it takes time and practice to develop authentic performance assessments that truly measure the desired learning outcomes. McTighe and Wiggins (2004) offered the GRASPS acronym, shown in the Check It Out textbox, as a strategy for collaborative teams seeking to develop performance tasks. Those interested in learning more about the use of GRASPS for performance assessments are encouraged to "dive deeper" by visiting Jay McTighe's blog.

Dive Deeper

Interested in using GRASPS and want to see sample performance assessments using the model? Dive into Jay McTighe's blog.

bit.ly/3YE0Ft3

Developing and evaluating authentic assessments is truly a collaborative activity. Several education experts have formulated criteria for evaluating the outcomes (e.g., McTighe, 2015; Overton, 2015). We have synthesized some of those guiding questions with suggestions for collaboration.

Evaluative Criterion:	Does the assessment require students to apply knowledge in a meaningful and authentic situation?

Collaborative Action: *Engage family members or community partners.*

Ask family members or community partners to review the assessment for relevance and accurate depiction of events that occur in their homes, workplaces, and community. Use the feedback to increase the authenticity of the assessment situation.

Evaluative Criterion:	Does the assessment clearly align with the targeted learning objectives?

Collaborative Action: *Engage fellow teachers.*

Ask fellow teachers, curriculum specialists, or even administrators to read the proposed assessment and identify the learning objectives that it addresses (McTighe, 2015). If the reviewers identify the learning objectives you intended to measure, the assessment is well aligned. If your targeted objectives are not identified, discuss options to bring those objectives to the forefront of the task.

Evaluative Criterion:	Does the assessment integrate skills from multiple content areas?

Collaborative Action: *Engage content-area teachers and specialists.*

Collaborate with content-area teachers or specialists (e.g., instructional technology, school librarian, nurse) to identify opportunities for cross-curricular connections. Many specialists are looking for opportunities to support cross-curricular integration. They may contribute ideas about how response items can be represented and how students can demonstrate knowledge across the curriculum. The integration adds relevance to the assessment.

Evaluative Criterion:	Does the assessment engage student interests and preferences?

Collaborative Action: *Assess student interests.*

In Chapter 5, we discussed the use of student interest surveys and group discussions as meaningful ways to understand learners when preparing for instruction. The information is equally valuable when planning authentic assessments. Use what you know about student interests and preferences to develop authentic performance scenarios and response options.

Evaluative Criterion:	Are expectations and criteria for success clear to students and teachers?

Collaborative Action: *Engage students and collaborating teachers.*

Consider a low-stakes trial run of an assessment as an opportunity to refine the expectations and criteria for success. Seek feedback from students after the assessment has been completed to guide future revisions. Seek student input about what was clear or unclear in the directions and grading. Co-teachers may also benefit from taking notes while grading the assessments and engaging in co-reflection to refine directions and grading criteria. This is an example of *interpreting student work* **[GE_HLP17]** to inform instruction and assessment practices.

Portfolio Assessment

Portfolios are collections of work products created over time. As an assessment tool, they either exemplify a student's best work related to a specific set of standards or demonstrate growth. Portfolios may include work samples generated from any of the previously discussed assessment formats. In this way, they naturally provide *multiple sources of information* **[SE_HLP4]** that educators can use to make informed decisions about student learning. Student self-assessment or self-reflection is a valuable element of portfolio assessment. By reflecting on their own growth or providing a rationale for why a specific work sample was chosen for a portfolio, students demonstrate knowledge of learning outcomes and expected performance. If you are incorporating student self-assessment, plan to explicitly teach young people how to compare their work to a known standard. Accurate self-assessment takes guidance and practice. A final benefit of portfolios involves their use to communicate authentic progress to students and families. Many schools invite family members to visit on special days, often toward the end of a school year, when their children can share portfolios and celebrate achievements.

One challenge with portfolios is that grading can be highly subjective. It is important that scoring be based on a well-defined rubric and that students have access to the rubric as the portfolio is being developed. Collaborating teachers can partner to decide what should be included in the portfolio and how to evaluate it. Community members can also play a valuable role in the development and evaluation of portfolios. They may share ideas about what an authentic skill application looks like beyond the school setting. This knowledge can be valuable in defining features of the portfolio as well as in establishing grading criteria.

Providing Feedback

No assessment is complete until student work **has been interpreted [GE_HLP17]** and feedback has been provided. The general and special education high-leverage practices both highlight the value of feedback, indicating that it needs to be **provided to students [GE_HLP18]** in **positive and constructive ways to guide student learning [SE_HLP22]**. We have already emphasized that summative assessment occurs after instruction has been completed, so the idea that it guides student learning may seem to be a contradiction. The primary use of summative assessment is to inform educators, students, and family members about student proficiency in performing taught skills. However, feedback on summative assessments also guides students and educators in planning for any future learning that will build upon the assessed skills (Wakefield et al., 2014). For example, information about student performance on summative assessments of multiplication may influence how educators teach division and how students practice it.

Two primary types of feedback are used with summative assessments: **grades**, which are usually associated with levels of proficiency, and **comments**, which can guide future actions (Koenka, 2022). To be meaningful, feedback needs to be responsive (see below). Because feedback can be delivered by educators in a variety of roles and from a variety of backgrounds, it is important that collaborative teams come to a consensus about features of responsive feedback they will use.

Responsive Feedback

When providing responsive feedback, educators need to consider when and how it will be delivered. Timing influences students' abilities to make connections between their actions and the feedback they received. If feedback is provided long after an assessment is completed, students may not recall the expectations of the task or the strategies they applied. Therefore, the feedback will have little influence on their future actions. When planning for co-assessment, educators should divide grading responsibilities in ways that ensure timely feedback. They may choose to divide students into equal groups, splitting the grading between the collaborating teachers. When doing this, it is important that groups are not formed based on service categories (e.g., special education, general education, ESOL). Remember that in co-taught settings, all students are the responsibility of all teachers. Collaborating teachers may also decide to divide grading responsibilities by breaking assessments into sections. For instance, the general education teacher might evaluate the nonfiction portion of all students' writing portfolios, while the ESOL teacher evaluates the fiction portion. Decisions about grading may also be based on teachers' confidence level regarding the content and on their other obligations (e.g., a specialist may have a week full of IEP assessments that preclude them from doing additional assessments). Co-teachers need to be willing to discuss these potential issues.

Educators also need to deliver feedback in ways that empower students (TeachingWorks, 2019). Grades and comments can make young people feel defeated or encouraged, depending on how the feedback is presented. As Dr. Rita Pierson (2013) stated in her inspirational TED Talk, a grade of "-18 sucks all the life out of you; +2 says, 'I ain't all bad'" (4:49). Talk with co-teachers about how to give empowering feedback. If in doubt, ask: "How would you feel if you received this comment on your paper?"

See It Yourself

Check out Dr. Pierson's powerful TED Talk by scanning this QR code.

https://bit.ly/41jlxGv

Educators must also be culturally responsive in delivering feedback. According to Hammond (2015), **culturally responsive feedback** supports students in progressing toward learning objectives without increasing anxiety. Failure to provide constructive feedback at all suggests low expectations and impedes growth, a problem that Hammond observed in her research on feedback provided to culturally diverse students. Providing feedback that is overly critical lowers student self-efficacy and also impedes growth. Delivering feedback well requires knowledge of students' individual and cultural preferences (Aceves & Orosco, 2014), which can be obtained through co-assessment for Differentiated Instruction, as described in Chapter 4. All educators involved in providing feedback, including paraprofessionals, need to be aware of students' individual and cultural preferences. This can be an important collaborative conversation among educators early in the school year with periodic updates planned across the year.

Grades

The process of interpreting student work on summative assessments invariably leads to grading. One of the most common concerns that teachers have about grading in inclusive settings is how to make it *fair*.

How can one system accurately describe the different levels of knowledge that students have and the varied supports learners use in demonstrating that knowledge?

Historically, teachers have formed their own systems for grading students with disabilities, English learners, and others with diverse learning needs. In their efforts to be fair, teachers often grade diverse learners by informally integrating points for academic knowledge, engagement, and persistence into the reported outcome (Brookhart , 2011). Unfortunately, these multifaceted systems are rarely described in sufficient detail to allow other educators to use them. The practice, while well intentioned, also means that the resulting grades don't have consistent meaning. The B on Dae-Hyun's report card may not mean the same thing as the B on Keenan's report card, even if it was given by the same teacher for the same class. The challenge of finding meaning in grades becomes even more complex when multiple educators are involved in grading the same assignments or students. Without a common practice for grading, student grades may be representative of who did the grading rather than the quality of learning.

Collaborating teachers seeking to grade accurately and equitably need to recognize three types of assessment criteria, evaluating and reporting them separately. Guskey and Jung (2009) identified these criteria as product, process, and progress. Criteria related to **product** (or performance, if using authentic assessment) evaluate learning based purely on demonstration of knowledge. Product criteria are all about academic skills. Collaborating teachers may also wish to assess **process**, which entails learning behaviors that students demonstrate. Process criteria may include information about student effort, work habits, collaboration, or engagement during the summative assessment and during the instruction that led up to that assessment. Finally, **progress** criteria document academic growth over time. Progress information is particularly relevant for students who are performing well below grade level. They may demonstrate a low degree of proficiency on product criteria but show significant growth on progress criteria. This information is meaningful for showing that instructional practices are working to close learning gaps.

Co-assessment, especially when done by co-teachers, provides greater opportunity to capture information in support of product, process, and progress grading. When developing grading criteria, collaborating educators should specifically identify assessment tasks that provide information about each criterion and consider these features in their grading process. Aligned assessments will naturally have product criteria covered. Co-teachers may need to be intentional about identifying or adding opportunities to evaluate process and progress.

These three sets of criteria can also help delineate active roles for each educator during assessment. For example, one educator may be focused on assessing the academic knowledge demonstrated in a performance task, such as a Socratic seminar. The other teacher might focus on process outcomes, such as collaboration or participation. Both teachers could use rubrics or checklists to ensure consistent grading of their assessment element. After the assessment is completed, the teachers could collaboratively compare student performance on the product and process criteria to prior performance in order to evaluate progress.

Accounting for Accommodations and Modifications in Grading

We have previously emphasized that accommodations and modifications are a required type of learning and assessment support for some students. We know that questions arise related to fair grading when these supports are used. The concerns often stem from a lack of understanding about the distinction between accommodations and modifications. As discussed previously, accommodations do not change the curriculum expectation or reduce the depth of knowledge required by a grade-level standard. Accommodations are adjustments intended to allow students to fully demonstrate their knowledge by reducing the impact of a disability or learning difference. Therefore, accommodations should have *no impact* on the grade that results from an assessment in which the accommodation was used.

Modifications, however, do alter the standard. They reduce the depth of knowledge, complexity, context, or amount of content assessed. When evaluating student performance on an assessment of modified standards, educators should establish clear criteria for what the modified learning outcome looks like and use those criteria for grading (Jung & Guskey, 2010). Because the criteria differ from the grade-level standard, formal documents such as report cards should note grades derived from modified standards. Details about modifications should be documented in formal learning plans, such as IEPs.

Although only modifications impact grading, it is a good practice to document accommodations or modifications provided on an assessment. This ensures that everyone knows how the grade was achieved. Collaborating educators may find it helpful to create a checklist of possible accommodations that can be marked and attached to completed assessments. Some teachers have even developed rubber stamps for this purpose.

Rubrics

Rubrics are an important tool for ensuring accurate and consistent grading when skills have subjective elements. Most educators are familiar with rubrics. They list the skills to be assessed and include detailed criteria by which each skill can be evaluated. Rubrics should be a staple for co-assessment!

Rubrics are beneficial to students when they are provided prior to or along with assessment tasks. They give students clear information about what is expected, and students can use them to self-assess before submitting an assignment (McTighe, 2016). Well-designed rubrics also benefit teachers. When developed prior to instruction, they serve to focus teaching methods. When used for scoring, they increase reliability across teachers. While rubrics are relatively simple to use, they can be challenging to design.

Clarifying Concepts

Learn more about rubrics and even get some excellent downloadable templates at the *Cult of Pedagogy* blog.

bit.ly/3S4SMua

There are three key elements of a rubric: the tasks or features of the assignment that will be evaluated, the levels of performance (or scale), and the performance indicators (Whittaker et al., 2001). These are usually arranged in a table with tasks running along the left column, levels of performance along the top row, and performance indicators filling in the remaining cells. Educators engaged in co-assessment will want to evaluate learning objectives and consider the assignment format to determine what tasks are important to evaluate. These may include product, process, and progress features. Next, three to five terms are selected to define the levels of performance. In general, these terms convey degrees to which the student meets standards, exceeds standards, or performs below standards. Finally, the performance indicators give detailed information about what each performance level looks like for each task.

Defining the performance indicators is one of the most challenging aspects of creating a rubric. Collaborating teachers may find that the performance indicator for "meets standards" is the easiest to define, as it will be largely based on the learning objective. To determine the performance indicator for "exceeds standards," collaborating teachers may find it helpful to examine prior student work looking for exemplary performance. Similarly, discussing challenges or common errors demonstrated by students may guide teachers in defining the performance indicators for "below standards." Rubrics can be used in multiple capacities and make it easier for teachers to engage in UDL activities. The more flexibility there is for students to demonstrate competency in the standards, the more universally designed the assessment is.

Reporting on Student Learning

The purpose of *all* assessment is to gather information to support educational decision making. Decisions are best made by **collaborative**

teams that include *education professionals*, students, and family members **[SE_HLP1]**. The cycle of assessment is not complete until information is shared and decisions are made. Report cards and IEP progress notes provide formal, but unilateral, means for sharing information about student progress with family members and others who may read the student's official record. They should be worded professionally and objectively and provide evidence of the collaboration involved in delivering instruction (e.g., names of all teachers, comments reflecting all teachers' observations).

Chapter Connections

Families are a key ingredient of student success! Learn more ways to meaningfully include them in planning and assessment efforts in Chapters 8 and 11.

Parent–teacher–student conferences provide a greater opportunity for truly reciprocal engagement between educators, family members, and students. Through these interactions, collaborative teams can make meaningful data-informed decisions that promote student success.

Chapters 8 and 11 provide additional information about engaging students and family members in meaningful conversations.

Summary

Co-assessment of learning involves the integration of ***multiple sources of information to understand student strengths and needs*** **[SE_HLP4]**. When educators approach summative assessment with an equity mindset, they ***select and design accessible assessments*** **[GE_HLP16]** and ***interpret student work*** **[GE_HLP17]** in ways that accurately document student learning. Through ***collaborative engagement with professionals***, students, and families **[SE_HLP1]**, educators provide ***meaningful and constructive feedback that guides future learning*** **[GE_HLP18, SE_HLP22]**.

Collaborating for Social, Emotional, and Behavioral Growth

Introduction to Section III

Collaborating for Social, Emotional, and Behavioral Growth

The role of education has become far more expansive than that time long ago when the so-called three Rs—"reading, 'riting, and 'rithmetic"—were the sole focus of instruction. In fact, when we consider the responsibilities of both educators and learners in schools today, it is difficult to imagine that there was ever a time when education was only focused on academic skills. Today, educators are responsible for engaging students in meaningful learning activities that promote critical thinking, collaboration, and real-world applications (Council of Chief State School Officers, 2013). This approach requires that students have the social, emotional, and behavioral competencies to interact with each other and with adults while learning academic content. To make this happen, educators are expected to teach social skills and provide support for students who have difficulty with these skills. This invaluable work is made more complex by the varied experiences and needs of students. Learners in U.S. public schools represent a broad array of cultural, linguistic, and academic backgrounds, which contribute to different values, expectations, and norms related to social interactions. Students and educators alike must learn how to respectfully engage with one another across these differences if learning is to occur.

An additional factor of relevance to the discussion of social, emotional, and behavioral growth is the increasing rate of mental health needs in the school-age population (U.S. Department of Education [USDOE], 2021b). Mental health diagnoses, which include anxiety, depression, and behavioral disorders, have been increasingly evident in school-age learners since 2009 (Centers for Disease Control and Prevention, 2019). Further, social isolation, financial insecurity, and the illness or loss of family members or friends resulting from the COVID-19 pandemic created traumatic experiences for nearly 50 million students in U.S. public schools (National Center for Education Statistics, 2021; USDOE, 2021b). Students who have experienced trauma and those with mental health diagnoses may need differentiated supports to meet the social emotional demands of the learning environment. When we think of the enormity of the task and the importance of developing students' interpersonal skills in coordination with their academic learning, it is clear that the work cannot be accomplished by a single individual, or even a single profession within the field of education (Maras et al., 2015). Promoting social, emotional, and behavioral growth requires collaboration.

In this section of the text, we focus on collaboration as a tool that allows educators to use best practices for promoting social, emotional, and behavioral growth. High-leverage practices, Multi-Tiered Systems of Support, and UDL, which have been integral to previous sections, are also important frameworks here. Additionally, we add Positive Behavioral Interventions and Supports, culturally responsive practices, and trauma-informed practices as key concepts woven into our discussion of social emotional learning. Table SIII.1 defines these concepts and provides a summary of their relevance to social, emotional, and behavioral growth.

TABLE SIII.1   Principal Concepts in Social, Emotional, and Behavioral Learning

RESEARCH-BASED PRACTICE	DEFINITION AND RELEVANCE
Positive Behavioral Interventions and Supports (PBIS)	Positive Behavioral Interventions and Supports is an evidence-based multi-tiered framework focused on creating a positive school climate and promoting social competence for all learners. Positive Behavioral Interventions and Supports is often the behavioral strand in Multi-Tiered Systems of Support. It establishes systems within a school for proactively teaching and reinforcing social expectations to all students. Increasingly intensive supports are layered for students who have difficulty meeting expectations. Positive Behavioral Interventions and Supports is not a set program. It must be customized to align with values of each school community and "is not fully implemented until it is culturally responsive" (Leverson et al., 2021, p. 6). In recent years, Positive Behavioral Interventions and Supports has also integrated trauma-informed perspectives (Filter et al., 2022).
Social Emotional Learning (SEL)	Social emotional learning describes the acquisition of skills that promote healthy emotional responses and positive interpersonal relationships (McKown, 2019). Social emotional competence, like academic competence, requires instruction. Instruction in social emotional learning typically addresses five areas of competency: self-awareness, self-management, social awareness, relationship skills, and responsible decision making (Collaborative for Academic, Social, and Emotional Learning, 2020). Research demonstrates that students who participate in

RESEARCH-BASED PRACTICE	DEFINITION AND RELEVANCE
SEL (continued)	school-based social emotional learning demonstrate improved social and emotional skills, more positive attitudes, increased academic performance, and decreased behavioral concerns (Durlak et al., 2011). Strategies for social emotional learning can be embedded into Multi-Tiered Systems of Support and Positive Behavioral Interventions and Supports frameworks.
Culturally Responsive Practice	Culturally responsive practice, sometimes described as culturally responsive teaching or culturally responsive pedagogy, is a framework dedicated to ensuring that culturally, ethnically, and racially diverse learners have "equitable academic success" through learning environments that recognize and integrate their cultural assets (Bennouna et al., 2021, p. 3). Culturally responsive practice is relevant to academic instruction, social emotional learning, and positive behavior support. The integration of culturally responsive practice with Positive Behavioral Interventions and Supports is proposed to decrease disproportionate exclusionary discipline for students from diverse cultural backgrounds (Bastable et al., 2021).
Trauma-Informed Practice	Educators engaging in trauma-informed practice understand ways in which traumatic experiences impact individual learners and apply that knowledge to address learner needs (Carello & Butler, 2015). Educators who lack understanding of trauma may identify students' behavioral symptoms of trauma as non-compliance or challenging behavior and respond with punitive or exclusionary discipline (USDOE, 2021b). Trauma-informed educators develop strategies for proactively supporting students in the classroom and connecting students with more intensive supports when needed (Rishel et al., 2019). Trauma-informed practice can be integrated into Multi-Tiered Systems of Support and Positive Behavioral Interventions and Supports frameworks.

The invaluable role of collaboration in each of these practices is discussed in depth in Chapters 8 through 11. The chapters progress through topics in a way that mirrors the experiences of the school year. We open with a discussion of collaborative strategies for assessing students' social, emotional, and behavioral needs in Chapter 8. Chapter 9 provides guidance for co-instruction to create a positive and responsive classroom climate aligned with student needs. Chapter 10 documents collaborative strategies for intensifying intervention. Finally, Chapter 11 closes the third section with a discussion of collaboration for evaluating and reporting social, emotional, and behavioral outcomes.

Co-assessment to Create a Positive Classroom Climate for All Learners

8

Take a moment and think back to the weeks leading up to your very first day as a teacher in your own classroom. There's a pretty good chance that you spent a considerable amount of time thinking about how to create a welcoming learning environment. You may have considered decorations for the walls, arrangement of the furniture, books to include in your classroom library, or fun "getting to know you" activities for the first day of school. Your preparations were likely geared toward creating a positive classroom climate before you even met your students. There is a good reason for this. The term **school climate** describes the way members of a school community perceive the school in terms of safety, belongingness, collaboration, and engagement (U.S. Department of Education [USDOE], 2019). Schools with positive climates are associated with higher student achievement, increased graduation rates, better overall attendance, and greater teacher satisfaction than schools with negative climates (USDOE, 2019). Whether you understood this from reading research, or just by instinct, a positive classroom climate is probably something that you value as an educator.

Classroom climate is determined by more than the physical features of the space and the welcoming attitude of the teacher. The climate of a classroom is created by the norms, beliefs, routines, and experiences that are represented and enacted every day (S. B. Stillman et al., 2018). Positive climates develop through patterns of experience that make all members of the classroom community feel physically and emotionally safe, supported, valued, and respected. In recent years, educators have come to understand the value of Positive Behavioral Interventions and

Supports (PBIS) and social emotional learning for fostering a positive climate. Activities that encourage social emotional learning can be embedded into Positive Behavioral Interventions and Supports or provided as stand-alone instruction in schools where the Positive Behavioral Interventions and Supports framework is not in place. Instructional practices promoting social emotional learning often target competencies that are viewed as foundational to lifelong development for all learners, not just those who have disabilities (Collaborative for Academic, Social, and Emotional Learning, 2020).

Chapter Connections

See Chapters 9 and 10 for more on co-instruction for social emotional learning and individualized supports for behavior.

Effective Positive Behavioral Interventions and Supports and social emotional learning require understanding of learners as individuals and as members of communities. If educators are to create environments where everyone feels safe, valued, and respected, they must understand what those terms mean to each member of the classroom community. Failure to recognize the perspectives and experiences of students who are not from the dominant culture, or those who have experienced trauma, can lead to marginalization (Leverson et al., 2021; USDOE, 2021b). The practices of Positive Behavioral Interventions and Supports and social emotional learning are most effective when they are customized to build on the assets of the community and address needs that reflect community values (El Mallah, 2022). To build on these traits, educators must understand them. That brings us to the topic of this chapter: co-assessment to create a positive climate for all learners.

Assessment, as mentioned before, involves collecting information from formal or informal sources for the purpose of making educational decisions (Overton, 2015). Educators do this all the time! Think about how you know that students are engaged (or not engaged) in a lesson. How do you know your students' favorite video games, sports teams, or television shows? How do you know about their families and communities? These are just a few examples of assessment related to social, emotional, and behavioral factors that educators use on a regular basis.

The high-leverage practices provide guidance for co-assessment that leads to a positive classroom climate. The general education high-leverage practices encourage educators to *learn about students* **[GE_HLP12]**, *communicate with families* **[GE_HLP11]**, and *build respectful relationships* **[GE_HLP10]**. The special education high-leverage practices define actions for doing that, documenting the need to use ***multiple sources of information to develop under-standing of strengths and needs* [SE_HLP4]** and to ***collaborate with families to support student learning and secure services* [SE_HLP3]**. In this chapter we discuss specific strategies for co-assessment that set the stage for social, emotional, and behavioral growth for all students and contribute to a positive classroom climate. We start by considering identity.

The Role of Identity

Positive classroom climate occurs when *all* members of the community feel safe, valued, and respected. This applies to students and educators. Therefore, assessment for a positive classroom climate requires information about students *and* educators. In their work on culturally responsive practices for Positive Behavioral Interventions and Supports, Leverson and colleagues (2021) describe the need for identity awareness. Although identity has become a topic for social media banter, the concept is bigger and more important than any meme can convey. **Identity awareness** refers to understanding cultures, values, and histories of educators and students as well as the impact of those characteristics on classroom culture. Educators engaged in co-assessment for identity awareness will want to identify

- values shared by community members that can lead to common expectations;

- assets that students, family members, and educators bring to the classroom that can foster learning and engagement;

- needs that require special consideration; and

- potential mismatches in values or experiences that need to be addressed to ensure a positive climate for all learners.

Self-Assessment of Educator Identity

In Chapter 1, we talked about the value of self-awareness and collaborative discussion for establishing parity. Educators' self-awareness is also important for creating a positive and responsive climate because it promotes the development of educator identity awareness. Teachers, like all members of the classroom, have expectations about appropriate, comfortable, and productive social behavior based on their own personalities, biases, and experiences (Foster et al., 2020). In some cases, these expectations align with the values and needs of the other members of the classroom community. However, because classroom populations have become increasingly diverse while the teacher workforce has remained primarily white, female, and middle class (Foster et al., 2020), the risk of mismatched values and expectations is still present. Historically, educators in U.S. schools have struggled to meet academic and social emotional needs of learners from diverse cultural and linguistic backgrounds. This is evident in disproportionately high rates of exclusionary discipline (i.e., suspensions and expulsions), placement in restrictive educational settings (e.g., self-contained classrooms, alternative education programs), and eligibility for special education (M. R. Brown et al., 2019; National Center for Learning Disabilities, 2020).

If expectations and practices are to be truly responsive to the needs of students, it is important for educators to reflect on their identities and the impact they have on classroom practices. It can be valuable for teachers to critically examine their own beliefs and practices to identify potential areas of bias.

The Check It Out box identifies some guiding questions that can help educators examine their beliefs and practices for cultural responsiveness. Engaging in this type of self-reflection is hard work. It can be uncomfortable to recognize personal biases and difficult to change long-standing practices. Collaborative, growth-focused discussions with a trusted co-teacher or other colleague can be helpful in making the changes needed for a positive classroom climate.

Check It Out

Guiding Questions for Self-Reflection

- What are my expectations for how students and teachers interact?

- What are my expectations for how students interact with each other?

- How might expectations of my students, co-teachers, and other collaborative team members differ from my own expectations?

- What social, political, or cultural experiences may influence my expectations? (Foster et al., 2020)

In some cases, collaborative teams may wish to work toward understanding their individual and collective educator identities. Leverson and colleagues (2021) share an activity called "Staff Elements of Culture," which can be useful for individual reflection and collaborative discussion. In the activity, educators are invited to consider the values and expectations that they held in childhood for social interactions, such as appropriate language, proximity during conversation, and gender roles. They are then asked to describe how their values and expectations have changed over time and finally consider how their current values may differ from those of their students and community members. The goal of this activity is to look for shared community values and to identify potential areas of conflict that could have an impact on climate or equity.

Dive Deeper

The Staff Elements of Culture activity and other materials for culturally responsive Positive Behavioral Interventions and Supports can be found on the Center for PBIS website.

bit.ly/3xtX3hp

The Co-Teaching SHARE worksheet by Murawski and Dieker (2004) described in Chapter 3 is another helpful resource for this type of collaborative discussion. By examining hopes, expectations, and roles, instructors can discuss elements of their educator identities that impact collaboration. Collaborative self-assessment activities, such as the Staff Elements of Culture and the SHARE worksheet, can play an important role in creating a positive school climate. If the activities are not conducted at the school level, co-teachers and paraprofessionals who share students may find them to be beneficial for smaller group discussion. As staff proactively engage in concrete and purposeful work to acknowledge and address their own preferences, beliefs, and identity, a culture of psychological safety will be created to benefit both staff and students.

Co-assessment of Student Identity

In addition to awareness of educator identity, teachers must develop understanding of student identity. The factors that contribute to student expectations and needs for a positive climate are vast and interconnected. They include cultural, academic, and social diversity; prior learning experiences; family values; experiences of trauma; personality traits; and physical characteristics. Each of these is relevant to the formation of student identity. When educators understand student identity, they can "validate the values of the students, families, and communities they serve" (Leverson et al., 2021, p. 9), thereby creating a positive school climate.

Student identity can be understood at the community level and at the individual level. **Community identity** encompasses shared values or experiences of groups, while **student identity** describes characteristics, values, and experiences of the individual. Educators can gather, analyze, and interpret information related to the school, groups of learners in a classroom, and individual students as part of their work to **_learn about students_** **[GE_HLP12]** and **_build respectful relationships_** **[GE_HLP10]**. While assessment is traditionally performed by school staff, co-assessment with a broad range of community stakeholders ensures that diverse perspectives are sought and understood.

Family or community liaisons (sometimes called "cultural liaisons") can play a valuable role in the co-assessment process, leading to a more responsive and positive climate (McLeskey et al., 2017). Liaisons are team members (staff or volunteer) who represent the diverse cultures and languages of a school community and seek to promote equitable school–family–community engagement (Jacques & Villegas, 2018). Liaisons can assist in developing and distributing assessment tools and ensuring that these tools are culturally responsive. The liaisons can also provide valuable insight when interpreting data. By engaging with family members, liaisons, and other community members, we use *multiple sources of information to develop understanding of strengths and needs* **[SE_HLP4]**; we also *collaborate with families* **[GE_HLP11]** *to support student learning and secure services* **[SE_HLP3]**. Schools that do not already have Family Centers or identified community liaisons should consider creating them to help build a collaborative, inclusive culture.

Co-assessment of School-Level Community Identity

School-level assessment refers to the collection of information for the purpose of *identifying patterns* **[GE_HLP4]** and trends related to the total school population that may impact community identity. School climate surveys are an example of school-level assessment because they are distributed to all members of the school community (e.g., staff, family members, students) for the purpose of understanding community perceptions about the climate and culture of a school. Data related to disciplinary referrals, suspensions, and attendance can also be used for school-level assessment when the information is analyzed for overall patterns, rather than for information about individual students. Recently, many schools have begun to adopt universal screenings of social, emotional, and behavioral well-being to support proactive intervention within Multi-Tiered Systems of Support or Positive Behavioral Interventions and Supports (Kilgus et al., 2018). Several validated screening tools exist for schoolwide use, including the Social, Academic, and Emotional Risk Screener (Kilgus et al., 2018), Social Skills Improvement System (Elliott & Gresham, 2008), and Student Risk Screening Scale—Internalizing and Externalizing (Lane et al., 2016).

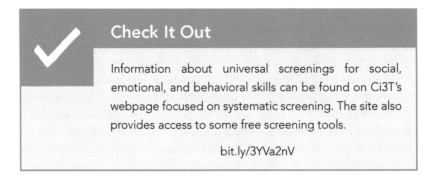

Check It Out

Information about universal screenings for social, emotional, and behavioral skills can be found on Ci3T's webpage focused on systematic screening. The site also provides access to some free screening tools.

bit.ly/3YVa2nV

Each of these tools is designed to quickly and systematically assess the entire student population of a school (or classroom) to identify young people who may need additional supports. The data obtained via these tools can also be used by collaborative teams to identify overall patterns related to student social, emotional, and behavioral competencies.

School-level assessment becomes more meaningful when it is collaboratively planned and interpreted. Administrators, educators in various roles, family liaisons, students, and family members may have valuable input in developing or selecting assessment formats to ensure that acquired information represents a broad range of school stakeholders. Many school divisions across the United States have established multidisciplinary stakeholder teams for the purpose of using data to promote equitable and inclusive school environments. We see a variety of names for these teams, including "School Site Council," "Equity Team," and "School or District Inclusion Committee." Teams such as these have the important role of analyzing school-level data to identify varied and inequitable experiences of groups within the school community. These teams can help identify important groupings for data analysis and guide the discussion about inequities to focus on system needs, rather than blaming groups or individuals (Leverson et al., 2021).

It is important to understand that data from school-level assessment do not measure specific social, emotional, or behavioral competencies. The trends in school-level data provide information about potential social emotional learning needs (McKown, 2019) and the strengths that can promote social emotional learning when integrated into the school culture. Collaborative interpretation of these data guide Tier 1 Positive Behavioral Interventions and Supports and social emotional learning strategies. The Connecting to Practice vignette provides an example of co-assessment completed by a School Site Council as they work with school climate data.

Connecting to Practice

Co-assessment of School Community Identity for Tier 1 Social Emotional Learning Supports

Teachers, administrators, and parents at Alexander Middle School had concerns about the overall well-being of students as they returned to in-person learning following the disruptions caused by the COVID-19 pandemic. The staff felt that they were dealing with levels of social

(Continued)

(Continued)

emotional needs that they had not previously experienced. However, they did not know how to quantify the differences that they felt or to determine what supports might be necessary. School leaders brought the concerns to the School Site Council, a multidisciplinary stakeholder team focused on school climate and equity. After investigating screening options, the Council determined that the Student Risk Screening Scale for Internalizing and Externalizing Behaviors (Lane et al., 2016) would be a useful tool for assessing schoolwide needs and it would allow the team to identify any students in need of individualized support. The administrator arranged for a brief training on the assessment to occur during a regularly scheduled staff meeting. Following the training, all teachers were asked to complete the rating scale for the students in their homeroom class. Once the screenings were completed, the data were analyzed by the School Site Council. The data revealed schoolwide concerns for internalizing behaviors, with over 80% of the students scoring in the moderate range of risk or higher. Further analysis revealed that peer rejection, anxiety, and depression were frequently marked as areas of concern on the screening tool. With this information in mind, the School Site Council recognized that Tier 1 supports within the school would need to be more focused on these specific social emotional needs. The School Site Council established a subcommittee that included the school counselors, school psychologist, social worker, as well as community mental health specialists to develop a plan for meeting these needs. The team planned to rescreen quarterly using the same tool to monitor progress toward meeting student needs.

Co-assessment of Classroom Community Identity

Class-level assessment, as it relates to identity and climate, is designed to identify specific assets, competencies, and challenges that are present in a classroom. Information about collective values and experiences of the group can be obtained through class activities, such as the co-taught lesson presented in Worksheet 8.1. In this lesson, students connect their own experiences and wishes for school climate to those of a character in a book. Co-assessment occurs with the co-teachers who develop the activity and monitor student responses, but the students themselves are also actively engaged in evaluating their collective wishes for how they want to feel when they are at school.

Worksheet 8.1

Co-teaching Lesson Plan for Social Emotional Learning and Language Arts

Subject Area: social emotional learning/language arts

Grade Level: 4

Content Standards: Students will "discuss and define developmentally appropriate core ethical and performance principles and their importance" with an emphasis on respect, fairness, kindness, and treating others as they wish to be treated (Kansas State Board of Education, 2018, p. 5).

Common Core RL 4.3: Describe in depth a character, setting, or event in a story or drama, drawing on specific details in the text (e.g., a character's thoughts, words, or actions).

Lesson Objective: Students will describe their values for school and classroom climate.

Essential Questions: How do we want to feel when we are at school? What choices can we make to influence how our school and classroom feel?

Key Vocabulary: community, positive feelings, uncomfortable feelings

Pre-assessment: N/A

Materials: Book *The Invisible Boy* by Trudy Ludwig, two sticky notes per student (two colors), construction paper, markers/crayons/colored pencils, laptops or tablets for individual student use

(Continued)

LESSON	CO-TEACHING APPROACH (CAN SELECT MORE THAN ONE)	TIME	GENERAL EDUCATION TEACHER / SPECIAL SERVICE PROVIDER	CONSIDERATIONS (MAY INCLUDE UDL OPTIONS, DIFFERENTIATION NEEDS, AND DATA COLLECTION STRATEGIES)
Beginning (may include Opening; Warm-Up; Review; Anticipatory Set)	☐ One Teach, One Support ☐ Parallel ☐ Alternative ☐ Station ☑ Team Teaching	5 min.	1. As students settle into their seats, **Teacher B** tells **Teacher A** that they had an awkward experience at a party the other night. They felt like everyone at the party knew each other and the teacher felt somewhat left out and awkward. **Teacher A** says they've felt that way before, too, and asks the class if anyone else has ever felt uncomfortable in a situation. 2. Together, both teachers introduce the purpose of the lesson: to develop an understanding of what the classroom community wants the school and classroom to feel like and to discuss specific actions that students and teachers can take to create that feeling. Explain that the book *The Invisible Boy* provides an example of how a young boy, Brian, feels at school and how his feelings are impacted by his peers. Tell students: "We will use the story to connect to our own ideas and experiences" (Team Teaching).	Use sound amplification device for Sarah. Either teacher can sign Beatte's Check-In, Check-Out (CICO) form at the beginning of a period. Display assigned groups and station rotations on the board.
Middle (may include Instruction; Checking for Understanding; Independent or Group Practice)	☑ One Teach, One Support ☐ Parallel ☐ Alternative ☐ Station ☐ Team Teaching	15 min.	3. **Teacher A** passes out two different-colored sticky notes (e.g., yellow and blue) to each student. **Teacher B** asks students to write on the yellow note a word that describes how they <u>want to feel</u> at school, and on the blue sticky note a word that describes a feeling they <u>don't want to have</u> at school. 4. **Teacher B** collects sticky notes and sorts them into two columns on the board as **Teacher A** gets the document projector and book ready.	Teachers circulate and assist students in writing or spelling words, as needed. Use document projector to display book clearly for all students while reading.

LESSON	CO-TEACHING APPROACH (CAN SELECT MORE THAN ONE)	TIME	GENERAL EDUCATION TEACHER	SPECIAL SERVICE PROVIDER	CONSIDERATIONS (MAY INCLUDE UDL OPTIONS, DIFFERENTIATION NEEDS, AND DATA COLLECTION STRATEGIES)
			5. Before **Teacher A** starts reading the book *The Invisible Boy* to the class, **Teacher B** advises students to pay attention to how the author's word choice and the illustrator's images convey the way Brian feels. **Teacher A** reads aloud, stopping on pages 11 and 12, where Brian draws during "choosing time," as **Teacher B** circulates.		Teachers circulate to encourage discussion, paying specific attention to students with communication differences; specific word choices are added to Jason's AAC device.
			6. After reading, **Teacher A** asks students in groups of four to discuss the following questions: a) How does Brian feel at school? b) What words or images from the text convey that idea? c) What causes Brian to feel that way? **Teacher B** circulates.		Directions for stations are on table tents for students to see and read.
			7. **Teacher A** asks groups to share key words that describe how Brian feels. **Teacher B** adds the words to the existing sticky note columns.		
			8. **Teacher B** reads the remainder of *The Invisible Boy*. **Teacher A** advises students to pay attention to how and why Brian's feelings change.		
			9. Ask students in groups of four to discuss the following questions: a) How do Brian's feelings change as the story progresses? b) What words or images from the text show the change? c) What causes Brian's feelings to change?		
			10. **Teacher B** asks groups to share the feelings that Brian seems to feel as the story progresses. **Teacher A** adds these words to the sticky note columns. Ask students what made Brian's feelings change.		
			11. **Teacher A** prepares students for Station Teaching activities, reviewing directions as **Teacher B** divides them into three groups by putting names on the board. Tell students: "The purpose of the stations will be to use examples from the story and our own experiences to define how we want our classroom to feel and to identify behaviors that we can use to make our classroom feel that way."		

(Continued)

LESSON	CO-TEACHING APPROACH (CAN SELECT MORE THAN ONE)	TIME	GENERAL EDUCATION TEACHER	SPECIAL SERVICE PROVIDER	CONSIDERATIONS (MAY INCLUDE UDL OPTIONS, DIFFERENTIATION NEEDS, AND DATA COLLECTION STRATEGIES)
	☐ One Teach, One Support ☐ Parallel ☐ Alternative ☑ **Station** ☐ Team	35 min. (10 min. per station)	Work with the **yellow** sticky notes that describe how students <u>may want to feel</u> at school. 12. Briefly discuss some of the common words that were used. 13. Ask each student to choose up to three words that best describe how they want to feel at school. 14. Have construction paper, drawing materials, and computers available. Ask students to select a way to show <u>positive examples</u> of desired class behaviors. They may choose to create a poster, a slide presentation, or a roleplay, or to write a story. Other options are available if students get approval from teachers.	Work with the **blue** sticky notes that describe how students <u>do not want to feel</u> at school. 12. Briefly discuss some of the common words that were used. 13. Ask each student to choose up to three words that describe how they don't want to feel at school. 14. Have construction paper, drawing materials, and computers available. Ask students to select a way to show <u>non-examples</u> of undesirable class behaviors. They may choose to create a poster, a slide presentation, or a roleplay, or to write a story. Other options are available if students get approval from teachers.	Different content Give sufficient time for Jason to participate with AAC. Be sure that Savannah participates, as she is extremely shy. Images/descriptions can be from student experiences or drawn from the story in the book. Students with fine motor or print disabilities may choose to complete the activity on paper or using a presentation application (such as Google Slides or PowerPoint).

LESSON	CO-TEACHING APPROACH (CAN SELECT MORE THAN ONE)	TIME	GENERAL EDUCATION TEACHER	SPECIAL SERVICE PROVIDER	CONSIDERATIONS (MAY INCLUDE UDL OPTIONS, DIFFERENTIATION NEEDS, AND DATA COLLECTION STRATEGIES)
			Independent station: Students will choose one of the following prompts for journaling: • Describe your best or worst day at school. • Describe your wish for this school year. • How did Brian and Justin help each other to have a positive experience at school?		Students may write and/or draw their responses in their journals. Students with fine motor or print disabilities may use word-processing tools with word-prediction software.
End (may include Closing; Assessments; Extension of the Lesson)	☐ One Teach, One Support ☐ Parallel ☐ Alternative ☐ Station ☑ **Team**	5 min.	15. Together, the teachers ask students to return to their desks; they invite students to share their creations within their small groups of four. 16. Together, the teachers close the lesson by summarizing common ideas for how students do and do not want to feel at school. Tell students that their creations and journals will be used to help define class expectations. Invite students to indicate if they want their creations shared on the hallway wall. They can put a checkmark on the back of their work if they want it to be shared or an X if they do not want it to be shared.		After collecting creations and journals, teachers will read them to identify common themes as well as individual concerns that need to be addressed through class or schoolwide social emotional learning. More specific needs can be met in future classes through Alternative Teaching.

Bottom of Form

Collaboration that aims to understand the community identity of a class-room can also occur between educators and family members. Remember that both the general education and special education high-leverage practices encourage ***communicating with families* [GE_HLP11] *to support student learning and secure services* [SE_HLP3]**. Traditional parent–teacher conferences are one way to engage families. However, other options may provide deeper collaborative engagement. Jacques and Villegas (2018) describe the use of group conferences as a supplement to traditional parent–teacher conferences. Group confer-ences, which include family members of all students in a class, occur multiple times a year and are designed to foster the mutual exchange of information between family members and educators and to build rela-tionships among all stakeholders. Group conferences focus on under-standing social emotional expectations in the community and in the school setting as well as on shared goals for student learning. Liaisons can support group conferences by sharing information about the process with community members, serving as meeting facilitators, and ensuring that needed resources (such as interpreters or childcare) are available during the conferences (Jacques & Villegas, 2018).

Understanding the community identity of the classroom through class-level co-assessment can help educators to create a respectful and accept-ing environment where students feel represented and valued. This may lead to better representation of student cultures and experiences in classroom materials as well as to practices that are built on family and community strengths. Classroom identity guides the refinement of Tier 1 social, emotional, and behavioral strategies to address specific assets and needs of students in the classroom. Information obtained through class-level co-assessment can also be used to identify students in need of Tier 2 or Tier 3 supports. The following Connecting to Practice vignette shows how group conferencing can help teachers better under-stand their classroom identity.

Connecting to Practice

Group Conferences in Action

Ms. Dessyatova and Mr. Drew are both new teachers in the school and community where they co-teach a fifth-grade class. They recognize the value of better understanding their students and communities in order to create a responsive classroom climate. Ms. Dessyatova asked Mrs. Kanaan, the school–family liaison, for suggestions about how to learn more. Mrs. Kanaan suggested that Ms. Dessyatova and Mr. Drew plan Back-to-School night in the form of a group conference rather than a presentation. She shared that a group conference invites collaborative input from all family members and that Back-to-School night would be a good opportunity for an initial group conference, because family attendance tends to be high on that evening. With Mrs. Kanaan's support, Ms. Dessyatova and Mr. Drew sent information to the families of all their students about the plan for Back-to-School night. Families were encouraged to think about their hopes and concerns for the coming school year, so the discussion could be centered around family and community goals.

Through the group conference, Ms. Dessyatova and Mr. Drew came to realize that the students in their classroom had very diverse cultural backgrounds. Many families wished to share experiences of their own cultures with the school community. The families hoped that some of their holidays and customs would be recognized alongside the holidays traditionally acknowledged in U.S. public schools. Some families also expressed concern about homework. Many reported that they didn't understand how math was being taught and they didn't know how to help their children with math homework.

Ms. Dessyatova and Mr. Drew recognized that the initial group conference provided surface-level information about their students and communities, but they were pleased to lay the foundation for positive collaboration with families. As a result of the conference, they worked to ensure that their classroom library included books representative of the diverse cultures of their students. They also began planning for ways to integrate multicultural celebrations into their curriculum. Additionally, they realized that the math curriculum was causing some stress and concern for families and students. Therefore, they began to work on a plan for helping families understand the math strategies being taught. The co-teachers planned ongoing collaboration with Mrs. Kanaan to engage families through group conferences and other forms of communication.

Co-assessment of Individual Student Identity

Co-assessment at the student level is focused on understanding characteristics, experiences, and values of a single student and their family members. Student-level assessment goes beyond examining *what* students do; it explores *why* they do it. Several sources of information can support understanding student identity. For example, co-teachers, administrators, and other school professionals can find important information by reviewing educational records. IEPs, Section 504 Plans, and other education plans provide detailed information about learning characteristics and experiences.

Because these records can be extensive, a divide-and-conquer co-assessment plan can be helpful. Collaborative team members will want to identify specific types of information that they are looking for. They may decide to develop specific questions to answer through the file review and to identify sources of information that can usually be found in the records. (Possible questions for a collaborative file review are listed in the text box with potential sources of information in parentheses.) Additionally, team members will want to have a plan for sharing and collaboratively evaluating the information for the purpose of understanding each student's strengths and needs.

Collaborative File Review Questions

1. Collectively, do the documents suggest that the student has had a generally positive, neutral, or negative school experience? (see awards/commendations, disciplinary referrals, home–school communication)

2. What academic successes, challenges, and/or supports are documented? (see report cards, transcripts, IEPs, 504 Plans, intervention plans, test scores)

3. What social, emotional, or behavioral successes, challenges, or supports are documented? (see awards/commendations, disciplinary referrals, suspensions/expulsions, home–school communication, intervention plans, attendance records)

4. What is the overall nature of documented communication with the family? Is it positive, neutral, negative, or nonexistent?

5. What family preferences are documented related to participation and engagement? (see enrollment records or teacher notes)

While information from a record review can be valuable, the best way to truly understand an individual's identity is to engage them and the people who know them best. Students can be engaged through informal interviews, interest inventories, or dialogue journals. There are countless "getting to know you" questionnaires and interest inventories available on the internet. These can be easily adapted to work with different grade levels, skill levels, and communication systems to be used in the first weeks of school.

Another strategy that provides a deep and ongoing assessment of student identity is the **dialogue journal**. Dialogue journals are designed to foster authentic communication between individual students and their teachers (J. Stillman et al., 2014). They have been effectively used with students across grade and skill levels, including emergent bilingual students and students with disabilities (Regan, 2003). When using dialogue journals, teachers and students engage in two-way written communication, much like writing letters to each other. Unlike traditional classroom writing, dialogue journals do not address classwide prompts. Teachers and students ask and answer questions and introduce new ideas to one another. Spelling and grammar conventions are not the focus and are not graded. However, teachers may specify that certain elements be included in the journals, such as a greeting and closing, minimum number of sentences, and responses to any posed questions (Regan, 2003). Any criteria that are specified apply to both the teacher and the student. Dialogue journals have been shown to foster relationship building and social emotional learning while simultaneously promoting literacy development, making them a particularly beneficial co-assessment tool (J. Stillman et al., 2014).

Adult collaboration can be helpful in using interest inventories, student interviews, and dialogue journals. The Alternative Teaching model can be used with co-teachers, teachers and paraprofessionals, or teachers and volunteers to provide time for more individualized student meetings. For example, one instructor might work with a large group of students, doing a class warm-up or review activity, while the other one completes small-group or one-on-one check-ins with students.

Station Teaching could be used with one teacher circulating and overseeing multiple independent student groups to provide an opportunity for the other teacher to read and respond to dialogue journals. Or, depending on the age of students and activities provided, both co-teachers could engage with the dialogue journals as students work independently in stations. Co-teachers may want to have designated student groups that they work with, dividing the students in half randomly or based on young people's interests. Remember that in co-teaching all educators have shared responsibility for all students, therefore the division should not be based on special education and general education, or any other special service. Additionally, with the focus on shared responsibility, it is important that collaborating adults discuss the obtained information so it can be used efficiently. There may also be times when teachers need to collaborate with other school professionals, such as school counselors or social workers, to determine how to respond to information shared by students.

Individualized connections with family members can also serve as a powerful co-assessment tool for understanding student identity. Parent–teacher conferences are the most traditional format for these engagements. While much less common, home visits provide another option for developing a deep understanding of student identity. Both meetings provide an opportunity to acquire information about a student that might not be available through any other assessment method. However, both strategies also have the potential to perpetuate deficit-focused beliefs about students and their families if they are not applied in collaborative and culturally responsive ways (Park & Paulick, 2021). Some key factors to promote collaborative and culturally responsive family–educator meetings have been identified through research on family engagement and home visits. We share these key factors below.

Family–educator meetings occur as dialogues

Meetings between educators and family members, whether they occur in the school, home, or elsewhere in the community, should affirm parity between the participants. Parity is established through a dialogue. Educators can learn about student and family values by listening to what family members share. Educators promote collaboration and engagement by actively listening, asking questions, and inviting family members to share ideas—not just giving the families a mini-lecture on their own child! When educators share information, they should balance discussions of student successes and challenges with opportunities for growth.

Family–educator meetings are flexible and adaptive

When planning meetings, it is important to be mindful of time, location, and communication needs. Conferences or home visits should be scheduled at mutually agreeable times. A variety of participation options, including in-person meetings, phone calls, and videoconferences, may help increase family engagement. Liaisons may be helpful in coordinating needs, such as childcare or interpreters. It is critically important that interpreters be used when language differences are present, rather than asking students to interpret meetings for their families. Culturally responsive educators will approach meetings with awareness of their own biases; they will actively seek to set those aside to view students and families with different cultural experiences through an assets-based lens (Park & Paulick, 2021).

Initial meetings are focused on sharing mutual aspirations

The Parent–Teacher Home Visits model advocates structuring the first visit around the theme of "hopes and dreams" (Venkateswaran et al., 2018). The focus on mutual aspirations centers the meeting, whether at home or at school, on the student and promotes collaboration toward a shared goal. Educators are encouraged to listen to family members first, before sharing their own hopes and dreams for the student. This foundational understanding can be used to connect to student interests and family values, as educators establish practices for social emotional learning. Additionally, any future concerns related to the student can be framed in the context of working toward the shared goals.

The three factors described above are applicable to both conferences and home visits. The Parent–Teacher Home Visits model (Venkateswaran et al., 2018) adds a few specific factors. First, educators are encouraged to visit in pairs. This promotes a sense of comfort for teachers as they meet families in new settings. While this is an obvious dynamic for co-teachers, even instructors who teach alone should find a collaborating partner with whom to visit homes; logical partners include the school counselor, psychologist, special education teachers, and coaches. Going in teams also provides an opportunity for educators to reflect and debrief after the visit, sharing their possibly diverse frames of reference.

Another factor that is particularly important for home visits is administrative support. Administrators need to ensure that educators have time for home visits and are compensated for any visits that occur outside of contract hours. This administrative support demonstrates a commitment to the process of home visiting and the value of co-assessing student identity. The knowledge acquired through educator–family meetings and other forms of co-assessment ultimately lead to positive classroom and school climates.

Summary

Classroom climate is a result of daily experiences of *all members* of the classroom community. Classrooms in which students and educators feel safe, valued, and respected are associated with positive academic and social emotional learning outcomes. Creating these positive climates requires deep understanding of students and educators as individuals and members of communities. Co-assessment strategies allow educators to ***learn about students* [GE_HLP12]** using ***multiple sources of information to develop understanding of strengths and needs* [SE_HLP4]**. Through these collaborative actions, educators ***build respectful relationships* [GE_HLP10]** and ***collaborate with families to support learning and secure services* [SE_HLP3]**.

Co-instruction for Social Emotional Learning

9

If you walk into two classrooms in any school on any given day, you are likely to see differences in the learning environment. You may see students working quietly, consistently raising their hands to speak, and following highly structured routines. Alternatively, you may hear the busy hum of students talking and see numerous on-the-fly adaptations. Both environments, and the countless variations between them, can promote academic and social emotional learning as long as all members of the classroom community feel safe, valued, and supported. Creating a positive and responsive classroom environment requires *teaching* social, emotional, and behavioral expectations in the same way that we teach academic expectations.

The high-leverage practices related to social emotional learning will come as no surprise to any practicing educator. Teachers are advised to establish **a consistent, organized, and respectful learning environment [SE_HLP7]** using **norms and routines for organization [GE_HLP8]**, **discourse, and work [GE_HLP5]** and to explicitly **teach social skills [SE_HLP 9]**. Through these practices **community expectations are established and maintained [GE_HLP7]**. These concepts are widely touted in the field of education and are likely familiar to novice and veteran educators alike. Positive Behavioral Interventions and Supports programs are built around teaching and reinforcing expected behaviors and routines throughout the school environment (Lane et al., 2019). Both general and special education teachers identify clear expectations and positive behavioral management plans as being essential practices that they are comfortable implementing to address social, emotional, and behavioral needs (Gable et al., 2012).

So, it seems like everything must be clear. No need to dedicate a book chapter to this topic, right? Well, it might be worth a second look. Here's the challenge. Even with the knowledge that educators have about classwide practices for positive behavior supports and social emotional learning, many students are not having their needs addressed or are experiencing a mismatch between their needs and educators' actions. In essence, our understanding of the practices and our effective implementation of the practices don't always line up.

Exclusionary discipline practices are a particular concern. These practices remove students from learning environments briefly (e.g., when a student is sent to the office) or for an extended period of time (e.g., suspensions or expulsions). They have a negative impact on academic progress and are ineffective at improving student behavior, yet they continue to be used extensively in public schools (Nese et al., 2021). An additional concern is the continued evidence that exclusionary discipline practices are disproportionately used with students of color, students with disabilities, and students from low socioeconomic status backgrounds (Nese et al., 2021; Sandomierski et al., 2022).

While most educators have good intentions, traditional preparation for classroom management insufficiently addresses the dynamics of culturally diverse learning environments (Moreno, 2021). This may lead educators to respond to behaviors that are outside of their own cultural expectations in ways that escalate student emotional and behavioral responses. Further, educators who don't recognize behavioral symptoms of trauma often utilize responses that intensify existing stressors (Rishel et al., 2019). These escalating responses may lead to exclusionary discipline, exacerbating the students' social, emotional, and behavioral needs instead of meeting them (Moreno, 2021).

In order to address these issues, it is important for educators to implement equitable classroom management practices through Positive Behavioral Interventions and Supports and to systematically embed social emotional learning into the classroom. The key word in that last sentence is *equitable*, meaning each student gets what they need.

Chapter Connections

Creating an inclusive, supportive, and culturally responsive climate is important. For strategies to create it, review Chapter 8.

In Chapter 8 we discussed co-assessment strategies for understanding what a positive and responsive classroom looks like based on strengths and assets of the community members. Here, we discuss how to bring that vision to reality by systematically teaching social emotional learning in ways that prepare young people for interactions in the classroom and beyond.

Student engagement in co-construction of social emotional learning is an important aspect of responsive instruction. However, it requires educators to be truly open to learning about and including elements of social emotional learning that diverge from their own norms. Further, as collaborating educators co-instruct elements of social emotional learning, they need to ensure that students receive consistent information. Young people may become confused by mixed messages from educators. A positive climate emerges when everyone knows expectations and applies them consistently.

Co-construction of Knowledge With Restorative Practices

Before digging deeper into co-instruction for social emotional learning, we want to share another framework that engages students in creating collective understanding of productive social emotional behaviors. **Restorative practices**, sometimes called "restorative discipline practices," are derived from restorative justice in the legal system. The intention of restorative justice is to shift from a focus on punitive consequences and toward repairing harm. In the school setting, **proactive restorative practices** are used to teach social skills and promote relationship building between and among students, educators, and family members. **Reactive restorative practices** are used for problem solving and repairing harm caused by wrongdoing or violation of social expectations (Garnett et al., 2022). As such, proactive restorative practices fit nicely into Tier 1 of Multi-Tiered Systems of Support or Positive Behavioral Interventions and Supports, while reactive restorative practices tend to be offered as Tier 2 or Tier 3 supports. Restorative practices include such activities as focused instruction in communication skills, use of affective language to communicate feelings and needs, peer mediation, student conferences, and restorative circles (Vincent et al., 2021).

Restorative circles are a hallmark feature of restorative practices. In these structured group meetings, participants sit in a circle and discuss a specific topic. A facilitator, often the teacher, *leads the discussion* **[GE_HLP1]** ensuring that everyone has an opportunity to be heard. A talking piece is passed around the circle, serving as a visible indicator of whose turn it is to speak. Proactive circles generally include the whole class. Reactive circles involve people who were somehow impacted by an incident or those who can offer support. Proactive and reactive circles are both powerful tools for engaging students in the co-construction of social emotional learning. Circles and other restorative practices integrate well with culturally responsive and trauma-informed practices due to the common emphasis on identifying and addressing unmet needs (Donaldson & Park, 2019).

Co-instruction that combines social emotional learning with restorative practices fosters collaboration among educators and students. In fact, teachers may find that collaborating with a school counselor, psychologist, or social worker may help them implement restorative practices. Co-teachers may opt to run a restorative circle together to ensure that different opinions and perspectives are heard or to use Alternative Teaching so that one teacher can run a reactive circle with a small group while the other teacher continues to engage the large group. The Connecting to Practice vignette found later in this chapter (page 178) documents the use of a restorative circle to engage students in resolving a problem related to unmet needs and classroom expectations.

Expectations

There has long been an understanding that students need to know what is allowed and expected in their classrooms. Traditionally, classroom discipline focused on rules that defined what students should or should not do. Violating rules resulted in punishment, which was intended to thwart future rule-breaking behavior (Lester et al., 2017). Below are examples of typical rules from the late 1800s.

One-Room Schoolhouse Rules
From the 1870s

1. Obey your elders.

2. Speak only when spoken to.

3. Idleness is sinful.

4. Busy hands make a quiet mouth.

5. Cleanliness is next to Godliness.

Source: Elkhart County Parks (2020).

As educators moved to more positive and proactive forms of classroom management with the Positive Behavioral Interventions and Supports movement, rules shifted to expectations. **Expectations** differ from rules in that they proactively set guidelines for responsible and productive behavior across settings (Lester et al., 2017). Expectations reflect the core values of the school and classroom community, as established through the co-assessment process. Three to five positively worded expectations are considered ideal. Schools using Positive Behavioral Interventions and Supports often establish schoolwide expectations around themes such as respect, responsibility, safety, preparedness, and collaboration. Schoolwide expectations are then translated into more specific expectations for different school settings, including classrooms, often using a tool called a "Behavioral Expectations Matrix." Sample Behavioral Expectation Matrices for elementary and secondary classrooms are provided in Tables 9.1 and 9.2. The class or schoolwide expectations are in the first column. The subsequent columns include **behavioral indicators** that tell students what the expectations look and sound like for specific settings or activities.

TABLE 9.1   Elementary Behavioral Expectations Matrix

	CLASSROOM	INDEPENDENT WORK	GROUP WORK
Be Responsible	• Use school materials safely and correctly • Follow directions • Clean up after yourself	• Do your best work • Ask for help when you need it • Choose a distraction-free workspace	• Do your part • Listen for transitions
Be Respectful	• Keep hands and feet to yourself • Listen when others are speaking • Follow directions	• Work quietly • Stay in your workspace	• Listen to others' ideas • Share materials • Give others personal space
Be Engaged	• Participate actively	• Use technology for learning • Stay focused (or refocus) on your work	• Share your ideas • Ask and answer questions

TABLE 9.2   Secondary Behavioral Expectations Matrix

	CLASSROOM	INDEPENDENT WORK	GROUP WORK
Be Responsible	• Take ownership of your choices • Bring required materials to class • Keep our classroom clean and organized	• Plan for due dates • Use strategies to stay focused • Complete assignments to the best of your abilities	• Contribute to the group outcome • Collaborate and problem solve • Provide thoughtful feedback in support of group goals
Be Respectful	• Honor our strengths and differences • Use polite language, tone, and actions • Follow directions	• Work quietly • Return materials when finished	• Listen to others' ideas • Provide a rationale for your opinions
Be Engaged	• Identify problems, resolve conflicts appropriately, restore relationships • Participate actively	• Use technology appropriately • Use time efficiently	• Participate actively • Ask and answer questions

Notice that, while the expectations in the two matrices are the same, the behavioral indicators are different. The behavioral indicators are customized to the learners and settings. When schoolwide expectations exist, teachers collaborate with students to define what each of the expectations looks like in their classroom. In schools that are not implementing schoolwide Positive Behavioral Interventions and Supports, individual teachers may collaborate with students and family members to identify expectations, then collaborate with students to define them. In all cases, systematic instruction is crucial to ensure that all students understand expectations and know how to demonstrate them. In responsive classrooms, educators are purposeful in teaching expectations through modeling, practice, and positive reinforcement. The Team Teaching approach is perfect for this!

When individualization is needed, expectations are customized to ensure an equitable and responsive climate. For example, the expectation of working quietly may look different for a student who has vocal tics. Similarly, students with attention difficulties may use any number of tools that differ from those needed by their peers to demonstrate engagement and stay focused. In classrooms with an equity mindset, students and teachers recognize and accept that everyone gets what they need.

Just as the posting of expectations should establish a positive and supportive environment, so too should the process of identifying consequences. Traditional posters related to rules and consequences identify infractions and what will happen if you break the rules. However, students are rarely treated to information that lets them know what will happen if they *follow* the rules! As teachers co-instruct students about the class norms and expectations, this is the ideal time to also reveal the positive outcomes associated with meeting these expectations. Examples and non-examples of class expectations and consequences are offered in the Check It Out box.

Check It Out

NON-EXAMPLE ☹		EXAMPLE ☺	
RULES	**CONSEQUENCES**	**EXPECTATIONS**	**CONSEQUENCES**
No chewing gum. No calling out. Bring your own materials to class. Stay in your seat. No talking.	1st infraction: Warning. 2nd infraction: Call home. 3rd infraction: Sent to office.	Enjoy food and gum outside of class. Be respectful of others. Be responsible. Be engaged.	Infractions may include warnings, individual conferences, calls home, contracts, etc. Meeting expectations may include smiles, positive calls home, good grades, stickers, reduced homework, more friends, happy teachers, etc.

Icon source: iStock.com/in8finity

Routines

When we think about all aspects that need to be managed to ensure that a classroom is safe, respectful, and efficient, three to five expectations do not seem to be enough. Most teachers, when asked, could come up with 50 expectations! Clearly, though, that would be overwhelming. How, then, do we help students engage in the safe and respectful behaviors that help learning occur? This is where routines come in. *Organizational routines* **[GE_HLP8]** are geared toward managing time, space, and materials (TeachingWorks, 2019). They are consistent procedures for common tasks and activities in a classroom. Organizational routines create predictability and structure, and reduce challenging behavior (Missouri Positive Behavior Supports, 2014). Routines that provide structured opportunities for choice are also supportive of a universally designed classroom. Many students with disabilities require the structure, while the flexibility provides opportunities for differentiation and multiple means of engagement. Once organizational routines are learned, their use allows teachers and students to devote cognitive energy to learning concepts rather than managing logistics.

Routines for discourse **[GE_HLP5]** are also important. These are content-driven practices for constructing and sharing knowledge (TeachingWorks, 2019). They demonstrate the interaction between academic and social emotional learning. Routines for discourse integrate class expectations into independent and collaborative learning behaviors. Some examples of routines that clearly integrate academic and social emotional competencies include asking students to provide evidence for an opinion, teaching them to analyze sources looking for the authors' purpose, and expecting all members of the classroom to express disagreement in a respectful way. On a simpler scale, group learning behaviors, such as hand raising or student discussions using Think-Pair-Share, are also examples of routines for discourse. Regardless of the complexity, these skills need to be clearly defined and systematically taught. Teachers cannot and should not assume that students at any age come to class with the same skills, expectations, or understandings.

Co-instruction of Expectations

The concept of **backward design** holds that the most effective instruction is developed with the end goal in mind (Wiggins & McTighe, 2005). This is true for academic and social emotional learning competencies. Educators use knowledge of community values obtained through co-assessment to establish the expectations for the classroom. Learning objectives for lessons focused on social emotional learning may include defining expectations and helping students understand and use behaviors aligned with these expectations across settings and events.

Collaboration and co-instruction are valuable in translating abstract expectations, like "respect," into observable and actionable behaviors. Engaging students in defining or even co-creating what expectations mean, as concepts and actions, promotes shared understanding and makes it more likely that young people will accept these expectations. Hollett (2022) reminds us that a truly justice-focused classroom does not assume that all students and teachers have the same understanding of what the term "respect" means or looks like. Recognizing how much of our typical expectations are based on tradition or a dominant culture provides an impetus for teachers to collaborate with others who may have a different perspective. For example, while one teacher may find students sitting quietly "respectful," another instructor may view interruptions and even disagreements as a demonstration of student engagement.

Teachers, all collaborating educators, and students in the classroom must come to a shared understanding of classroom expectations. The co-taught lesson plan in Worksheet 9.1 provides an example of how educators and students can come to a shared understanding of the expectation "be respectful." While in this example the lesson is delivered by a general educator and special educator, it could also be taught through a variety of other co-instruction configurations, such as multiple general educators, a general educator and paraprofessional, a teacher and counselor, and so on. Other expectations, such as responsibility, kindness, or safety, could be explored through a similar activity. The lesson is intended for middle school students. However, it could be adjusted for older or younger students by using different options for reading, writing, or speaking and by shifting the vocabulary level.

Worksheet 9.1

Co-teaching Lesson Plan on Respect

Subject Area: social emotional learning

Grade Level: middle school

Content Standard: Students will "illustrate and discuss personal core principles in the context of relationships and of classroom work" (Kansas State Board of Education, 2018, p. 5).

Lesson Objective: Students will identify examples and non-examples of respectful behavior.

Essential Questions: What does respectful behavior look like? How do we differ in our understandings of respectful behavior?

Key Vocabulary: respectful, disrespectful

Pre-assessment: informal conversation between co-teachers regarding observed behaviors in class

Materials: interactive whiteboard application such as Google Jamboard, or paper sticky notes if technology is not available; computer or tablet access for groups, if available; laptops or tablets for individual student use

(Continued)

LESSON	CO-TEACHING APPROACH (CAN SELECT MORE THAN ONE)	TIME	GENERAL EDUCATION TEACHER	SPECIAL SERVICE PROVIDER	CONSIDERATIONS (MAY INCLUDE UDL OPTIONS, DIFFERENTIATION NEEDS, AND DATA COLLECTION STRATEGIES)
Beginning (may include Opening; Warm-Up; Review; Anticipatory Set)	☐ One Teach, One Support ☐ Parallel ☐ Alternative ☐ Station ☑ **Team**	10 min.	1. Introduce purpose of lesson: to get student input on the development of the class expectations related to the idea of "respect." 2. Explain that respect has been chosen as a schoolwide core value based on input from staff, students, and community members. 3. Invite students to use provided technology (or personal devices) to look up various definitions of respect. 4. Provide personal examples to show that perceptions of respectful behavior differ (even between the two teachers) and that class input is needed to define what respect does and does not look like for this classroom community.		Students may write or draw to record their ideas about respectful and disrespectful behavior. Notes will not be collected. Use of technology to search for definitions of respect will allow for screen readers or materials in the first language of emergent bilinguals.
	☐ One Teach, One Support ☐ Parallel ☑ **Alternative** ☐ Station ☐ Team		5. Give students (large group) brainstorming time to list examples of respectful and disrespectful behavior they have seen in person or in media that could be relevant to school.	5. Allow some students (small group) to come to the back table if they would prefer to dictate aloud examples of respectful and disrespectful behavior.	Create a culture where students are comfortable going to a back table when they would prefer to talk something out over writing it. Either teacher could work with the large or small group.
			6. Divide students into two groups for Parallel Teaching.		

LESSON	CO-TEACHING APPROACH (CAN SELECT MORE THAN ONE)	TIME	GENERAL EDUCATION TEACHER	SPECIAL SERVICE PROVIDER	CONSIDERATIONS (MAY INCLUDE UDL OPTIONS, DIFFERENTIATION NEEDS, AND DATA COLLECTION STRATEGIES)
Middle (may include Instruction; Checking for Understanding; Independent or Group Practice)	☐ One Teach, One Support ☒ **Parallel (same content, same way)** ☐ Alternative ☐ Station ☐ Team	20 min.	7. Ask students to share examples and non-examples of respectful behavior from their individual brainstorming. 8. Facilitate group discussion to determine where there is agreement or disagreement about what is respectful or disrespectful. 9. As a group, choose four examples of respectful behavior and four examples of disrespectful behavior that are most relevant to school. Create interactive whiteboard sticky notes that can be sorted by the group led by the other teacher. 10. Switch whiteboard slides and collaboratively sort sticky notes into categories "Respectful," "Disrespectful," or "It Depends."	7. Ask students to share examples and non-examples of respectful behavior from their individual brainstorming. 8. Facilitate group discussion to determine where there is agreement or disagreement about what is respectful or disrespectful. 9. As a group, choose four examples of respectful behavior and four examples of disrespectful behavior that are most relevant to school. Create interactive whiteboard sticky notes that can be sorted by the group led by the other teacher. 10. Switch whiteboard slides and collaboratively sort sticky notes into categories "Respectful," "Disrespectful," or "It Depends."	Use Parallel Teaching to break whole class into smaller groups in order to allow more students to have a voice in the discussion. Ensure that all examples of respectful behavior are validated, even if they differ from what is typically expected in the school setting. As the discussion progresses toward defining classroom expectations for respect, teachers should explain the concept of "situationally appropriate" to help students recognize that different representations of respect are valued in different settings (Leverson et al., 2021). Make sure Matthias knows where to locate the terms "Respectful," "Disrespectful," and "It Depends" on his communication device.

(Continued)

LESSON	CO-TEACHING APPROACH (CAN SELECT MORE THAN ONE)	TIME	GENERAL EDUCATION TEACHER	SPECIAL SERVICE PROVIDER	CONSIDERATIONS (MAY INCLUDE UDL OPTIONS, DIFFERENTIATION NEEDS, AND DATA COLLECTION STRATEGIES)
End (may include Closing; Assessments; Extension of the Lesson)	☑ **One Teach, One Support** ☐ Parallel ☐ Alternative ☐ Station ☐ Team	15 min	11. Write a sentence frame on the board (UDL). Provide a hard copy, as needed, for emergent bilinguals or students with language/writing disabilities. *We will demonstrate respect to ___ by ___.* 12. Take note of themes related to respect and disrespect from the group discussion. Support individual students in participating, as needed. 13. Assist students who need support in recording their statements. Provide hard copies of the sentence frames to students, as needed. Assist with technology needs.	11. Lead a group discussion about the behaviors that were sorted into the "It Depends" category or about any disagreements. Seek clarifications that allow the group to come to consensus. 12. Invite students to work in pairs or to write up to three statements individually describing what they believe respectful behavior should look like in the classroom. 13. Explain that the teachers will read all statements and use them to establish the official expectations for respect in the classroom.	Put a timer on Jada's desk so she knows to limit the sharing of her opinions verbally to one minute. Encourage word-prediction or speech-to-text options for students with writing disabilities. Have copies of sentence frame available as needed.

Bottom of Form

Lesson plan template format compliments of www.2TeachLLC.com

The sample lesson initially leads the group to a shared understanding of the concept of "respect," acknowledging different experiences and perceptions that students may have. The activities also lead to examples of observable respectful behaviors and guide the students to describe their vision of respectful behaviors in the classroom. Engaging young people in this way promotes a culturally responsive, trauma-informed classroom climate. The outcome of this lesson is a shared understanding of what respect looks like as a broad expectation for the class. Co-teachers would co-analyze the students' final written responses to synthesize behavioral indicators for the category "be respectful." The indicators would be documented in the classroom section of a Behavioral Expectations Matrix and/or made visible in some other format, such as printed posters or even a short video that is accessible online or on a class website.

Once specific behavioral indicators are identified, they need to be shared with students and explicitly taught to them. **Responsive explicit instruction** in a behavioral skill includes (1) explaining the purpose or a value of the skill, (2) modeling the skill with examples and non-examples, (3) providing guided practice with feedback, (4) creating visuals or other supports that promote independent use of the skill, and (5) providing independent practice with feedback.

When students play an integral role in defining and elaborating the expectations in an initial lesson, co-teachers can easily integrate examples and non-examples provided by young people when teaching the expectations. Students may also be engaged in creating the visual reminders. Whether students or educators make the visuals, it is important that they are accessible to all students (TeachingWorks, 2019). Therefore, teachers should be mindful of vocabulary level and may want to pair images with words as an element of UDL.

The sample co-taught lesson in Worksheet 9.1 provides the overall expectation of what respect means and looks like in the classroom. However, students may need additional clarification to understand what respectful behavior looks like when entering and exiting the classroom, when using shared resources, when playing, when disagreeing with a peer or adult, or in any number of other events that happen in or around a classroom. While generalization to other contexts is desirable, it cannot be expected or assumed. When students need detailed information about how to demonstrate classroom expectations in a specific situation, a routine may be warranted.

Co-instruction of Classroom Routines

There are countless routines that could be established in the classroom. Collaborating educators will want to prioritize those that promote physical and emotional safety, followed by routines for high-frequency activities. These high-priority routines are taught at the beginning of the year. Additional routines can be developed and taught over time. Routines for organization and discourse integrate classroom expectations into high-frequency classroom activities. When developed with student assets and needs in mind, routines give all learners equitable access to materials and instructional time (TeachingWorks, 2019).

Organizational routines are often developed for activities such as turning in papers, indicating lunch preference, recording homework assignments, entering/exiting the classroom, and transitioning between activities. In considering which organizational routines to prioritize, collaborating teachers may want to ask: What tasks or activities occur most frequently in the classroom? When do we find ourselves repeating directions? What activities need additional structure or predictability to ensure safety (physical and emotional) or efficiency? What types of differentiation options might we need to proactively identify so we are prepared when flexibility is required?

Routines for discourse are often evidenced in learning standards. For example, the Common Core State Standards hold the expectation that kindergarteners will engage in group reading activities, third graders will distinguish their own point of view from an author's point of view, and fifth graders will write to express and support an opinion (Common Core State Standards Initiative [CCSSI], 2010). Standards for students in grades 6–12 require collaboration with others, including those whose backgrounds differ from their own, to discuss a variety of texts and issues (CCSSI, 2010). These standards require social emotional competencies to be integrated into academic routines.

With time, teachers become adept at recognizing the routines that need to be taught early in the school year. Newer teachers may find it helpful to collaborate with experienced teachers to identify the routines that are needed for specific grade levels or content areas. Informal and formal mentoring is a wonderful application of collaboration in schools. Even with collaboration, however, there will often be situations where the need for new routines becomes evident through student behavior. The following Connecting to Practice vignette illustrates a situation when student needs revealed that a new routine was necessary.

Connecting to Practice

Time for a Routine!

Mrs. Mouring, an experienced special educator, and Ms. Peyton, an experienced third-grade teacher, co-teach math. Both have extensive knowledge of the third-grade math curriculum and have a strong collaborative relationship. They share beliefs about classroom climate and about positive behavioral supports. They've worked together with students to establish overall classroom expectations and teach routines. They've integrated some restorative practices, such as restorative circles and student conferences, into their classroom routines to promote a positive and responsive classroom climate.

A few months into the school year, Mrs. Mouring and Ms. Peyton realize that a significant amount of instructional time is lost to behavioral concerns during the math block. They note that it is difficult to keep students engaged and there are multiple arguments between students every day, often about minor concerns like, "James is tapping his pencil too loudly" or "Kinzie rolled her eyes at me." The class just seems to be "off" during the math block in ways that differ from the rest of the school day. Discussing the situation, the teachers speculate that the behaviors have something to do with recess, which occurs immediately before the math block. They decide to hold a classroom circle to get input from students about what might be going on.

Ms. Peyton and Mrs. Mouring open the circle by sharing that math time isn't going as well as they would like. They briefly highlight the importance of math skills and their concerns that classroom expectations for respect and responsibility aren't being met. They explain that the purpose of the classroom meeting is to understand student perspectives about what is and isn't working during math time and to engage the whole class in making the math block better for everyone. They give the students a few minutes to think about behaviors during math class that align with class expectations and behaviors that don't, before inviting them to share. Ms. Peyton reminds the students to share their ideas using "I statements" and provides the following sample sentence starters on the board: "I feel _____," "I think _____," "I've noticed _____." Mrs. Mouring shows the students the talking stick, reminding them that it will be passed around the circle and that the person holding the talking stick gets to speak. Those who do not have the talking stick are asked to listen thoughtfully and respectfully. As Mrs. Mouring facilitates the circle discussion, Ms. Peyton makes notes of students' ideas.

As the students talk, it becomes apparent that the transition from recess immediately into the structured math class is challenging for a couple of different reasons. Some students are disappointed about leaving recess and want to continue playing, so they enter the room feeling grumpy. Others feel full of energy after recess and have a hard time settling down. A third group expresses feeling tired and wanting a break. Finally, some students share that they just don't like math or they think that math is hard. After students share their feelings and observations, Ms. Peyton leads the circle in a problem-solving discussion asking, "What needs to happen to make this better?" After Kiernan suggests, "How about we skip math altogether?" and the students laugh, another student, Amari, shares, "We just need five minutes of peace before we start math!" Ms. Peyton

(Continued)

(Continued)

and Mrs. Mourning thank the students for their input and tell them that they will work on a plan to help with the transition from recess to math.

After reviewing the information provided by students in the circle, Ms. Peyton and Mrs. Mouring decide to build on Amari's suggestion of "Five Minutes of Peace." They think that a transition routine that incorporates student self-monitoring and self-regulation activities will help students be ready for math class. They plan to turn down the lights and play quiet music as students return from recess. They also plan to teach students how to self-monitor their energy level and readiness to learn, then engage in a quiet activity to "gear up" or "settle down" for math class. Ms. Peyton and Mrs. Mouring schedule a follow-up classroom circle to engage students in defining the steps in the transition routine and making a list of quiet activities. The routine and list of activities generated by the follow-up discussion are turned into classroom posters that are placed strategically around the classroom.

AFTER-RECESS TRANSITION ROUTINE "FIVE MINUTES OF PEACE"	"GEAR UP" OR "SETTLE DOWN" CHOICES
1. Enter the classroom quietly. Voices should be no louder than a whisper. 2. Self-check your energy level using the visual on the bulletin board. 3. Choose an activity to "gear up" (increase your energy) or "settle down" (calm your energy) so you can be ready to work. 4. Put the activity away when the lights turn on.	• Read • Write or draw in your journal • Color • Rest with your head on your desk • Do "lazy 8 breathing" or some other breathing exercise • Work quietly at the puzzle table • Use a sensory tool from the sensory basket • Do push-ups at the back of the room

Ms. Peyton and Mrs. Mouring know that telling students the routine is not the same as teaching the routine. They explicitly prompt and model the steps of the routine for a few days, fading their prompts and encouraging the students to use the posted visual. They provide positive reinforcement to students for following the routine and prompt students who need additional support. Over time, the students become independent at completing the routine. Mrs. Mouring and Ms. Peyton know that they will need to continue to monitor student use of the routine and its impact on behaviors during math time.

The Connecting to Practice vignette offers another example of what co-instruction and co-construction can look like when working to create *a consistent, organized, and respectful learning environment* **[SE_HLP7]**. Note that in this activity for building a routine, students were actively engaged in co-constructing meaning. Collaboration is evident between educators and students. The co-instruction included the following steps:

1. Provide a rationale for the chosen routine.

2. Explicitly teach the routine with models, examples, and non-examples.

3. Create visuals to promote independent use of the routine.

4. Offer supports and reminders when students need them.

5. Reinforce use of the routine.

6. Evaluate the effectiveness of the routine and adjust, as needed.

You'll notice that the last step takes us back to co-assessment. Collaborating teachers will want to collect information to determine if the routines are working (TeacherWorks, 2019). Questions for consideration include: Do students understand the routines? Are they able to follow the routines independently (more or less)? Are the routines contributing to the desired outcome for classroom climate? Are the routines promoting equity, or are specific students or student groups benefitting less than others? Do teachers need to differentiate their support for understanding and learning the routines?

Secondary educators who see students for only one class period may question the use of precious time to engage in the co-creation of expectations and routines, the participation in restorative circles, or the dialogue required to get students' opinions and reactions. However, not only do these activities promote a more equitable and culturally responsive class culture, but they also lead to improved behavioral and academic outcomes (Klevan, 2021). Student choice and voice are major components of a universally designed classroom; moreover, as students age, their need for asserting their own choice and voice grows as well (Murawski & Scott, 2019). In a nutshell, middle school and high school teachers can choose to spend a few periods throughout the year dedicated to establishing norms, expectations, and routines proactively—or risk the loss of far more time while responding to inappropriate behaviors, addressing issues, and re-explaining directions.

Moving Beyond Classroom Management With Social Emotional Learning

Educators who establish, teach, and reinforce classroom expectations and routines create the foundation for a positive classroom climate in alignment with the high-leverage practices for social emotional learning. *Teaching social skills* **[SE_HLP9]** includes teaching expectations and routines, but there is so much more to social emotional learning. Positive classroom climate is about more than safety and efficiency. It's about promoting the social emotional skills that make all students feel valued, welcomed, and supported. Collaboratively planned routines and expectations can strategically foster self-awareness, self-management, and decision making. However, instruction needs to be integrated into other aspects of the school day as well. This does not mean that teachers need to schedule a separate block of instruction for social skills. In fact, educators are encouraged to look for opportunities to integrate instruction for social emotional learning into collaborative and project-based learning across content areas.

Consider how skills like goal setting, planning, predicting consequences, conflict resolution, and problem solving are needed when students work on projects. Rather than assuming students have these skills, it is important to provide explicit instruction in connection to the activities when they are applied. This aim might be achieved by collaborating with a social emotional learning specialist, such as a school counselor, school psychologist, or special education teacher. These individuals may provide consultation and ideas for integration, or they may even be able to co-teach a lesson or unit. It is also important to recognize that sometimes students need a little extra support or incentive to use newly taught skills. Supports may be provided using Alternative or Station Teaching when smaller groups need differentiated amounts of practice or explanation. Positive reinforcement is needed to ensure that newly taught skills are applied. Incentives can be offered individually and at the class level through group contingencies (see below).

Reinforcement to Support Social Emotional Learning

Learning and applying a new social emotional skill can be challenging in some situations, even with effective instruction. It can be particularly challenging for students to replace an existing behavior or habit with something new. This is why feedback and reinforcement are important elements of social emotional learning. You'll recall that we opened this chapter with a discussion of old-school rules that were maintained through punishment. We know now that rewarding desired behavior is far more effective than punishing misbehavior. When behavior is governed by punishment, people generally exhibit the desired behavior only when the risk of punishment is immediately present. (Consider the difference in highway driving speeds when a police officer is present compared to when one is not present!) Rewards do not have to be tangible, but students must get clear feedback and reinforcement if a new behavior is to be continued and expanded.

Reinforcement can occur naturally, as when peers want to socialize with a child who offers to share a toy. Reinforcement can also be intentionally added to the environment when natural reinforcement is not enough. Verbal praise, a form of social reinforcement, can meet this need. Sometimes activity-based reinforcement or tangible rewards are needed in combination with verbal feedback to help a student recognize the value of a new behavior. Conversely, students need constructive feedback when they are not performing the expected behavior. We want to be very clear that constructive feedback never involves shaming students or diminishing their standing in front of peers, as it often happens with color charts (e.g., Bobby is on "red") or lists of punitive consequences. Constructive feedback involves prompting or reteaching the expected behavior so the student can perform it successfully. Through such feedback, young people have the opportunity to successfully perform a desired behavior and earn reinforcement. It is important for collaborating educators to discuss reinforcement strategies that will be used with students. When learners need more customized reinforcement, instructors should collaborate with young people (and, in some cases, with their family members) to identify meaningful options.

At times, multiple students will need added reinforcement to develop and apply a new behavioral skill. **Group contingencies** are a specific type of positive reinforcement that can be helpful in establishing a positive classroom climate. Group contingencies are intended to reinforce desired behaviors, while simultaneously promoting student collaboration. When using group contingencies in the classroom, teachers establish a goal for the whole class or for groups of students within the class. When learners achieve the goal, they collectively earn a desired reinforcement.

In the spirit of positive behavior supports, the goal should be positively worded. For example, a high school teacher who has noticed that students are on their phones during instructional time might set a goal that phones will be kept in backpacks for the duration of class for five days, as opposed to simply posting a "No Phones Allowed" policy. She would collaborate with students to identify the reward to be earned when the goal is achieved. Young people would work in collaborative teams, supporting each other with reminders and prompts to help them achieve the goal. Once achieved, the entire class would earn the desired activity (e.g., no homework on Friday). Through the group effort, new behaviors would be learned, practiced, and reinforced.

Summary

Creating a positive classroom climate requires that expected *social skills are explicitly taught and reinforced* **[SE_HLP9]**. Educators need to collaborate with each other *and* with students to create classroom climates that are truly responsive to the needs and experiences of diverse learners. Social emotional learning can be fostered through restorative practices, co-constructed understandings of expectations and routines, co-instruction of expectations, and positive reinforcement systems. Through these actions, *a consistent, organized, and respectful learning environment* **[SE_HLP7]** with *norms and routines for organization* **[GE_HLP8]**, *discourse, and work* **[GE_HLP5]** can be created.

Collaborating for Individual Behavioral Support and Intervention

10

Perhaps you have opened this chapter eager to enhance your already well-equipped behavioral support tool kit with collaborative strategies, or perhaps you've come feeling overwhelmed by student behavioral needs. Whether one of these descriptions fits you, or whether you find yourself somewhere between these two positions, we know that challenging student behaviors can be a significant source of stress. There is a lot at stake when learners demonstrate socially unexpected, disruptive, or potentially harmful behaviors in school. As educators, we worry about physical and emotional safety, as well as about learning outcomes, for all our students when behaviors of concern are present.

Chapter Connections

See Chapters 8 and 9 for more on creating a positive classroom culture and fostering social emotional learning.

In previous chapters we discussed collaborative strategies for understanding students' social emotional needs and how to create a classroom culture that fosters social emotional learning for all students. These foundational strategies fall under Tier 1 supports in Multi-Tiered Systems of Support models and are expected to meet the needs of about 80% of our students. It doesn't take much effort to realize that this means about 20% of students will need additional support.

While educators generally feel confident implementing Tier 1 classroom management strategies, many feel far less prepared to provide the more individualized behavioral intervention needed for the 20% of students in

Tiers 2 and 3 (Flower et al., 2017). Even special education professionals, who are likely to have additional training in behavioral support strategies, identify professional development in this area as a top priority (Bullock, 2018). In this chapter, we discuss function-aligned intervention as a valuable evidence-based practice for individualizing and intensifying behavioral support. We also examine the critical role of collaboration in designing and implementing function-aligned intervention.

The general and special education high-leverage practices are well aligned when it comes to addressing social, emotional, and behavioral needs. The general education high-leverage practices encourage educators to *elicit and interpret student thinking* **[GE_HLP3]**, specifically seeking to *understand patterns* **[GE_HLP4]**. A process for understanding student thinking is described by special education high-leverage practices, which encourage educators to *conduct Functional Behavior Assessments to develop behavior support plans* **[SE_HLP10]**. The high-leverage practices further detail what elements should be documented in those support plans, including *agreements about behavior* **[GE_HLP7]** and *positive and constructive feedback to guide students' behavior* **[SE_HLP8]**.

Evidence-Based Practices for Individualized Behavioral Support

You might be asking yourself what types of behavior require individualized intervention, or how behavioral needs may differ in Tiers 2 and 3. The answer to the first question is fairly straightforward. Whenever typically effective classroom or schoolwide behavioral supports, implemented with fidelity, are ineffective for meeting a student's unique needs, this student requires some degree of individualization. In other words, if we have developed and consistently taught classwide expectations, as described in Chapter 9, and some students are still not experiencing success, they may need individualized intervention. The degree of individualization and intensity of that support is what distinguishes Tier 2 from Tier 3. While Tier 2 behavioral supports are more prescriptive than those used for the entire school, their customization may be limited to meeting the needs of groups of learners who share similar characteristics. Tier 2 behavioral supports may be appropriate for students who demonstrate socially unexpected or unproductive behaviors that do not pose a safety risk.

Conversely, Tier 3 behavioral supports are highly customized to meet the needs of an individual student with more significant support needs. Tier 3 supports are provided at a higher level of intensity (e.g., more frequently or for longer duration) and may be used to address safety concerns or complex behaviors that have not been effectively managed by Tier 2 supports. Although intervention plans are often developed by behavior specialists or school psychologists, general and special education teachers have reported that they assume the bulk of responsibility for implementing

Tier 2 and Tier 3 behavioral support and that this can feel overwhelming (Allday et al., 2011). As the complexity of student behaviors and intensity of intervention increase, teachers need collaborative support to collect and analyze data as well as to implement behavioral supports.

Function-aligned behavioral intervention is a collaboratively imple-mented evidence-based practice that is effective in addressing both Tier 2 and Tier 3 behaviors of concern (Gage et al., 2012). **Function-aligned interventions** are grounded in the premise that every repeated behavior has a purpose. In behavioral terms, that purpose is called the **function** of the behavior. Socially expected behaviors, positive coping strategies, and behaviors of concern are purposeful. While we may not be able to immediately understand the purpose of a concerning behavior, it is important to recognize that it is somehow working for the student who employs it. Behaviors of concern will continue to be present as long as they meet a need and there is no more effective alternative in the stu-dent's behavioral repertoire. Educators wanting to change a behavior of concern must *teach* an effective and efficient replacement behavior that meets the same need. This process of teaching and reinforcing socially acceptable replacement behaviors is considered function-aligned inter-vention. Before we can intervene, we must understand the function of the behavior (i.e., its purpose).

Functional Behavior Assessment and Function-Based Thinking

Unfortunately, students aren't always forthright in sharing the func-tions of their behavior. In fact, they often don't recognize the functions themselves. Additionally, the various individuals who work with a stu-dent throughout the day may have a variety of theories about the func-tion of a behavior. How, then, are we supposed to collaborate to develop function-aligned intervention? The answer lies in the high-leverage practice identified in both general and special education research. The general education high-leverage practice tells us to **elicit and understand student thinking [GE_HLP3]**, and the special edu-cation high-leverage practice defines a process for doing that—**using Functional Behavior Assessment [SE_HLP10]**.

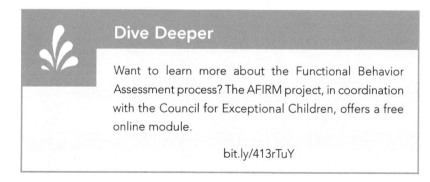

Dive Deeper

Want to learn more about the Functional Behavior Assessment process? The AFIRM project, in coordination with the Council for Exceptional Children, offers a free online module.

bit.ly/413rTuY

If you are a special educator, you have probably heard of Functional Behavior Assessment. Depending on your role, you may have had extensive experience or very little experience with the process. If you are a general educator, you may be under the impression that this assessment is only used for students with disabilities. The truth is, Functional Behavior Assessment is an intensive and time-consuming process that is probably best reserved for behaviors requiring Tier 3 support. When implemented with fidelity, it involves multiple team members who have been trained in behavioral data collection and analysis. Although the effort is intensive, when the assessment is done by a truly collaborative team, it can be truly life-changing for students. (Trust us! We've seen it in action!)

As an alternative to Functional Behavior Assessment, collaborative teams wanting to develop function-aligned interventions for Tier 2 behaviors of concern may choose to use a process called **Function-Based Thinking**, which is sometimes described as a "basic FBA" (Strickland-Cohen et al., 2016, p. 237). This systematic process adopts some of the key features of Functional Behavior Assessment but is less time-consuming and requires fewer trained professionals (Hershfeldt et al., 2010). In both cases, collaborative teaming is important. Functional Behavior Assessment and Function-Based Thinking are consistent in including four critical steps, which are identified in Figure 10.1.

FIGURE 10.1	Steps for Conducting a Functional Behavior Assessment or Function-Based Thinking

1. Operationalize the behavior of concern.

Define the behavior in a precise way that is measurable and observable. When a behavior is clearly operationalized, its occurrence or absence will be immediately recognizable to all collaborative team members, allowing for accurate data collection. When it comes to operationalizing a behavior, the only difference between Functional Behavior Assessment and Function-Based Thinking is the number of people who may be involved in the process. There are likely to be more people in a Functional Behavior Assessment. That said, no matter how many people are involved, clear communication between collaborating colleagues is key to ensure that everyone has the same definition of the behavior of concern.

2. Gather information about the behavior of concern.

When conducting a Functional Behavior Assessment, data are gathered through direct observations at various times of day and in various settings. This is not easily done by a single person; therefore, collaboration is particularly important to determine when, where, and how data should be collected. Data collection includes observations focused on the antecedent–behavior–consequence (ABC) sequence, often using a tool called an "ABC chart." Direct observation data may also be collected using frequency counts, duration recording, or latency recording, as appropriate for the specific behavior. In addition to direct observation data, the Functional Behavior Assessment usually includes at least one form of indirect data, such as an interview with a student, family member, or teacher. (The AFIRM module listed in the Dive Deeper box includes detailed information about these data collection procedures.) With Function-Based

Thinking, the information-gathering process is simpler. While ABC chart data are often collected, there will be fewer sources of new and direct observation data. Additional information may be acquired through existing sources, such as attendance or tardiness records, work completion, office referrals, or number of suspensions (Hershfeldt et al., 2010). Function-Based Thinking may require fewer professionals; however, collaboration is still necessary to determine what data are needed, how these data can be accessed, and what meaningful information can be pulled from those sources.

3. **Use the data to hypothesize a function.**

Once information has been collected, a collaborative team will analyze it with the goal of identifying the function of the behavior. In Functional Behavior Assessment, this is often done by the full IEP team and may also include additional specialists. In Function-Based Thinking, the team may include only a teacher and one or two other individuals who are familiar with the student (such as a family member, special educator, or paraprofessional). A hypothesis about an assumed function of the problematic behavior is created to be tested through function-aligned intervention.

4. **Develop a function-aligned Behavior Intervention Plan.**

With a hypothesized function in mind, the team can begin to plan interventions that teach and reinforce a safe and productive behavior that replaces the behavior of concern. The Behavior Intervention Plan is where high-leverage practices related to *establishing community behavioral expectations* [GE_HLP7] and *including positive and constructive feedback to guide students' behavior* [SE_HLP8] come into play. In Tier 2, the Behavior Intervention Plan may take the form of a structured intervention, such as Check-In, Check-Out (Drevon et al., 2019), "Check, Connect, and Expect" (Cheney et al., 2010), or social skills instruction. In Tier 3, the intervention will have increased individualization and intensity. (See the Connecting to Practice vignette examples later in this chapter for descriptions of how Check-In, Check-Out can be used for Tier 2 and Tier 3 support.) In both cases, the collaborative team will continue to collect data while the plan is being implemented to verify that their hypothesis about the function was accurate and that the behavior is improving.

Collaboration in the Behavior Intervention Process

Functional Behavior Assessment and Function-Based Thinking offer two pathways for collaborative teams to understand the function of a student's behavior and develop function-aligned Behavior Intervention Plans. Both processes are clearly documented as team efforts in the literature, but we know that the collaboration element sometimes breaks down in practice (Walker & Barry, 2017). In our experience, it is not uncommon to hear educators say that the behavior specialist, school psychologist, case manager, or some other specialist is responsible for "completing the Functional Behavior Assessment" or "writing the Behavior Intervention Plan."

We understand that the team approach requires time, which always seems to be in short supply for educators. We also understand that team members may be unfamiliar with the process and unsure how they can make meaningful contributions. However, the investment of time and collaborative input from team members with diverse perspectives can make a real difference. Let's talk about some of the common challenges associated with conducting Functional Behavior Assessment/Function-Based Thinking and developing a Behavior Intervention Plan, as well as collaborative strategies that can address these challenges.

Challenge: Some team members see the student's behavior as a major concern. Others aren't particularly worried about it.

Collaborative Strategy:	Describe and contextualize the severity of the problem.

Every educator has different experiences with, and tolerance levels for, student behaviors. One educator might describe a behavior as mildly annoying, while another describes the same behavior as a major disruption to learning. Family members and school team members may also have varying levels of concern about a behavior. What should a team do if some members express significant concern while others do not? A collaborative conversation is a good starting point. When a team comes together to discuss behavior, the discussion should address the presence and severity of the problem in different contexts. Team members often recognize that behaviors are present in some settings but not in others; however, participants do not always consider that a behavior could be completely acceptable in one setting and dangerous in another one. For example, a behavior that is safe and productive in theater class could be dangerous in a science lab.

The discussion of severity and context can lead the team to different assessment and intervention options. If the behavior is observed across a variety of settings and is described as highly concerning by multiple team members, a full Functional Behavior Assessment may be warranted. If the team reports that the behavior occurs in only a few settings or has mild intensity, participants may choose Function-Based Thinking. Finally, if the behavior is concerning in only one setting, a more informal support strategy may be more useful. For example, the team may decide to clarify expectations of different settings for the student or provide individualized coaching to the team member for whom the behavior in question is the most concerning. Each of these options demonstrates respect for individual experiences and promotes productive behavior across settings.

Challenge: Collecting data across times and settings is difficult.

Collaborative Strategy:	Prioritize, divide, and conquer.

Collecting data from multiple sources across times and settings is a hall-mark feature of Functional Behavior Assessment. This valuable process can feel overwhelming, given educators' busy schedules. When develop-ing the data collection plan, it is important to remember that we don't need to be collecting data all day long, several days in a row. We need to collect a *sampling* of data that allows the team to ***identify patterns*** and functions **[GE_HLP4]**. Strategically planned observations that last 15–20 minutes in purposely selected contexts often address this need. The data collection plan can be developed by reviewing existing data sources and having conversations to obtain insight from each other about when and where behaviors are likely to occur. This information helps the team prioritize when and where to collect data. Data collection in the settings where the behavior is likely to occur can help the team identify antecedents and consequences. A few observations in settings where the behavior is unlikely to occur can allow the team to identify skills that the student may already have and to develop supports that can be helpful in changing the behavior in question.

Strategic data collection helps to save time on this stage of the process, but it can still feel overwhelming if one or two people are responsible for it. Many school administrators find it helpful to build and train a standing Functional Behavior Assessment/Behavior Intervention Plan team. Members of the standing team collaborate with student-specific team members to collect and interpret data. Don't forget to include family members, especially parents, as key partners in data collection. Sharing the responsibility this way reduces the burden on any single team member and increases the validity and reliability of the data (Walker & Barry, 2017).

Challenge: A clear pattern is not evident in the student's behavior.

Collaborative Strategy:	Include indirect data sources.

We've already discussed that students behave differently across times, settings, and people. In addition, young people may experience thoughts or sensations related to the behavior in question, which are not observ-able to others. With all these variables in place, it makes sense that there will be times when teams can't pinpoint patterns in behavior or may have different theories about patterns and functions. That's okay! Collaborative discussions around questions and hypotheses help team members recognize missing pieces of information, which may lead to additional strategic data collection.

Up to this point, we've focused on data obtained through direct observa-tion. In some cases, more direct observation is needed to clarify patterns.

However, when there are questions or divergent hypotheses about patterns, indirect data collection can be very beneficial. Interviews with the student, parents, and others who interact with the student are considered indirect data. Several generic interview protocols are available online. However, consider that a conversation framed around the data, and questions that build on the data, can sometimes be more helpful than general interview forms.

The student is an important source of information. (Remember that one of the general education high-leverage practices encourages us to *elicit student thinking* **[GE_HLP3]**!) The student is the only team member who can accurately share what they are thinking and feeling when a behavior occurs. Therefore, a strategic conversation with the student can lead to powerful insights. Even young children or children who don't use spoken language can be supported in communicating their feelings. Engaging the student in the process also fosters self-determination and self-advocacy, which can go a long way toward creating positive behavior change.

Interviews with parents and various educators can also be helpful. Family members may share events from the home or community that set the stage for behavior before students arrive at school. For example, changes in sleep patterns and family routines often affect student behavior. Educators often would not know about these changes unless they collaborate with family members. Interviews with various school personnel (e.g., bus drivers, cafeteria workers, school counselors, paraprofessionals) may also provide information that can help to clarify patterns. By interviewing individuals who have different experiences with a student, the team can learn about unique features of settings or interpersonal relationships that impact student behavior. These details may clarify inconsistencies in the direct observation data. For example, the team may discover that a student is less likely to engage in a behavior of concern when working with a teacher who incorporates student choice into assignments.

Challenge: This behavior plan will never work!

(Other variations: "I don't know how to implement this strategy," "We don't have enough staff," and "The intervention is too complex/unrealistic.")

Collaborative Strategy:	Ensure team development of the Behavior Intervention Plan and training for all team members.

Behavior support is not about paperwork; it's about practice. A detailed, function-aligned Behavior Intervention Plan that is written to include evidence-based behavioral supports will fail if it can't be implemented with fidelity. As mentioned in Section II, fidelity means that the intervention is implemented as intended, not just when time and resources are available to do it. Earlier we mentioned that we often hear that the behavior specialist or some other individual holds sole responsibility for writing Behavior Intervention Plans for a school. While having a specialist for this task seems to save time with paperwork, this tactic often presents real challenges for the *practice* of behavior support.

Specialists may be skilled in implementing a vast array of research-based interventions; however, they may not understand contextual challenges of implementing an intervention in a given setting. A strategy that works well with small groups or one on one may be almost impossible for a teacher in a class of 30 students. To remedy these concerns, the team should collaborate in developing the Behavior Intervention Plan from the beginning. It is crucial that team members who will have core responsibilities for implementing the plan have a say in its development. It is also essential that the student and their family members have a voice in the process. Specialists may come to a Behavior Intervention Plan meeting with ideas and suggestions; however, the whole team needs to evaluate these ideas and suggestions for value and functionality before they become part of the plan.

Key questions to help the team assess the *value* of an intervention include the following:

- Is this intervention well aligned with the function of the behavior?

- Does this intervention teach a productive, socially expected behavior that can be used across settings?

- Does research support the use of this intervention with students who have characteristics similar to this student and under similar circumstances?

Similarly, in addressing the *functionality* of an intervention in a setting, the team may ask the following:

- Do we have the time, staffing, and materials to implement this intervention?

- Do all team members know how to implement the intervention?

- Is everybody on the team, including the student and their family members, open to trying the intervention?

If a strategy has high value but low functionality, the team should determine if training or additional resources are available to address the concerns. These supports should then be documented in the plan. If the necessary training and/or resources are not readily available, the team should consider other interventions that may have equal value but greater functionality. There is almost always more than one way to provide effective behavioral support. The team has the goal of finding the best match for a given situation.

Once the Behavior Intervention Plan is written, it is essential that every team member who is responsible for implementation receive training. Training is often required for individuals who were not originally involved in the development of the plan. To identify these individuals, the team should consider when the interventions might need to occur and who will be present when this happens. Behavior Intervention Plan implementation team members may have a variety of roles. Some participants might teach new skills to the student, others may cue the use of the skills across settings or provide additional reinforcement. A few will likely be engaged in all of these roles. A simple form that documents the Behavior Intervention Plan and the responsibilities of each team member can assist with training and fidelity of implementation. The Competing Pathways Framework is one such document.

Competing Pathways Framework

Documentation of a full Functional Behavior Assessment is often a multi-page technical report. Accessing and interpreting this report may not be practical for all team members involved in providing behavioral support to a student. One way to facilitate collaboration is to use a form that summarizes the key information in an easy-to-read, easy-to-implement format. To accomplish this goal, O'Neill and colleagues (1997) developed a tool called the "Competing Pathways diagram." It is designed to help teams translate findings of the Functional Behavior Assessment or Function-Based Thinking into function-aligned Behavior Intervention Plans. Collaborative roles for each stage of the process are identified in our adapted version of the diagram found in Figure 10.2. This graphic representation of the Functional Behavior Assessment is designed to foster conversations about events surrounding behaviors of concern, then guide the team in identifying alternative behaviors and developing supports needed to elicit these alternative behaviors.

The middle row of the diagram, marked with the large continuous arrow, is used to document the original path of behavior as identified through the Functional Behavior Assessment or Function-Based Thinking process. This row concisely summarizes the **setting events** (sometimes called "slow triggers"), the **antecedent** that predicts the behavior of concern, the **behavior** itself, and the maintaining **consequence** (i.e., function). When developing function-aligned intervention, the collaborative team will want to identify **alternative behaviors** that the student can demonstrate given the same setting and antecedent events. These behaviors are documented in the two alternative pathways of the Competing Pathways diagram.

The top row of the diagram, marked with a curved arrow and dashed lines, is used to describe the desired behavior and consequences that occur naturally in response to that behavior. When selecting a desired behavior, the team will want to consider what is socially expected when the setting and antecedent events occur. Input from a variety of teachers and other school support staff (e.g., bus drivers, paraprofessionals, recess monitors) can help the team determine the types of responses that are expected of the student's peer group in educational settings. Collaboration with the student and their family members can help the team determine what is expected at home and in the community. It is important to understand that the desired behavior pathway marks the best-case scenario. Moving from the behavior of concern to the desired behavior is a pretty big jump. It is not realistic to expect a student to immediately progress from the first pathway to the second. Therefore, the Competing Pathways diagram includes a third path called the **acceptable alternative**.

The bottom row, marked with a curved arrow and dotted lines, represents the acceptable alternative. In this pathway, the team identifies a replacement behavior that meets the original function of behavior in a safer or more socially acceptable manner. For example, if a student's behavior of concern involves arguing and refusing to complete a math assignment in order to escape a frustrating task, an acceptable alternative behavior might involve the student in negotiating a reduction in the number of math problems to be completed. This is not an ideal replacement behavior, but it is more accessible to the student than the desired behavior and it represents an improvement over the original behavior of concern.

It can sometimes be challenging for teams to settle on an acceptable alternative behavior. There may be concerns about "giving in" or encouraging a behavior that is not ideal. In considering the options, it is important for teams to weigh the increase in safety or decrease in disruption that will occur with the acceptable alternative against the challenges associated with the behavior of concern. It is also important for team members to understand that the acceptable alternative is a crucial first step toward the desired behavior, not the end goal. The intervention plan designed around these behaviors must systematically teach and reinforce both options, as described in the high-leverage practices. Once again, the need for team members to be willing to communicate, share concerns, describe options, and generally be open to one another's frames of reference will be key to identifying and establishing possible options for replacement behaviors.

FIGURE 10.2 Competing Pathways Diagram With Collaborative Actions

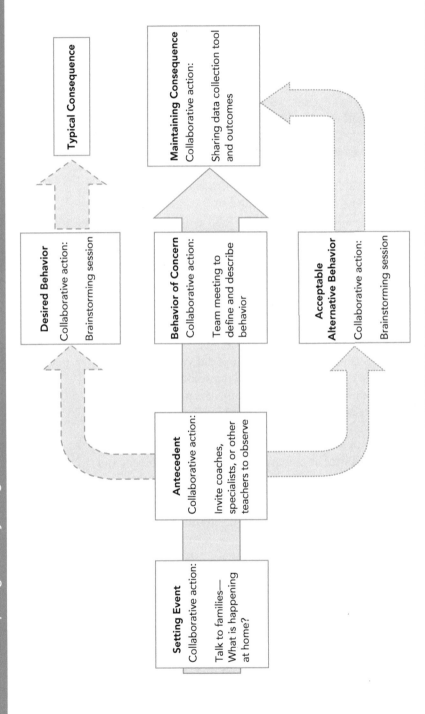

Setting Event
Collaborative action:

Talk to families—
What is happening
at home?

Antecedent
Collaborative action:

Invite coaches,
specialists, or other
teachers to observe

Desired Behavior
Collaborative action:

Brainstorming session

Typical Consequence

Behavior of Concern
Collaborative action:

Team meeting to
define and describe
behavior

Maintaining Consequence
Collaborative action:

Sharing data collection tool
and outcomes

**Acceptable
Alternative Behavior**
Collaborative action:

Brainstorming session

Source: Adapted from *Functional assessment and program development for problem behavior: A practical handbook* (O'Neill et al., 2015). Cengage Learning Inc. Reproduced by permission. www.cengage.com/permissions

The Competing Pathways diagram includes a second section that is meant to help translate the three pathways into a collaborative Behavior Intervention Plan. This section facilitates ***providing positive and constructive feedback to guide students' learning and behavior* [SE_HLP8]**. When planning an intervention, a team should consider the Competing Pathways diagram in columns (setting, antecedent, behavior, consequences) and identify supports for each stage of the sequence.

The collaborative team begins by looking at the setting and antecedent events to identify supports that either inhibit the occurrence of behavior triggers or increase the chance that the student will respond to them using the acceptable alternative or desired behavior. After considering setting and antecedent supports, the team identifies systematic ways to *teach* the acceptable alternative and desired behaviors. Finally, the team discusses the column of consequences and identifies strategies that reinforce the use of the desired behavior and acceptable alternative. They also articulate ways of withdrawing reinforcement for the behavior of concern. Team engagement is crucial to ensure that the considered options are appropriate in all necessary settings and that those who will implement the interventions have the knowledge and support to do so. As previously stated, a well-written plan means nothing if the team cannot implement it!

When collaboratively developing the Behavior Intervention Plan, it is helpful to systematically describe who will be responsible for each aspect of the intervention. We've added guiding questions to the planning template, as shown in Table 10.1, to help teams consider what should be done in each stage and who will be responsible for doing those things. Once the Competing Pathways diagram and intervention plan have been completed, they can be distributed to all members of the collaborative team to concisely summarize the plan and each team member's responsibilities.

TABLE 10.1   Competing Pathways Intervention Planning Template

SETTING INTERVENTIONS	ANTECEDENT INTERVENTIONS	BEHAVIOR INTERVENTIONS	CONSEQUENCE INTERVENTIONS
How will you work to prevent setting events or minimize their impact? Who is responsible?	How will you set the stage for success? Who is responsible?	How will you teach the acceptable alternative and desired behaviors? Who is responsible?	How will you reward the acceptable alternative and desired behaviors? How will you withdraw reinforcement for the behaviors of concern? Who is responsible?

Chapter Connections

Once specific roles are identified, refer back to Chapter 3 for ways to delegate and document responsibilities!

Remember that Chapter 3 emphasized how identifying individual strengths and skills can then be utilized to have educators select roles that match those strengths and skills and lead to increased parity and agreement. If each team member feels valued for what they bring to the collective table, they will be more likely to follow through with their part of the plan.

The Connecting to Practice vignettes provided here demonstrate instances of collaborative teams using the Competing Pathways diagram to provide Tier 2 and Tier 3 behavioral supports. The vignettes provide clear examples of roles that different collaborative team members can take to support student behavior. They also demonstrate how specific evidence-based behavioral support strategies can fit into a comprehensive Behavior Intervention Plan.

Connecting to Practice

Tier 2 Support With Check-In, Check-Out

Aparicio is a 10th-grade student who came to the attention of his school's Student Support Team through a universal screening of risk indicators. Aparicio had failing grades in all of his core academic classes for the first and second marking periods. The team has been particularly diligent in monitoring students as they returned to in-person learning after over a year of virtual instruction required by pandemic protocols. Prior to the pandemic, Aparicio had been an average student, earning Bs and Cs in his core subjects and As in his art electives.

Aparicio's history of grade-level achievement led the support team to question whether his 10th-grade performance was due to a loss of skill, behavioral changes, or some combination of the two. Quick check-ins with Aparicio's teachers and a review of the online gradebook revealed that Aparicio's failing grades were largely due to missing assignments. When he did submit work, he generally earned Bs or Cs. Teachers reported that Aparicio demonstrated knowledge of taught concepts during group discussions. Collectively, his teachers felt that Aparicio was capable of the work but choosing not to complete it. The Student Support Team met with Aparicio's parents and decided to use Function-Based Thinking to understand the situation better.

The team used information from the gradebook, disciplinary referrals, and an interview with Aparicio as indirect data sources. They also asked each of Aparicio's teachers to complete a simple form to track the antecedent, behavior, and consequence when he was given assignments in class for one week. A pattern emerged indicating that Aparicio rarely completed worksheets or anything that involved writing more than a paragraph. This was true of in-class assignments and homework. Aparicio was more likely to complete assignments that allowed him to integrate art or technology, or to share his knowledge orally. Analysis of the ABC data revealed that, when given a written assignment in class, Aparicio often ignored the assignment and listened to music while drawing. Aparicio had one disciplinary referral that was issued because he yelled and cursed at a teacher who pressed him to complete his work and took away his drawing.

During the interview, Aparicio reported that most assignments are "stupid and pointless because you are never going to use that stuff in the real world." He shared that he was planning to be a graphic designer because he could create art and make good money. When asked what happened on the day he received a disciplinary referral, Aparicio shared that he lost his temper because the teacher took a drawing that he had been working on for several days.

With this information, the support team hypothesized that the primary function of Aparicio's behavior was to **gain access** to a preferred activity (drawing). A secondary function was to **avoid** tasks that he perceived as pointless. This hypothesis is documented in the middle row of the Aparicio's Competing Pathways diagram (Figure 10.3).

(Continued)

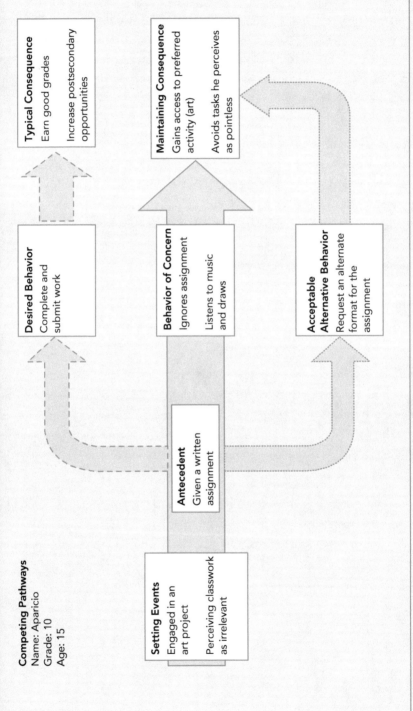

FIGURE 10.3 Competing Pathways for Aparicio

Competing Pathways
Name: Aparicio
Grade: 10
Age: 15

Setting Events
Engaged in an art project

Perceiving classwork as irrelevant

Antecedent
Given a written assignment

Desired Behavior
Complete and submit work

Typical Consequence
Earn good grades

Increase postsecondary opportunities

Behavior of Concern
Ignores assignment

Listens to music and draws

Maintaining Consequence
Gains access to preferred activity (art)

Avoids tasks he perceives as pointless

Acceptable Alternative Behavior
Request an alternate format for the assignment

Source: Adapted from Functional assessment and program development for problem behavior: A practical handbook (O'Neill et al., 2015). Cengage Learning Inc. Reproduced by permission. www.cengage.com/permissions

The team determined that the desired behavior was for Aparicio to complete his work, which would eventually lead to better grades. Aparicio's graphic design teacher offered to show Aparicio some postsecondary graphic design programs and help Aparicio see the connection between good grades in his core content classes and being accepted in those graphic design programs. The team determined that an acceptable alternative behavior would be for Aparicio to request an alternative format for assignments, allowing him to use art, technology, or spoken responses to demonstrate his knowledge. The team decided to implement Check-In, Check-Out, with the graphic design teacher serving as Aparicio's coach. Aparicio would collaborate with his coach to set daily goals for work completion in standard and alternative formats. He would earn access to specialized graphic design software for achieving those goals. The graphic design teacher would also use the coaching sessions to discuss postsecondary options for graphic design with Aparicio and meet with Aparicio's core content teachers to suggest alternative assignments that would meet their objectives while also fulfilling Aparicio's desire to engage in technology use and drawing. Table 10.2 is Aparicio's Competing Pathways intervention plan.

TABLE 10.2 Competing Pathways Intervention Planning for Aparicio

SETTING INTERVENTIONS	ANTECEDENT INTERVENTIONS	BEHAVIOR INTERVENTIONS	CONSEQUENCE INTERVENTIONS
Morning Check-In, Check-Out Routine The graphic design teacher will check in with Aparicio each morning. Aparicio and the graphic design teacher will discuss art projects that are in progress and identify appropriate times to work on them. Aparicio and the graphic design teacher will establish daily goals for completing work as assigned and for requesting alternative formats.	When passing out assignments, teachers will quietly remind Aparicio that he can have time to work on art projects when his classwork is completed. Aparicio will keep a list of possible alternative formats for assignments in his binder. The graphic design teacher will meet with other teachers and the school counselor to proactively brainstorm alternative assignments that would also meet content objectives. This will help teachers feel more comfortable with the plan going forward when Aparicio requests alternative formats.	The school counselor will collect information from Aparicio's teachers to establish guidelines about when assignment formats can or cannot be changed. The school counselor and Aparicio will discuss possible format changes for different types of school assignments. The school counselor and graphic design teacher will teach Aparicio how to request alternative assignment formats politely. The graphic design teacher will talk with Aparicio about post-secondary programs in graphic design and discuss admission requirements. All teachers will prompt Aparicio to consider format options when they notice he is not working.	All teachers will consider Aparicio's requests for alternative format options when the proposed option allows them to evaluate his knowledge or explain why the requested alternative format won't work. All teachers will note Aparicio's progress toward his daily work goals on a Google Form. *Afternoon Check-In, Check-Out Routine* The graphic design teacher will check in with Aparicio at the end of the day to see how he made progress toward his daily goals. Aparicio will be able to use graphic design software after school when he has met weekly work completion goals.

Connecting to Practice

Tier 3 Support With Intensified Check-In, Check-Out

Samantha is a fifth grader who was found eligible for special education as a student with autism and a learning disability in reading. In previous school years, she engaged in high rates of self-injury (hitting or biting herself) or property destruction (flipping desks, pulling items off walls or shelves) when she was overwhelmed by academic content or noisy settings, or when she lost a game. She has been receiving all academic instruction in the special education setting with Ms. Reagan for the last year and a half. Ms. Reagan and a collaborative team (including Samantha, her parents, the school counselor, and the instructional technology teacher) successfully developed and implemented a function-aligned behavior intervention that extinguished Samantha's self-injury and reduced the frequency of property destruction to less than one incident per month. As Samantha's behaviors of concern decreased, she made significant academic gains. Her decoding skills improved from a kindergarten level to a second-grade level and her math skills improved to grade level. The IEP team, including Samantha's parents, decided to transition her into a co-taught general education math classroom so she could receive increased exposure to grade-level math content.

While Samantha was initially excited about the plan, her behavior quickly deteriorated. After one week of being in the general education classroom, Samantha began expressing concern that people thought she was "stupid." In the second week, she ran away from the general education classroom on four occasions and left the school building twice. Although Samantha's team tried applying the strategies from the original Behavior Intervention Plan, Samantha's behavior escalated. When she was unable to run from the classroom, she would flip desks and throw objects until an administrator or special education teacher came to remove her from the classroom. The collaborative team decided to update the Functional Behavior Assessment to get a better understanding of the patterns and function associated with Samantha's behavior. The findings of the Functional Behavior Assessment are depicted in the middle row of Figure 10.4. Essentially, Samantha was triggered to run from the classroom when she made a mistake or feared she made a mistake. The function of the behavior was hypothesized to be **escape** from the challenging content and her perception that peers were judging her.

The team determined that the desired behaviors (top row of Figure 10.4) would be for Samantha to calmly accept making a mistake or to ask for help when she was feeling uncertain about content. The team recognized that it would take time for Samantha to develop these skills. They decided that teaching Samantha to take a break in or outside of the classroom would be an acceptable alternative to running from the room or school building (bottom row of Samantha's Competing Pathways diagram). This would meet the escape need while ensuring that Samantha and other students remained safe.

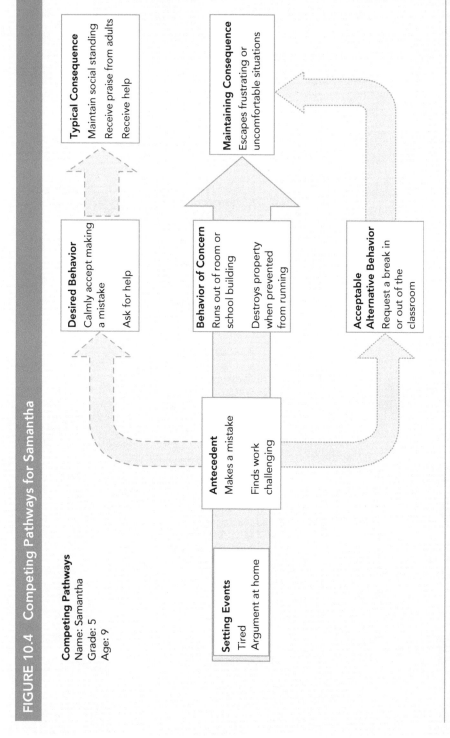

FIGURE 10.4 Competing Pathways for Samantha

Competing Pathways
Name: Samantha
Grade: 5
Age: 9

Setting Events
Tired
Argument at home

Antecedent
Makes a mistake
Finds work challenging

Desired Behavior
Calmly accept making a mistake
Ask for help

Typical Consequence
Maintain social standing
Receive praise from adults
Receive help

Behavior of Concern
Runs out of room or school building
Destroys property when prevented from running

Maintaining Consequence
Escapes frustrating or uncomfortable situations

Acceptable Alternative Behavior
Request a break in or out of the classroom

Source: Adapted from *Functional assessment and program development for problem behavior: A practical handbook* (O'Neill et al., 2015). Cengage Learning Inc. Reproduced by permission. www.cengage.com/permissions

(Continued)

(Continued)

The team also recognized that no individual member could address Samantha's needs across the phases of the behavior. They developed a plan that involved parent communication, an intensified Check-In, Check-Out process with the instructional technology teacher serving as Samantha's coach, systematic instruction in the replacement behaviors provided by the special education teacher and school counselor, and collaborative prompting and priming provided by all of the teachers and paraprofessionals who worked with Samantha as well as her classroom peers. The plan is documented in Samantha's Competing Pathways intervention plan (Table 10.3).

TABLE 10.3   Competing Pathways Intervention Planning for Samantha

SETTING INTERVENTIONS	ANTECEDENT INTERVENTIONS	BEHAVIOR INTERVENTIONS	CONSEQUENCE INTERVENTIONS
Parent will email or call the special education teacher when Samantha has had disrupted sleep or an argument at home before school. *Morning Check-In, Check-Out Routine* The instructional technology teacher will check in with Samantha as she gets off the bus to see how she is feeling and whether she is ready to go to class immediately or needs to use self-regulation strategies before joining the group. The instructional technology teacher will collaborate with Samantha to establish a daily goal for time in the general education setting.	The general education teacher will post visual cues at Samantha's desk to prompt requesting a break or asking for help. *Intensified Check-In, Check-Out Routine* The instructional technology teacher or special education teacher will check in with Samantha before her general education math class to see if she needs to use any self-regulation strategies. Before Samantha enters the general education classroom each day, the instructional technology teacher or special education teacher will remind her of how she can request a break or ask for help.	The special education teacher will work with Samantha to identify safe and comfortable break locations in the general education classroom and at least one location outside of the classroom. The special education teacher will work with Samantha to develop verbal and nonverbal cues that she can use to indicate that she needs to access one of those break spaces. Both co-teachers will be familiar with the cues. The special education teacher will roleplay safe transitions to the break spaces with Samantha.	All teachers and paraprofessionals will respond to Samantha's requests for help or requests for a break immediately and consistently. *Afternoon Check-In, Check-Out Routine* The instructional technology teacher will check in with Samantha at the end of the day to see how she made progress toward her daily goal. The instructional technology teacher will play a game with Samantha during bus call on the days when she has met her daily goal. Alternatively, the teacher will coach Samantha through strategies for future implementation on days when the goal was not met.

SETTING INTERVENTIONS	ANTECEDENT INTERVENTIONS	BEHAVIOR INTERVENTIONS	CONSEQUENCE INTERVENTIONS
	The general education and special education co-teachers will provide Samantha with two questions that will be asked during group work, so she will have a chance to preview those questions and be prepared to respond with correct answers when class begins. With Samantha's family's permission, Samantha's class peers will be taught ways to provide positive feedback when she attempts to answer a question, to increase positive feedback and decrease Samantha's perception that her peers are judging her negatively.	The school counselor and a group of selected classroom peers will engage in social skills instruction related to making mistakes and asking for help. All teachers and paraprofessionals who work with Samantha will use the same phrasing to prompt Samantha to ask for help. Samantha's peers will be taught to use the same phrasing to ask for help in class.	

Summary

There are times when students require individualized support to learn safe and productive behaviors. ***Function-aligned behavioral intervention*** **[SE_HLP10]** is both an evidence-based and a high-leverage practice. Functional Behavior Assessment, Function-Based Thinking, and the behavior plans that derive from those processes are inherently collaborative. Through these processes, educators ***elicit and interpret student thinking*** **[GE_HLP3]**, ***establish community expectations for behavior*** **[GE_HLP7]**, and identify supports to provide ***positive and constructive feedback to guide students' behavior*** **[SE_HLP8]**.

Co-assessing and Sharing Social Emotional Learning Outcomes

11

Which came first, assessment or instruction? Yes, it is the ol' chicken-and-egg conundrum. While we cannot say definitively which one comes first, we *know* that the most effective instruction begins and ends with assessment. This is true of both academics and social emotional learning. Throughout this book we have discussed the three elements of co-teaching: co-assessment, co-planning, and co-instruction. They occur in a continuous cycle, as shown in Figure 11.1, which is why both the second and the third sections of this book open and close with chapters on co-assessment.

FIGURE 11.1   Co-teaching Cycle

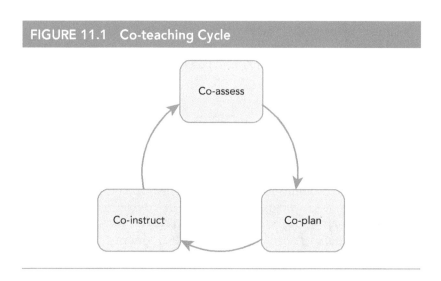

The purpose of co-assessment *prior to* social emotional instruction differs from the purpose of co-assessment that occurs *after* instruction and intervention for social emotional learning have begun. Think of the initial co-assessment as establishing a baseline. Its purpose is essentially to answer the question, "Where are we starting?" which should lead to the follow-up question, "Where do we want to be?" These elements of co-assessment for social emotional learning are addressed in Chapters 8 and 9 of the book.

Co-assessment that occurs *after* instruction has ended (e.g., summative assessment) answers the question, "Did we achieve our desired outcome?" We would suggest that true summative assessment is uncommon when working toward social emotional competencies, because educators continuously raise the bar of developmental expectations and continue teaching. However, there are times when they assess the outcome of an intervention using a summative assessment, for example, to report on an IEP goal. Formative assessment is far more common with social emotional competencies. In this case, it answers the question, "Are we making progress toward our desired outcome?" Thus, it is often called **progress monitoring**. Co-assessment for the purpose of monitoring the progress of social, emotional, and behavioral growth is the focus of this chapter.

As with co-assessment that occurs to set the stage for a responsive classroom climate or to identify needs for individualized intervention, co-assessment for progress monitoring can involve a variety of collaborative interactions. Co-teachers, paraprofessionals, school specialists, administrators, parents, and students themselves may all contribute in meaningful ways. Collaboration for assessment may occur when teams are (1) identifying social emotional goals and selecting aligned measures, (2) collecting assessment data, (3) interpreting these data, and (4) reporting outcomes.

Administrators have a particularly important role in supporting co-assessment of social emotional learning. Research indicates that teachers find assessment of behavior and social skills to be more challenging than academic assessment (Ruble et al., 2018). Teachers express a need for training in social, emotional, and behavioral assessments as well as time to conduct the assessments and collaboratively analyze outcomes. Administrators have an important responsibility to ensure that these opportunities are provided.

The progress monitoring cycle is an example of the high-leverage practice *use student assessment data, analyze instruction, and make adjustments* [SE_HLP6]. Other high-leverage practices from general and special education are closely aligned with progress monitoring through co-assessment. These include *prioritizing goals* [SE_HLP11], *interpreting student work* [GE_HLP17] in ways that identify *patterns of thinking* [GE_HLP4], *providing feedback to students* [GE_HLP18], and *collaborating with profession-als to increase student success* [SE_HLP1]. Below we discuss the integration of high-leverage practices, steps of progress monitoring, and collaborative opportunities that exist in each of these steps.

Progress Monitoring and Data-Based Decision Making

Progress monitoring is a form of recurrent formative assessment used to measure the development of skills associated with long-term outcomes. Progress monitoring requires frequent and systematic use of measures that are sensitive to student growth. The intention of progress monitoring is to *interpret student work* [GE_HLP17] and quickly *make adjustments* [SE_HLP6] to ensure that instructional practices are meeting student needs.

Collaborative teams conduct assessment to monitor progress toward social emotional learning outcomes in all tiers of Multi-Tiered Systems of Support or Positive Behavioral Interventions and Supports. Team members collect and analyze group data to evaluate the effectiveness of Tier 1 supports for creating culturally responsive and positive school or classroom climates. Individualized data must be collected to evaluate the effectiveness of Tier 2 and Tier 3 interventions. Multi-Tiered Systems of Support and Positive Behavioral Interventions and Supports both emphasize collaborative data-based decision making as a requirement for equitable and responsive outcomes. Educators in schools that are not implementing these frameworks can still benefit from collaborating with colleagues across the phases of assessment for social emotional learning.

Collaboration to Establish Goals and Select Progress Monitoring Measures

Before progress monitoring can occur, educators must select or create the assessment tools that will be used. Integral to that selection is understanding the social, emotional, or behavioral outcome that is to be measured. We can't determine if we are making progress if the end goal is unknown! Goals must be quantitatively measurable and objectively stated. Progress monitoring measures must be accurate, efficient, and aligned with the goals.

When establishing goals and selecting measures of individual student progress in social emotional competencies for Tier 2 or Tier 3 interventions, goals often become apparent through the Functional Behavior Assessment or Function-Based Thinking processes, as described in Chapter 10. The desired and acceptable alternative behaviors become the outcomes that need to be measured.

> ### Chapter Connections
>
> Time to go back and revisit Functional Behavior Assessment and Function-Based Thinking processes in Chapter 10. Look back over the examples with Aparicio and Samantha at the end of that chapter.

For example, in Chapter 10 the desired behavior for Aparicio was to complete and submit his classwork. A specific goal aligned with this behavior might be for Aparicio to complete and submit 95% of his work by the due date in all classes for four consecutive weeks. In this case, the goal makes the measure clear: tracking the percentage of assignments completed and submitted on a weekly basis. The wording of the goal also makes it easy to determine if it has been achieved.

Sometimes in the early stages of developing goals for class or schoolwide social emotional learning, a positively worded measurable goal is difficult to articulate. Teams may have a broad sense of what they want to work toward, but be unable to describe it in precise or measurable ways. For example, the goal of "improving school climate" could mean any number of things. Perhaps it means increasing parent and community engagement, which could be measured by tracking participation in school events. Or it may mean increasing students' perceptions of safety, which might be measured through a student survey or focus groups. If it is about improving actual safety, this outcome could be measured by tracking acts of bullying or aggression through disciplinary referrals. Before finalizing their goals, teams need to discuss what the desired outcome looks like and how it could be measured.

In addition to having broad goals, school teams are sometimes focused on naming the behaviors they want to decrease as opposed to the specific behaviors they want to increase. Positively worded goals are helpful in guiding teams to think about instructional strategies as opposed to punishment strategies for addressing social emotional outcomes. The shift to positive goals can occur by collaboratively identifying sources that specify what desired behavior looks like. Teams may build goals around social emotional learning standards, if applicable to the state. Specialists, such as school counselors or social workers, may have detailed knowledge of those standards, making them valuable collaborators in setting goals and identifying assessment measures. Collaboration with students, families, and community members can help teams identify goals that have value beyond the school setting, as discussed in Chapters 9 and 10.

Goals and progress measures built around community input are more likely to have community support. For example, in Chapter 9 we identified using polite language, tone, and actions as a behavioral indicator for the expectation "be respectful" in secondary classrooms. A collaborative history and social science team wanting to reduce students' use of personal insults during discussions of controversial topics could frame a behavioral goal in the context of using polite language and tone of voice (as opposed to merely saying, "Don't be rude or disrespectful"). The goal might be to have students use the civil discourse strategy known as the Assertion Reasoning Evidence method for constructing an argument (Shuster, n.d.). Precisely measuring progress toward this type of goal requires direct observation, which is discussed later in this chapter. Alternatively, progress toward the overall goal of decreasing insults could be measured by tracking data on the use of insults that lead to disciplinary referrals. With this measure, the team must intentionally focus on increasing respectful behavior to decrease the disciplinary referrals.

Universal Assessments of Social Emotional Learning

We've mentioned discipline referrals as a data source a few times already. Tier 1 social emotional learning outcomes often focus on creating a positive climate that keeps learners safely engaged in school. Therefore, Positive Behavioral Interventions and Supports experts advocate for the use of office disciplinary referrals and school climate data to monitor the effectiveness of Tier 1 supports. While school climate data are typically collected only a few times a year, office disciplinary referrals can be analyzed monthly and serve as a form of schoolwide progress monitoring. (If we analyze data monthly, we have opportunities to make changes during the school year. If we only collect data at the beginning and end of the school year, we have to wait until the next year.)

When using office disciplinary referrals to evaluate progress toward positive, culturally responsive schools, the referrals must include data that allow collaborative teams to determine where and when additional supports may be needed. For example, are there certain settings or times of day in which referrals are more likely to be issued? If so, the team needs to examine expectations and routines for those settings and determine if revisions are required or if additional instruction is needed. The referrals also need to have information that allows data to be disaggregated to identify inequitable experiences. In other words, collaborative teams want to be able to determine if certain groups of students are more likely to receive office disciplinary referrals than others, or if certain staff members are more likely to make referrals. This is a critical step toward creating culturally responsive, trauma-informed school cultures.

The Center on PBIS (n.d.) identifies the following as important elements of an office disciplinary referral:

- Date and time of the event

- Student name and ID number

- Name of referring staff member

- Student grade level

- Location of the event

- Behavior

- Action taken

Additional data related to gender, race/ethnicity, and disability are often captured in the analysis, though not specifically recorded on the forms completed by school staff.

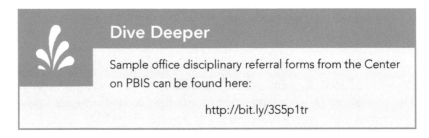

Dive Deeper

Sample office disciplinary referral forms from the Center on PBIS can be found here:

http://bit.ly/3S5p1tr

When schoolwide systems do not exist for progress monitoring social emotional learning practices, collaborating teachers may want to evaluate their own use of disciplinary referrals. Co-teachers and grade-level or content-area teams can look for trends related to students who receive referrals, educators who issue referrals, times of day, and settings. Through collaboration, educators can use this assessment data to create responsive classrooms, even in the absence of schoolwide practices. This process is a form of *interpreting student work* **[GE_HLP17]** and *using assessment data to analyze instruction and make adjustments* when needed **[SE_HLP6]**.

Teachers can also seek student input to monitor progress toward a positive classroom climate. While schoolwide climate surveys are typically administered once or twice a year, teachers can survey students using informal tools much more frequently. This strategy provides ample opportunity to *identify patterns of student thinking* **[GE_HLP4]**. Students can be asked to rate their perceptions of factors that align with a positive climate such as feeling safe or respected. Learners can also self-report feelings associated with climate. For example, young students might rate their feelings of stress using a visual scale, such as the one depicted in Figure 11.2. (Note that allowing students to generate their own images or terminology for concepts on a scale can make the tools more meaningful.)

FIGURE 11.2   Visual Scale of Stress

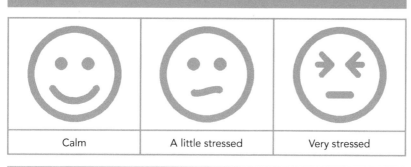

| Calm | A little stressed | Very stressed |

Icon source: iStock.com/in8finity

Digital tools, such as Google Forms or polling options available in many learning management systems, including Canvas and Blackboard, allow students to respond anonymously. Teachers can also use low-tech options, such as having students place a token in a jar or sticky note on a poster to indicate their perspectives about classroom climate. Small-group or individualized check-ins with students also provide valuable information. However, educators need to think about how they will consistently collect data from those check-ins as part of progress monitoring. A tally sheet used as co-teachers apply OTOS or alternative groupings could be a quick and easy tool for turning those personal connections into quantitative data.

There is also a wide range of published measures available to assess Tier 1 social emotional learning. Many of them are not designed for the type of repeated use that is required for progress monitoring, but they can still be effective for overall assessment of climate. In the Check It Out box below you can find a searchable bank of social emotional assessment tools provided on the Collaborative for Academic, Social, and Emotional Learning website.

 Check It Out

The Collaborative for Academic, Social, and Emotional Learning (www.casel.org) has a searchable list of social emotional learning assessments that can be found here:

http://bit.ly/3lyBmmz

Assessments of Individualized
Social, Emotional, and Behavioral Growth

As noted previously, students receiving Tier 2 or Tier 3 supports for social emotional learning have individualized goals based on the skills that were targeted for growth. Measuring progress in individualized skills often requires individualized assessment. Assessment of social, emotional, and behavioral skills can be done through direct or indirect measures. **Direct measures** involve observations of students to assess a specific set of behaviors.

Chapter Connections

In Chapter 10, we provided a link to the AFIRM module, which offers more information about using direct measures. Feel free to revisit it!

http://bit.ly/413rTuY

Examples of direct measures include frequency counts, latency recording, duration recording, and time sampling. These measures are precise, repeatable, and highly sensitive to student progress (F. G. Miller et al., 2014). In fact, they are ideal for progress monitoring in many ways. However, accurate data collection with these measures requires training and a considerable amount of practice. **Indirect measures** don't require focused observations of students. The most common type of indirect measure used for progress monitoring is a rating scale. Individuals familiar with a student are asked to rate the young person's behavior based on general knowledge, rather than specific events. Rating scales are easy to complete but can be more subjective than direct observations. Additionally, many rating scales require training for officially interpreting the results.

A third type of measure, which blends elements of direct and indirect measures, also exists. It is called a **hybrid measure**. One such tool, the Direct Behavior Rating–Single Item Scales (Chafouleas et al., 2012) asks teachers to rate student engagement, respectful behaviors, and disruptive behaviors immediately following a brief, focused observation (F. G. Miller et al., 2014). Exploring the validity and reliability of this measure, Chafouleas and colleagues (2012) found that it accurately describes student behaviors across settings and times of day and that it is sensitive to change.

Check It Out

Get free access to the Direct Behavior Rating–Single Item Scales through the Evidence-Based Intervention Network (missouri.edu).

http://bit.ly/3lBiz0S

Different observers are highly consistent in assigning ratings when students demonstrate behaviors with high intensity or frequency and when the behaviors are of minimal concern. There is more variability across observers when student behavior is inconsistent or in the more moderate ranges of intensity. Therefore, when using this measure, it is beneficial to have consistent observers who are familiar with the student. The Direct Behavior Rating–Single Item Scales tool is available for free through the Evidence-Based Intervention Network.

Collaborating to Collect Assessment Data

In addition to direct, indirect, and hybrid observation tools, co-assessment for social, emotional, and behavioral growth can use tools that are embedded into instruction and intervention. As we shared in Chapter 10, educators may feel overwhelmed by the prospect of collecting data alone. That is one reason why *co*-assessment is so valuable for ensuring that information is gathered efficiently and accurately. Co-teaching and other forms of collaboration with staff, and even students, can make progress monitoring of social emotional learning manageable.

The OTOS co-teaching model is ideal for progress monitoring through direct and hybrid observation. While one teacher leads instruction, the other educator can observe one or more students to collect data. In fact, the teacher in the support role can even collect data on the whole-class use of a strategy. For example, in the previously mentioned secondary social studies class, where teachers are working on decreasing insults and increasing the use of the Assertion Reasoning Evidence method for civil discourse, the educator in the support role could collect data on how often students use the Assertion Reasoning Evidence method during a group discussion. The co-teachers could plan for this assessment activity to occur twice a month for 15 minutes to allow for continuous progress monitoring. By co-teaching using OTOS, the teacher in the support role can dedicate their attention to observing student behavior, without the distraction of managing content. This is important for accurate assessment, particularly when collecting frequency, latency, or duration data. Either teacher might take the role of data collector as the other leads instruction.

Collaboration for co-assessment can also occur outside of the co-teaching relationship. You may recall that we discussed Check-In, Check-Out in Chapter 10. It's a research-based intervention in which students collaborate with a coach at the beginning and end of the school day to set and track goals for their own growth. The student uses a Daily Progress Report, on which teachers document student progress toward goal behaviors and provide brief feedback throughout the day (Drevon et al., 2019). The Daily Progress Report integrates multiple high-leverage practices including ***providing feedback to students*** **[GE_HLP18]** and ***collaborating with professionals to increase student success*** **[SE_HLP1]**. Check-In, Check-Out is relatively easy to implement and has the added benefit of incorporating data that can be used for progress monitoring into intervention itself. No extra steps required! Teachers, Check-In, Check-Out coaches, and the student monitor progress by tracking the frequency with which the student achieves the daily goal.

Other daily reports can be used in a similar fashion. For example, Table 11.1 shows a Daily Behavior Tracker used in a secondary setting to simultaneously remind a student of expectations for demonstrating engagement and monitor their progress in doing so. The version represented in Table 11.1 was developed for Michael, a high school student who was referred to his school's Student Support Team because he was failing classes and getting multiple low-level discipline referrals. The team identified two consistent behaviors of concern that were contributing to his difficulties. These behaviors included not bringing needed materials to class and engaging in disruptive, off-topic discussions during instruction and independent work. These behaviors prevented Michael from completing and submitting work. The team decided to set and track three goals that were incompatible with his behaviors of concern. He received instruction in expectations for these goals. The tracker reminded him of the expectations, provided an opportunity for teachers to give him feedback during each instructional period, and offered a source of data for progress monitoring. (We will come back to the intervention and progress monitoring used with Michael later in this chapter.)

While the form is customized to Michael's goals, this type of tracker is easily adaptable. A paper behavior tracker is easy to produce and requires no technological expertise from the receiving teachers. However, paper forms sometimes get lost. Digital versions using Google Forms or a similar technology can also be used and don't get lost as easily. However, without a tangible reminder, students sometimes forget to get the forms marked. Some educators have found it useful to give a student a QR code that they can share with teachers when it is time to check in. Whether using this type of tracker on paper or as a digital form, collaboration is important. Teachers and students need to select the format that works for everyone, make sure that the behaviors being tracked are clearly defined and understood by all parties, and determine when the student should ask teachers to complete it.

The Daily Progress Report and Daily Behavior Tracker both include opportunities for student self-monitoring. Self-monitoring can occur outside of these interventions as well. **Self-monitoring** is a research-based intervention that raises student awareness about the frequency of a behavior. The intervention is a self-assessment strategy. It serves two purposes—changing behavior and tracking behavior—which allows for easy progress monitoring. When using self-monitoring as an intervention, students collaborate with adults to define behaviors that they want to change and set goals for how often desired behaviors should occur.

TABLE 11.1 Daily Behavior Tracker for Secondary Student Engagement

Name: _____ Week of: _____

Note for teachers: Please mark "yes" or "no" to indicate the student's performance of the goal behaviors.

DAY	Arrived in class with all required materials including homework			Completed and turned in all work assigned for the period				Was quiet during instruction and independent work time			
	PERIOD 1	PERIOD 2 OR 3	PERIOD 4 OR 5	PERIOD 6 OR 7	PERIOD 1	PERIOD 2 OR 3	PERIOD 4 OR 5	PERIOD 6 OR 7	PERIOD 1	PERIOD 2 OR 3	PERIOD 4 OR 5	PERIOD 6 OR 7
Monday	Yes/No	Yes/No	Yes/No	Yes/No	Yes/No	Yes/No	Yes/No	Yes/No	Yes/No	Yes/No	Yes/No	Yes/No
Tuesday	Yes/No	Yes/No	Yes/No	Yes/No	Yes/No	Yes/No	Yes/No	Yes/No	Yes/No	Yes/No	Yes/No	Yes/No
Thursday	Yes/No	Yes/No	Yes/No	Yes/No	Yes/No	Yes/No	Yes/No	Yes/No	Yes/No	Yes/No	Yes/No	Yes/No
Friday	Yes/No	Yes/No	Yes/No	Yes/No	Yes/No	Yes/No	Yes/No	Yes/No	Yes/No	Yes/No	Yes/No	Yes/No
Saturday	Yes/No	Yes/No	Yes/No	Yes/No	Yes/No	Yes/No	Yes/No	Yes/No	Yes/No	Yes/No	Yes/No	Yes/No

Total number of "yes" responses earned for the week: _____ /60

Parent Signature: _____

The goal can be to increase or decrease the frequency of a behavior. For example, in Chapter 10, Samantha's team wanted to increase the frequency with which she asked for help and decrease the frequency of running from the classroom. In this case it would make sense to set goals for the behavior the team wants to encourage—asking for help. Samantha would track the number of times that she asked for assistance during her math class by making a tally mark each time she did so. She would work toward achieving realistic daily (or weekly) goals that she established for herself in collaboration with her teachers. When she had achieved her goals, a reinforcement would be provided.

Self-monitoring can be used for a wide variety of behaviors such as staying on-task, using friendly greetings, following organizational routines, and countless other social emotional expectations. As an alternative to using frequency counts, students can self-monitor using "yes" or "no" questions at the end of a designated period. An example of a lunchtime self-monitoring ticket is shown in the Clarifying Concepts box.

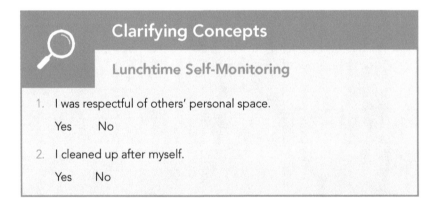

Clarifying Concepts

Lunchtime Self-Monitoring

1. I was respectful of others' personal space.

   Yes   No

2. I cleaned up after myself.

   Yes   No

An essential feature of self-monitoring is that students are rewarded for accurate reporting of the goal behavior, independent of goal achievement. We want students to truthfully acknowledge how frequently a behavior occurs, then work on changing the frequency. When self-monitoring is introduced, students and teachers usually co-monitor and check with each other to verify the counts. When mismatches are present, the collaborating teacher and student discuss differences in perspective until they reach a consensus. When student self-monitoring is reliable, it can become a tool for progress monitoring.

Organizing and Interpreting
Social Emotional Learning Assessment Data

Co-assessment does not stop once assessments have been administered. Assessment data only become valuable when educators can use the ***patterns identified*** **[GE_HLP4]** to make informed decisions. Positive Behavioral Interventions and Supports frameworks provide important guidance about who should be involved in organizing and analyzing social emotional learning assessment data, when the data should be analyzed, and how data can be interpreted.

Literature on Positive Behavioral Interventions and Supports often talks about the "Leadership Team" as the group that makes schoolwide decisions. The team could be called a variety of other names. Some examples include "School Site Council" or "Equity Team." In responsive schools, these collaborative teams include administrators, teacher leaders, and other key stakeholders who represent values of the community. The team that makes decisions for the school, a grade level, or a classroom should include people who have knowledge of students and school values *and* who have the authority to implement decisions made by the team. The collaborative team that convenes to organize and interpret Tier 2 or Tier 3 data for individual learners also needs to include individuals who have detailed knowledge of the young people. Parents and students are important members of these teams.

Positive Behavioral Interventions and Supports literature is clear that progress monitoring data should be collected frequently so supports can be adjusted in a timely fashion. It is recommended that progress monitoring occur at least weekly for students receiving Tier 2 or Tier 3 social emotional intervention (Missouri Department of Elementary and Secondary Education, 2017). Data analysis should occur every four to six weeks during intervention. In all cases, teams need a minimum of three data points to be able to draw meaningful conclusions about the effectiveness of an intervention.

We previously said that co-assessment for progress monitoring needs to result in quantitative data. Educators are often skilled at sensing if an intervention is working, but years of research show that we cannot merely rely on intuition for making culturally responsive decisions about social emotional learning. Even the most skilled and best-intentioned educators sometimes demonstrate bias when reporting on social emotional outcomes. Sometimes a student has just pushed buttons for so long that it is hard to see change. In other cases, we hope for change so much that we overestimate the effectiveness of our interventions. Quantitative assessment data discussed by a collaborative team help to reduce bias and ensure the best outcomes for students. Graphing data are particularly helpful because they give a visual representation of trends.

Graphing and interpreting data can feel a bit overwhelming. In fact, it is an area where teachers report having low self-efficacy (Espin et al., 2021). There are elaborate ways to precisely evaluate growth in comparison to target goals over time. A link to a great module from the National Center on Intensive Intervention is provided in the Dive Deeper box if you are ready to use that level of data analysis.

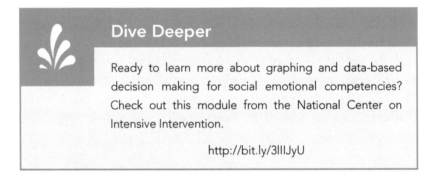

Dive Deeper

Ready to learn more about graphing and data-based decision making for social emotional competencies? Check out this module from the National Center on Intensive Intervention.

http://bit.ly/3IIIJyU

However, there is a simpler option that is still very effective. It requires three things: (1) the student's starting point before intervention, also known as baseline; (2) the end goal for performance; and (3) a progress monitoring measure.

It is possible to create paper-and-pencil graphs of this information to help with decision making. However, if you are spreadsheet savvy, you can create your own documents in Excel or Google Sheets. Better yet, the Missouri Department of Elementary and Secondary Education (2017), in coordination with university partners and the Office of Special Education Programs, has created free templates in Excel and Google that are very easy to use. You can find them by following the link in the Dive Deeper box on the next page. The Advanced Tier Spreadsheet is a user-friendly tool for tracking and graphing student data.

Dive Deeper

Want easy-to-use data analysis tools for progress monitoring behavior? Visit the Missouri Schoolwide Positive Behavior Supports website at

https://bit.ly/3xtTcRo

We felt that a demonstration would be the best way to explain how baseline data, an end goal, and progress monitoring data come together in a graph to facilitate collaborative decision making. So, let's discuss Michael a bit further. Michael's case is provided in the Connecting to Practice box, along with his Daily Behavior Tracker and progress monitoring examples.

Connecting to Practice

Michael

Michael was receiving Tier 2 intervention for not having materials and engaging in disruptive off-task behavior in his classes. His intervention team decided to use the Daily Behavior Tracker shown in Table 11.1.

The school counselor, Ms. Jennings, took the lead role in collaborating with Michael and his teachers to implement the intervention developed by the Student Support Team. The team, including Michael, set a goal for him to earn 80% of the possible points on his tracking sheet each week for six consecutive weeks. In the first week, ending 3/7/22, Michael brought the tracking sheet to each of his classes to establish baseline data. No other supports were used during that week. This approach resulted in a baseline score of 20 out of 69 possible points for the week.

Ms. Jennings entered the data point into the Advanced Tier Spreadsheet and added a notation in the phase-change column. This action created a vertical line on the graph separating the baseline phase from subsequent intervention phases. She also entered the goal of 80% into the spreadsheet, which created a horizontal goal line across the top of the graph (Figure 11.3).

(Continued)

FIGURE 11.3   Progress Monitoring Intervention 1

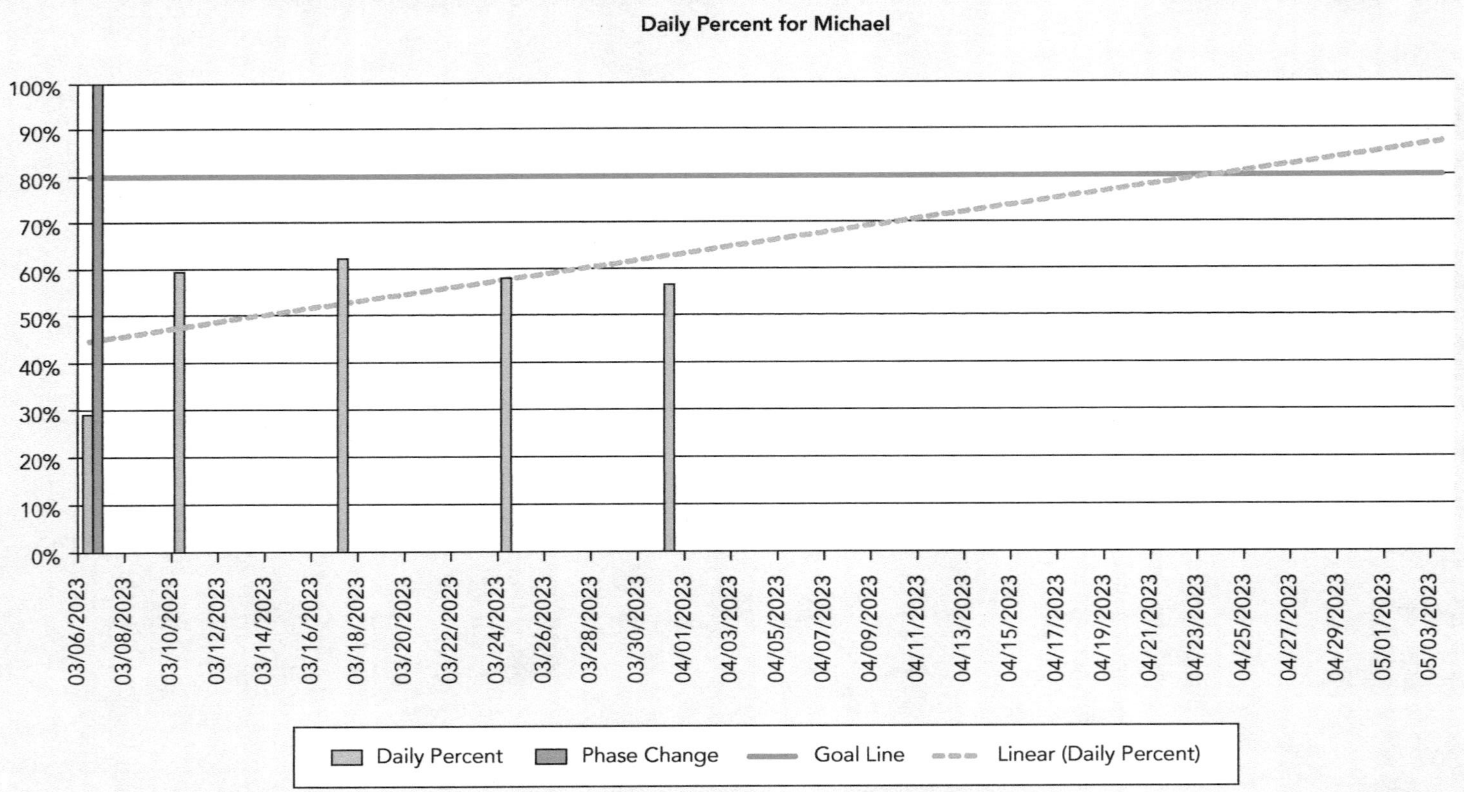

Daily Percent for Michael

Progress Monitoring of Engagement Expectations for Michael—Intervention 1

After the week of baseline data collection, Ms. Jennings met with Michael to give and receive feedback related to the form. She and Michael discussed specific strategies for organizing his binder and locker so he would be more likely to bring all required materials to class. Ms. Jennings also encouraged Michael to quickly review the tracker as he entered each class to remind himself of the goals he was working toward. Michael continued to use the tracker for the next four weeks, checking in with each teacher at the end of class and meeting with Ms. Jennings at the end of the week. Ms. Jennings continued to enter Michael's weekly data into the Advanced Tier Spreadsheet. His weekly points improved to about 60% of points possible, but the graph showed that Michael was not making further progress. Ms. Jennings reconvened the Student Support Team to discuss Michael's progress-monitoring data, engaging the collaborative team in the high-leverage practice **use student assessment data, analyze instruction, and make adjustments [SE_HLP6]**.

The team acknowledged the improvement evident when comparing the baseline and intervention phases of Michael's graphed data. They talked about the dotted trendline that went upward after Michael began using the tracking sheet, but also noted that the four data points in the intervention phase didn't change much after the initial improvement. The team looked at Michael's weekly data sheets and noticed that he was consistently earning points for having his materials, but inconsistently earning points for being quiet and turning in his work. Michael reported that it is "just hard to be quiet" in class, especially during independent work. He shared that the room is "too quiet to think" and that talking to friends is more interesting.

The team discussed options that might help and decided to try allowing Michael to listen to music through his earbuds during independent work and to choose seating that would minimize distractions. The team documented the plan, and Ms. Jennings distributed it to Michael's teachers, making sure they could envision viable options for implementing the supports in their classrooms. Michael continued to use his tracking sheet and meet weekly with Ms. Jennings. She continued entering his weekly data into the Advanced Tier Spreadsheet, adding a vertical phase-change line to show the beginning of the second intervention. In her weekly meetings with Michael, Ms. Jennings used the graph to show Michael how he was progressing toward his goal of six consecutive weeks earning at least 80% of the possible points (Figure 11.4). Ms. Jennings scheduled a follow-up meeting with the Student Support Team to discuss next steps for Michael.

(Continued)

(Continued)

FIGURE 11.4 Progress Monitoring Intervention 2

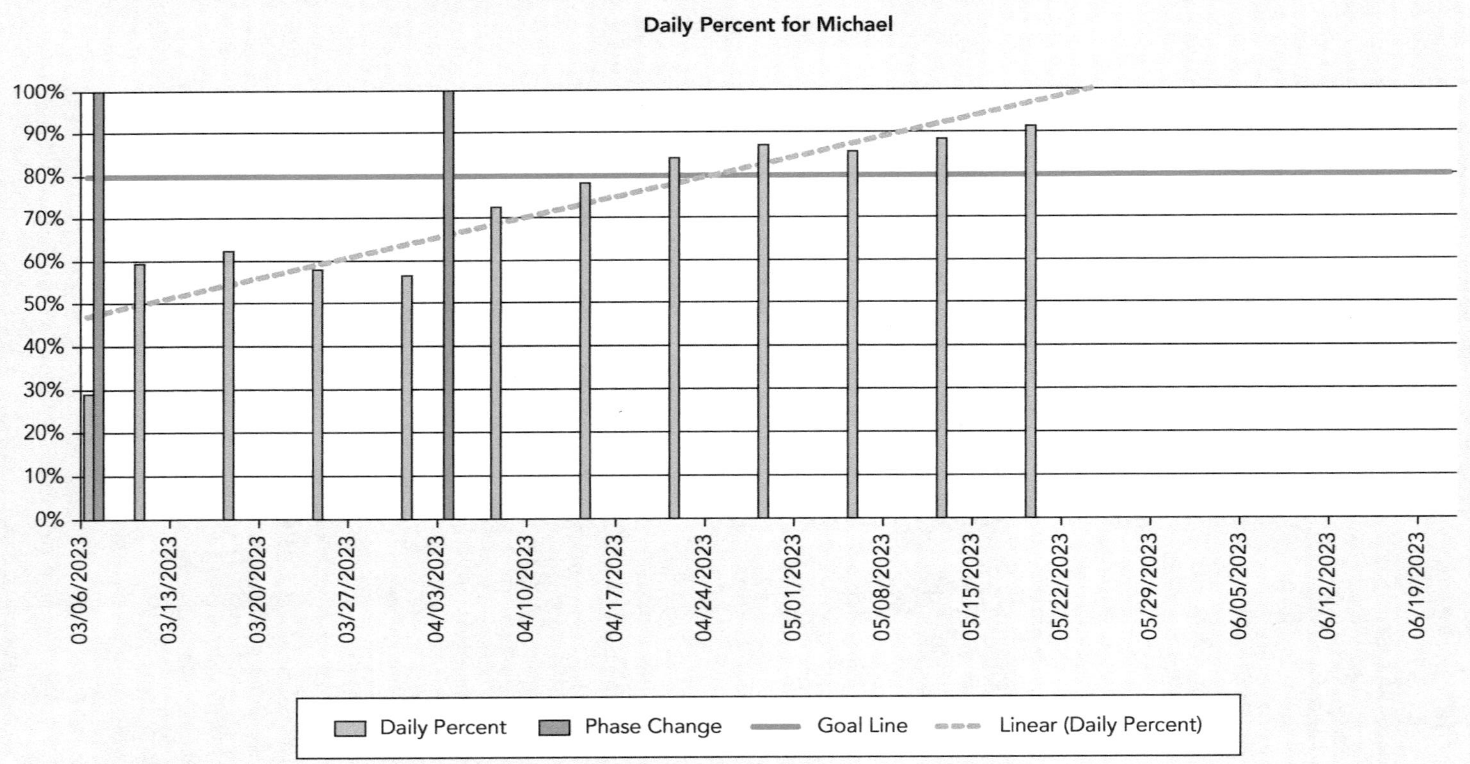

Daily Percent for Michael

Legend: Daily Percent | Phase Change | Goal Line | Linear (Daily Percent)

> ### Progress Monitoring of Engagement Expectations for Michael—Intervention 2
>
> At the follow-up meeting, team members congratulated Michael and asked for his ideas about what was working well and whether he felt that he could continue to be successful without the supports he was receiving. Through discussion, the team determined that it would be appropriate to raise Michael's goal to 90% of weekly points and shift the use of the tracker to three days per week for the remainder of the school year. This would give the team the opportunity to see if Michael could continue to be successful while reducing the level of supports. The ultimate goal would be for Michael to continue to bring materials, work quietly, and turn in work without needing immediate feedback from his teachers after each period.

Sharing Outcomes

Team meetings are one way that progress monitoring results can be shared and discussed. Information about student progress toward social emotional goals can also be shared through other informal and formal means. When conducting co-assessment, information is shared with students, family members, and other educators to ***increase student success*** **[SE_HLP1]**.

Providing Feedback to Students

Providing feedback to students **[GE_HLP18]** is an important tool for guiding student growth in social emotional and academic skills. Feedback stems from formal or informal assessment. **Feedback** is the sharing of "information that allows learners to compare their actual performance with that of a standard to which they aspire, *and* that enables them to take action to remedy the gap between the two" (Atkinson et al., 2021, p. 442). Effective feedback is intrinsically collaborative. It is an *exchange* between teachers and students for the purpose of facilitating learning. Feedback can be provided in written or verbal formats. However, it is *truly* feedback only if the learner has an opportunity to take the information provided and use it to adjust their performance. Therefore, true feedback is part of formative assessment rather than summative assessment.

TeachingWorks (2019) highlights the importance of providing feedback that is focused on a specific skill, designed to empower learners, and delivered in ways that do not diminish student standing with their peers. When providing feedback for social emotional competencies, it is important to stay focused on skills aligned with established goals. Often, when we observe student behaviors, we see many skills that could be improved. It is important to limit feedback to the target skill so students don't become overwhelmed. It is also important to make sure that feedback acknowledges strengths *and* challenges that learners experience. It can be very easy to focus on what went wrong. This may cause the student to feel defeated.

When meeting with students, educators should discuss what is working and where breakdowns are occurring using specific examples from students' real experiences. Talk with young people about how they can build on their strengths to address their challenges. Finally, consider how and where feedback is given. It may be necessary to give behavioral feedback in public forums—the classroom, hallway, cafeteria, and so forth—though it is preferable to have conversations in private. Educators should consider their tone of voice and the use of language. A calm, assertive voice paired with positively stated expectations helps to maintain the student's status with peers while providing immediate corrective feedback when it's needed. Educators may also find that it is helpful to collaborate with students to identify subtle ways to provide feedback in public settings. A whispered reminder or inconspicuous gesture may cause a young person to use a taught strategy without drawing the attention of their peers.

The use of **specific feedback** maximizes student learning. Specific feedback precisely describes a behavior with detailed information about how it is aligned with a desired outcome, whereas **general feedback** provides no detailed connection to the observed behavior (Royer et al., 2019). For example, when providing feedback to Samantha (see Table 10.3 in Chapter 10) related to her goal of asking for help, her teachers would be providing specific feedback if they said, "Samantha, you raised your hand to ask for help twice during math today. Good job!" Conversely, the feedback would be general if the teachers said, "Good job in class today."

Behavior-specific praise, in which observed actions that represent desired behavior are purposely acknowledged, has been demonstrated to be effective in addressing social emotional (and academic) competencies in grades K–12 (Royer et al., 2019). Behavior-specific praise contributes to social emotional learning by positively acknowledging observed actions that represent desired behavior. Collaborating teachers wishing to increase their use of specific feedback and behavior-specific praise may want to observe each other and discuss strategies, essentially giving each other feedback on the use of feedback!

Informal Communication With Family Members

Families of students who receive Tier 2 or Tier 3 intervention for social, emotional, or behavioral skills often experience a significant amount of negative communication about their child's behavior at school. While it is important to keep family members informed, it is not always necessary to report *every* misbehavior. We have worked with families who were so inundated by negative behavior reports that the appearance of the school phone number on caller ID caused significant anxiety.

Educators can nurture collaborative relationships by establishing a communication plan with family members. Discuss what behaviors necessitate an immediate phone call or written notification. Talk with families about their preferences for phone calls, emails, or communication logs. Finally, think of family communication as another form of feedback that has the goal of fostering student growth. Communicate to share both successes and challenges. Make sure that concerns are shared as objectively as possible and that family members have the opportunity to share ideas for growth but don't feel obligated to "solve the problem" on their own. These informal interactions can go a long way to building community and strengthening social emotional skills.

Formal Reports of Social Emotional Learning

Beyond informal interactions with families, educators often have formal progress reporting requirements for students receiving Tier 2 or Tier 3 social emotional intervention. Formal progress reports may be shared at team meetings, provided to parents with report cards, and/ or included in the student's cumulative academic record. Therefore, it is crucial that the reports be objectively stated and based on assessment data. If collaborative teams have started with an end goal in mind and used progress monitoring tools aligned with the end goal, the progress reports are easy to generate.

Using Michael as an example, you'll recall that the goal established by his collaborative team was to earn 80% of the weekly points possible on his Daily Behavior Tracker for six consecutive weeks. The weekly behavior tracker could be sent home to his family as one form of communication about progress. Data from the Advanced Tiers Spreadsheet would be summarized for formal written reports. For example, a formal report generated on April 4 in preparation for the first meeting might read:

> Michael has increased the percentage of points earned on his weekly behavior tracker from just under 30% before intervention to an average of 59% over the last four weeks of intervention. Michael has not yet achieved the goal of earning 80% of the possible points for a week.

This report is data-driven and objective. It recognizes that growth has occurred while simultaneously documenting that Michael has not demonstrated the level of growth needed to achieve the goal.

If the progress report was intended to document the team meeting, it might go on to describe the additional supports that the team selected. A progress report generated for the meeting on May 23 might read:

Michael is on track to achieve the goal of earning 80% of the weekly points possible for six consecutive weeks. He has earned 80% or higher for five consecutive weeks and has earned an average of 83% of points possible over the six-week period since the intervention was revised in April.

It can be tempting to add comments or anecdotes to formal written reports. These are best reserved for conversations, preserving the formal progress report as an objective record in the student's cumulative file.

Summary

Collaborative teams engage in co-assessment to determine if instruction and intervention for social emotional skills have been effective. Ongoing progress monitoring allows the teams to **use student assessment data, analyze instruction, and make adjustments [SE_HLP6]** to efficiently meet student needs. Collaboration is beneficial in identifying the goals for social emotional learning and selecting measures for progress monitoring. Multiple educators and individual students may be involved in collecting the assessment data to **increase student success [SE_HLP1]**. It is important that collaborative teams come together to **analyze and interpret** social emotional learning data **[GE_HLP17]** to ensure culturally responsive outcomes. It is also essential that students receive **feedback [GE_HLP18]** that supports them in adjusting their own behavioral responses. Finally, formal and informal reports on social emotional learning outcomes should be shared in objective and responsive ways.

Synthesis and Analysis

Co-reflecting and Co-planning for Improvement

12

To reflect or not to reflect? It does not seem like this should even be a question. Throughout this text, we have encouraged you to build reflection into your practice as you seek to improve inclusive instruction through collaboration. Why then did we start our final chapter by asking this question, other than because it is always cool to give a nod to Shakespeare?

Believe it or not, the use of reflection is not always accepted as a positive or essential practice. While teacher education has traditionally included reflection as an integral component—think of the journals or discussion forums you engaged in as a student teacher—its use has also been criticized (e.g., Beauchamp, 2015; Benade, 2012). Too often, teachers complain that they are weary of being asked to reflect on a topic, with little to no guidance "in terms of what reflection involves, what the results of reflection should look like, and how reflection can help them learn to teach" (Russell, 2013, p. 81).

To address these concerns, we must transition from **reflection** solely as a consideration of one's actions and toward **reflective practice**. Reflective practitioners actively seek to reduce the gap between what they know to be effective from formal education, research, or textbooks and what they see or do on a daily basis. Thus, as we bring together the main ideas of this book and leave you with key concepts on which to reflect, we also want to ensure that reflection moves beyond a superficial examination of topics learned and into **reflection-in-action** (Russell, 2013). Let's not just think about collaborating to help schools become more inclusive; let's do something about it!

Critical Reflection

Critical reflection is a subset of reflective practice (Fook, 2015). It is focused on unearthing and examining deeply held assumptions and then being open to transforming those assumptions. In essence, it means to reflect in a way that results in change. Critical reflection is required if the goal is to identify why gaps exist between knowledge and practice, where they are, and how to make connections that help bring schools to the desired inclusive outcomes that research has identified as possible.

To do that, we first need to examine fundamental assumptions we may have made, then use this knowledge to enact change. For example, have you assumed that students with disabilities are having their needs met in your school? Many general education teachers report that they feel unqualified to meet the needs of students with disabilities, and that is the reason they prefer to have those students in special education classes (Wehmeyer et al., 2021). Clearly, this rationale is well meaning, but those teachers may not be aware that self-contained or segregated special education has consistently been found to provide inadequate access to grade-level content, high-quality instruction, or social interactions with age-appropriate peers (Wehmeyer et al., 2021).

Another assumption general educators may make is that special education paraprofessionals are better equipped to work with students with disabilities than they are, so they defer to those individuals in the general education class. In fact, paraprofessionals often have little training in working with students, with or without disabilities (Massafra et al., 2020)! Yet another assumption is that administrators have had training in co-teaching or know how to build a master schedule to support it. That is often not the case. These are just a few examples of assumptions that we might find if we begin to truly reflect on our district, school, or classroom's present level of inclusive performance.

Another key aspect to critical reflection is awareness of how power operates. Fook and Askeland (2007) suggest that change cannot occur without this awareness. They state that critical reflection needs to involve positioning one's personal experiences within social, cultural, and structural contexts. Think about it. (Oh no. Did we just ask you to *reflect?*) Are your responses to such questions as "Is your school collaborative?" or "How inclusive is your school currently?" based on your position of power or relationships you have with others? Might these responses be different if you were answering as a parent, paraprofessional, self-contained special education teacher, or specialist? Might they be different if you were responding as a nonnative English speaker or an individual with a disability yourself? Does the superintendent share the same perspective as all teachers on their staff? With almost every question, educators will have different experiences, different views, and different responses based on those different frames of reference. Each of these questions emphasizes the role that context and identity play when engaging in critical reflection (Beauchamp, 2015).

Context and Identity

In his work on teacher education, Shandomo (2010) explained that critical reflection is a "process by which adults identify the assumptions governing their actions, locate the historical and cultural origins of the assumptions, question the meaning of assumptions, and develop alternative ways of acting" (p. 102). In recognizing that our assumptions are grounded in our own identities and that our actions stem from those assumptions, we can begin to question and change our practices, becoming more responsive to those with differing identities. Consider the application to inclusive education; the vast majority of individuals making decisions about it are those who do *not* have disabilities!

Educators' identities, assumptions, and actions impact students, families, colleagues, and administrators with whom educators interact. Our actions impact those students we help to include—and those we do not. Clearly, then, teachers need to spend the necessary time examining their own contexts and considering the creation of their own professional identity. Critical reflection can help determine our identity as educators; it can help us position our philosophy of inclusion and establish identity as collaborators and co-teachers. Sharing our experiences, assumptions, and even mistakes with others can help us learn from our colleagues and recognize power struggles we have not personally experienced (Kohli, 2019).

Social Connections to Aid Critical Reflection

This is not merely a book on why inclusion is so important for today's schools and society. It is specifically a book about how collaboration can support those inclusive practices. It would be a mistake not to bring this conversation back to how collaborating with others can help this process. Chang (2019) identified five themes related to how critical reflection can impact learning. He wrote that it (1) increases the depth of knowledge, (2) helps to identify areas that are missing or deficient, (3) personalizes and contextualizes knowledge, (4) provides comparative references in learning, and (5) helps build structural connections in knowledge and social connections. Let's focus on this last piece.

When educators have the space to share reflections, contexts, identities, and assumptions through collaborative activities, we increase knowledge, bridge gaps, make connections, and ultimately make the changes that need to be made. Throughout this text, we have offered numerous suggestions for making connections within school communities. Journaling and engaging in asynchronous discussion forums are also options, though some find those time-consuming or too slow. As an alternative, web-supported groups can be created or joined for those who have not found a critically reflective community in their own schools. We identify a few existing communities in the Check It Out textbox that you may want to explore.

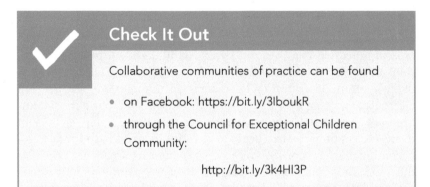

Check It Out

Collaborative communities of practice can be found

- on Facebook: https://bit.ly/3lboukR
- through the Council for Exceptional Children Community:

    http://bit.ly/3k4HI3P

Reflecting on an important problem, such as inclusion, and subsequently trying to make change can be daunting. Where do you start? How do you collaborate with others when their contexts and identities vary from your own? While educational literature and the internet offer many excellent options to help educators organize their reflection and subsequent actions, the model explained below is specifically focused on collaborative practices.

Collaborative Teaching Improvement Model of Excellence for Critical Reflection

The Collaborative Teaching Improvement Model of Excellence (CTIME), was outlined by Murawski and Lochner (2018) in their book *Beyond Co-Teaching Basics: A Data-Driven, No-Fail Model for Continuous Improvement*. The CTIME model is a culmination of the best research in the field for systemic improvement of co-teaching. It features evidence-based practices including reflection, data collection and analysis, microteaching, feedback and collegial support, and collaborative group work—all geared toward a recursive continuous improvement process for collaborative teaching and inclusion. The CTIME model focuses on both schoolwide and team-level processes.

The model has six basic steps. In *Beyond Co-teaching Basics*, the authors describe each step in detail and provide supporting flowcharts, forms, and templates. In essence, the steps are as follows:

1. Self-Reflections (Team Level) and Teacher Observations (School Level)

2. Schoolwide Analytics and Action Planning

3. Personalized Teacher Development Based on Team Data and Communities of Practice

4. Conducting and Managing Microteaching Sessions

5. Studying Microteaching and Schoolwide Outcomes

6. Repeat as a Continuous Improvement Process

In Step One, communities of practice, structured around grade- or content-area teams, engage in reflection through self-surveys. Family members and students also provide feedback through surveys to ensure that reflections on co-teaching and inclusion represent varied perspectives. At the school level, teacher observations are conducted using the Co-Teaching Core Competencies (Murawski & Lochner, 2018).

Dive Deeper

Read about the 22 Co-teaching Core Competencies in "Observing Co-Teaching: What to Ask For, Look For, and Listen For" (Murawski & Lochner, 2011) or check out all 120 Co-teaching Competencies in the Co-Teaching Competency Framework (Murawski & Lochner, 2018).

www.2TeachLLC.com

In Step Two, teams collaboratively evaluate the data aggregated from the self-reflections and teacher observations. Teams seek to identify and agree upon a problem of practice, asking, "Based on the data, what needs to be done at the school and team levels?" Fook and Askeland (2007) suggest that it is acceptable for the group to simply "sit" with the problem for a while and see how data continue to unfold, rather than immediately jumping to deal with the issue.

As data continue to tell a story and educators have time to reflect on its meaning and impact on their own situation, professional development can be identified to bridge gaps and make meaningful connections for teachers (Step Three). Many instructors report needing additional training in co-teaching, in how to provide academic adaptations and differentiation, and in other strategies for supporting diverse learners in the inclusive classroom. The information gleaned from the data collection and analysis can help determine what kind of professional development is most needed.

Step Four of the CTIME process involves microteaching. Microteaching has been around since the 1960s; it is a non-evaluative technique used for practice, personal reflection, and skill development (Murawski & Lochner, 2011). Many teacher training institutions and organizations, like the National Board for Professional Teaching Standards, use microteaching to provide educators with a technique for analyzing and reflecting on their own teaching, with the goal of making a positive change. Microteaching for the purpose of critical reflection on co-teaching and inclusion involves educators co-planning a lesson, videotaping themselves co-teaching the lesson, and then co-reflecting on that lesson as they watch the video with other educators who also co-teach (Step Five).

Once all those data have been compiled and analyzed, the CTIME process repeats in a continuous learning and improving cycle (Step Six). At the school level, professional learning communities focused on co-teaching or inclusion collect and analyze data to get a big picture perspective. Murawski and Lochner (2018) write:

> We hear a lot about data-driven decision making, but more often than not, we work with schools that have had absolutely no data collection related to their co-teaching or inclusive practices. It's understandable, then, that many teachers and other staff members may become frustrated. (p. 29)

Unfortunately, we must concur. This is where professional learning communities can help.

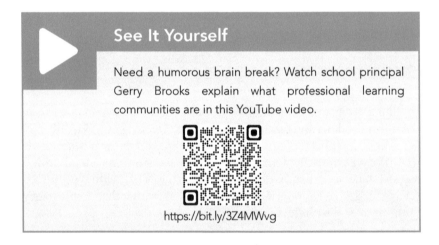

See It Yourself

Need a humorous brain break? Watch school principal Gerry Brooks explain what professional learning communities are in this YouTube video.

https://bit.ly/3Z4MWvg

Educators often complain that professional learning communities have simply become one more meeting or an excess of paperwork (if you agree, you may want to watch the video in the See It Yourself box). However, the goal of the professional learning communities is to be "an inclusive group of people, motivated by a shared learning vision, who support and work with each other to inquire on their practice and together learn new and better approaches to enhance student learning" (Stoll et al., 2006, p. 224). Sounds like shared critical reflection, reflective practice, and reflection-in-action, doesn't it? Looking at data together with our various contexts and identities will help us take action to address concerns, resulting in a more inclusive environment for all!

Using Assessment to Improve Instruction and Social Emotional Learning

While processes like CTIME can help educators improve their collaboration and co-teaching, critical reflection and analysis of assessment data are also important in improving instruction and social emotional learning as aspects of inclusive practice. In fact, ***analyzing instruction***

***for the purpose of improving* [GE_HLP19]** is a general education high-leverage practice. As we have mentioned previously, we feel that academic instruction and social emotional learning should be interwoven. They are integrally connected. Despite the fact that we separated them in the rest of this book to adequately address them, this final chapter focuses on using assessment data to reflect and make change for both academic and social emotional improvement. We should ***interpret and communicate assessment information with stakeholders to collaboratively design and implement educational programs* [SE_HLP5]**.

Making a positive change in a classroom, school, or district—especially on a major social justice issue like inclusion—will not be easy, nor will it be quick. As we consider the assessments we conduct, the data we collect, the stakeholders we include, and the way in which we use our findings to design and implement change, we also need to remember that this is a journey. The journey to inclusive education began in 1975 with the passage of the Education of All Handicapped Children Act, and it continues to evolve with laws like the Americans with Disabilities Act (1990) and the Every Student Succeeds Act (2015). Each new law, policy, or iteration of existing laws emphasizes a belief in the importance of more inclusive practices for all learners. Despite its significance, this change is a slow process.

The journey of school improvement involves many variables. While McLeskey and Waldron (2007) specifically recognized that each school and district has its own unique culture as it relates to inclusion, the process of school improvement in general can be linked to various features. For example, research has found that patterns of school improvement are associated with student composition, school size, school level, location, and performance trajectory (i.e., stable, declining, improving) (Hallinger & Heck, 2011). Even more importantly, while features of the school context are a factor and work together to present unique challenges, a major catalyst for change is strong, collaborative, learning-directed leadership (Hallinger & Heck, 2011).

Schools that are most successful in their improvement journeys engage in collaborative leadership that over time diffuses throughout the organization, "transforming from an individual characteristic (e.g., the principal) to an attribute of a team, and finally into an organizational property," resulting in a state of school improvement where "everyone is a leader" (Day et al., 2010, p. 23). Clearly, then, the work does not lie on the shoulders of one person. If shared leadership practices can help the analysis, meaning-making, and dissemination of instructional and social emotional learning data, what stakeholders may need to be included in school improvement leadership?

Identifying Stakeholders

By now, you should be familiar with the range of educational stakeholders with whom you might collaborate to embed inclusive practices into your setting. Families, specialists, administrators, paraprofessionals, support staff, and other educators should immediately come to mind. We also mentioned the importance of collaborating with students themselves. But what about the broader educational community? Other possible stakeholders are academic researchers and authors from local universities, federal and state politicians, state boards of education, as well as educational and parent organizations. Each of these individuals and entities would have a different role in helping a district **_interpret and communicate assessment information to collaboratively design and implement educational programs_** [GE_HLP5].

Academic researchers can help identify best evidence-based practices in inclusion while helping districts investigate reliability and validity of findings for their settings. Politicians can learn from educators about the impact that inclusive education has on academic and social emotional outcomes for students with and without disabilities. Ideally, politicians should then use this knowledge to pass laws and create policies that have a social justice lens supporting inclusion. State boards of education regularly identify and then often mandate specific educational programs; they, too, need to hear from districts and schools about how those programs are—or, more frequently, are _not_—accessible to diverse learners. Educational and parent organizations are created for the purpose of advocacy and often serve as direct conduits to change. We need to engage these organizations in conversations about our experiences on the journey toward collaboration and inclusive practices. Some community and family-focused organizations are listed in the Check It Out box.

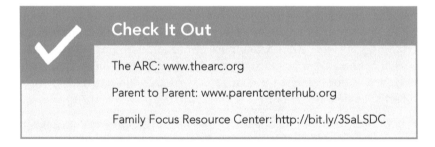

Check It Out

The ARC: www.thearc.org

Parent to Parent: www.parentcenterhub.org

Family Focus Resource Center: http://bit.ly/3SaLSDC

Though the need to collaborate and communicate actively with families has been emphasized throughout this book—and, hopefully, in just about any text dedicated to school improvement and inclusive education—we would like to emphasize it yet again. Research abounds documenting the positive outcomes for students when parents and educators collaborate (e.g., Powell et al., 2010; Topor et al., 2010). This collaboration can be neither taken for granted nor assumed. Prior to IDEA, families of students with disabilities had very little active role with schools, other than attending IEP meetings and essentially being told what would be occurring for their children. This lack of involvement was part of what led parents to take strong advocacy roles and form organizations to support other families and to make an impact on policy, curriculum, instruction, and inclusion!

Woods and colleagues (2018) noted that most communication between educators and parents still appears to be one-sided. This is so despite the recognition of how positively impactful collaborating with families can be and despite the general agreement that families and educators should play equally active educational decision-making roles. Teachers share information with parents and not the other way around. Parents rarely seem to initiate interaction without teacher invitation, and engagement with families is much higher in elementary than secondary school, despite the fact that families of older students report less satisfaction with the communication they have with schools (Woods et al., 2018; Zablotsky et al., 2012). Let us consider this situation as yet another call to action! Use the suggestions in Table 12.1 to spark some ideas for actively engaging families in the analysis of assessment data in order to design and implement educational programs that will *directly impact their children.*

TABLE 12.1	Collaborating With Families Around Assessment for Academics and Social Emotional Learning
ASK A QUESTION	**FIND MEANINGFUL WAYS TO INCLUDE FAMILIES**
What problems exist at our school?	Create surveys in English, Spanish, and other common languages. Send them in the hard-copy format home with students, distribute on the web and through email, post in parent centers on campus. Allow for anonymous responses. Offer translation services and allow for responses to be provided in a variety of formats (languages other than English, signed videos, pictures, meetings with administration).
How are we doing in [name the **instructional** area: writing instruction, literacy, math, general test-taking skills, etc.]?	Ask for volunteers to form focus groups of family members and educators to brainstorm areas/ways to collect assessment data. Encourage participants to review existing data (e.g., test scores, student sample products) and offer feedback. Provide options for feedback (anonymously, online, hard-copy, narrative, Likert scale 1–5, alternative views of what might be considered meeting a state standard).
How are we doing in [name the **social emotional learning** area: self-advocacy, social skills, reduction in bullying, teaching responsibility, etc.]?	Set up "Coffee With the Principal" meetings one morning a week and have interpreters present. Keep each meeting focused on a particular topic and let families and teachers direct the discussion. Invite external groups in to conduct diagnostics that include interviewing students and asking them questions. Ask the school counselors/psychologists/paraprofessionals to share any trends or issues they keep seeing or hearing in their daily work.
How can we use these data to design inclusive, accessible educational programs?	Invite families and community members to review existing programs (curricula, texts, instructional materials, social emotional learning programs) to give feedback to the district. Ensure that there are family representatives in each workgroup. Depending on age, students with and without disabilities could be invited as well. Have options for workgroup meetings (e.g., virtually, after work hours, on weekends, asynchronously).

Deciding What to Assess

Just as education should not be solely focused on academic success, we are not advocating that the pendulum swing to only focus on social emotional learning either. Part of the argument in support of inclusive education and collaboration is that people are different; we all have strengths and areas of need. Focusing on the "whole person" involves recognizing that students bring all of those strengths and needs to the classroom and that educators cannot ignore the integration of academic and social emotional learning (Caparas, 2021). In their research brief on educating the whole child, Darling-Hammond and Cook-Harvey (2018) found that addressing social emotional and academic needs through a whole-student approach results in improved student attendance, participation, engagement, social emotional well-being, and academic achievement.

These are wonderful, concrete, clear outcomes. They help inform our practice and our decision making. But while attendance, math scores, and grades are easily quantifiable and collectable by teachers, some question the value of data on engagement, social emotional health, and other social emotional outcomes. In his 2008 keynote address to the Collaborative for Academic, Social, and Emotional Learning, neuroscientist Richard Davidson asserted that "social emotional learning changes the brain" (00:52).

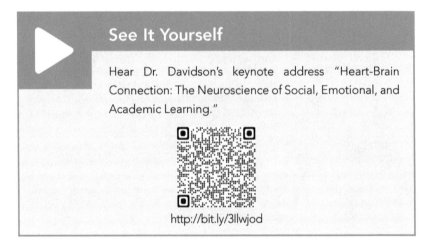

See It Yourself

Hear Dr. Davidson's keynote address "Heart-Brain Connection: The Neuroscience of Social, Emotional, and Academic Learning."

http://bit.ly/3llwjod

He went on to discuss how the brain is built to change in response to experience. He displayed brain images showing positive changes that are evident in the brain as the result of social emotional learning. Davidson concluded that social emotional learning not only benefits social emotional wellness, it also improves academic performance and physical health. Most teachers will not have access to MRI machines—or know what to do with them if they do! So, though there are ways to design empirical research around social emotional learning, most of us will stick to evaluating outcomes in more functional ways. For example, "After teaching this social skill, is Freddy able to make a friend?" and "After using this schoolwide Positive Behavioral Interventions and Supports curriculum, have our referrals for disciplinary action reduced?"

Using Assessment Data. With so many high-leverage practices focused on assessing and analyzing data, it is clear that these are important and impactful actions. Yet, in a study for the National Institute for Learning Outcomes, Blaich and Wise (2011) found what many educators already know. We have plenty of data already—but we simply do not use all we collect! Teachers nationally rail against a seemingly never-ending list of tests they need to administer. We hear constant complaints that they do not have time to teach because they are so busy testing! Maybe, then, this is not about doing *more* assessments, but rather using what we have and identifying the areas where we *need* more information. See the Clarifying Concepts box, adapted from Blaich and Wise (2011) for the steps of using assessment data efficiently.

Clarifying Concepts

Using Assessment Data More Effectively

1. Perform thorough audits of useful information about student learning and experience that your institution has already collected. *What do you already have available?*

2. Set aside resources for faculty, student, and staff responses to the assessment information before assessment evidence is distributed around campus. *What will different stakeholders need to have the data make sense to them?*

3. Develop careful communication plans so that a wide range of representatives have an opportunity to engage in discussions about the data. *How can we make sure everyone has a voice?*

4. Use these conversations to identify one or two outcomes on which to focus improvement efforts. *How can we narrow our focus so we can actually accomplish something?*

5. Be sure to engage students (and families!) in helping you make sense of, and form responses to, assessment evidence. *What does all of this mean and what are we going to do with it?*

What if the data already collected were not created to specifically provide feedback on inclusive practices? No worries. A collaborative team of individuals with different perspectives might look at math data, for example, and hypothesize that the reason students with disabilities collectively scored so low might be due to the fact that the test was timed, no accommodations were offered, test anxiety was high, no study skills were taught proactively, and so on. This could lead to the designing of additional components to the math curriculum and to developing a pacing plan. Together, the team could determine how data will be collected to ascertain if these new components made an impact on the math results for students with and without disabilities.

There may also be new areas for which timely and focused assessment is needed. For example, as schools moved to virtual instruction due to the COVID-19 pandemic, assessment on the transition from physical to online learning and its impact on students needed to be assessed. Another major area of increased focus after the pandemic relates to creating trauma-informed classrooms to recognize and address social emotional needs that increased during this time.

Individual teachers and co-teaching teams may also want to try new instructional techniques with their own students and collect data on improvement. Just because the whole school is not collecting data on the use of Station Teaching in social studies, for instance, does not mean teachers cannot craft their own mini-research studies. Working together to identify a classroom problem or goal, determine how results can be measured, collect the data, and then analyze the results can be a meaningful project for collaborating educators; in fact, collaborators could include not only teachers, but also paraprofessionals, adult volunteers, and the students themselves!

Building Educator Skills Around Assessment

Worried that you have not been trained in formal research methodologies? Worry not. The internet is chock-full of templates, examples, lists, and suggestions. One resource we like is the *Instructional Improvement Cycle: A Teacher's Toolkit for Collecting and Analyzing Data on Instructional Strategies* (Cherasaro et al., 2015).

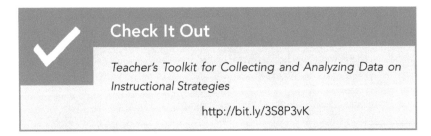

Check It Out

Teacher's Toolkit for Collecting and Analyzing Data on Instructional Strategies

http://bit.ly/3S8P3vK

In this free resource, the authors offer three tools to help teachers use data from their classroom assessments to evaluate promising teaching practices: a planning guide to compare an experimental group with a comparison group, a preprogrammed Excel spreadsheet to collect the data, and a reflection guide to interpret and make meaning of the results. This tool can also be adapted to address social emotional learning needs and strategies.

Professional development and collaboration can support teachers' provision of social emotional learning and high-quality inclusive, universally designed instruction. Describing the connection between science and practice in education, Riley and colleagues (2008) highlight the fact that teachers often engage in what they consider best practices, without actually being able to explain the research behind their action. Thus, it is definitely important that educators receive more professional development and support in learning about academic and social emotional assessment and instruction so they are able to generalize and maintain inclusive strategies.

A Call to Action

As you near the end of this book, having read and internalized each word we are sure, what does all this mean for you? How will you reflect critically? How will you use your newfound knowledge to connect collaboration and high-leverage practices to support academic and social emotional success for all students in inclusive settings? What are your next steps?

Let us be so bold as to suggest some baby steps. Figure 12.1 offers a flow chart for collaborative decision making about how to use this information to make a change. Please note that there is no option for "take a nap," "put my head in the sand," or "keep the status quo." We have not done our job sufficiently if you are walking away from this text thinking that all is well in education. With a like-minded group of potential change agents, start looking at the matrix and determine if your decisions (initially) are due to data you have been reviewing, observations you have made, or simply your gut instincts. Do not discount the latter! If you feel that your instruction is inaccessible to some learners or that there is a real need for focus on improved social emotional skills, go with it. The data will come.

After selecting an area on which to focus (academic or social emotional skills), identify all the possible strengths and challenges you have in these areas. This is when it will be helpful to have colleagues and other stakeholders weigh in with their varying frames of reference. Something you may have considered a strength may be viewed as a challenge by another individual, and vice versa. Feel free to use more space than we have provided in our template! After brainstorming your strengths and challenges (remember the rule of brainstorming: all input is counted as valid and equal), determine whether you might like to come up with improvement strategies related to co-planning, co-instructing, or co-assessing. Not sure what that might look like? Figure 12.1 is a tool to help your team decide where to focus, while Table 12.2 offers some examples of action steps. We also encourage you (nudge, nudge) to look back at the text for the ideas and suggestions we have provided throughout. Now that you are ready to take action, some of these ideas may really resonate.

FIGURE 12.1   Taking Action: A Decision-Making Matrix

Based on ☐ data, ☐ observations, or ☐ our gut feeling, we want to focus on:

ACADEMICS

SOCIAL EMOTIONAL LEARNING

Based on our selection above, the following are our current strengths and challenges:

STRENGTHS

CHALLENGES

Based on our strengths and challenges above, we want to focus our efforts on:

☐ Co-planning

☐ Co-instructing

☐ Co-assessing

Based on our focus area above, some actions we might take are:

TABLE 12.2 Collaborating to Improve Inclusive Practices: Ideas for Taking Action

COLLABORATIVE STRATEGIES	CO-TEACHERS/ CLASS-LEVEL TEAMS	SCHOOL/DISTRICT-LEVEL TEAMS
FOCUS ON CO-PLANNING		
Academic	Co-teachers can plan universally designed lessons that provide options for students to access content.	Always have at least one Curriculum and Instruction team member focused on ensuring that needs of students with disabilities, English learners, and others with access issues are identified and discussed.
Social Emotional	Classroom teachers can meet with school counselors to plan ways to provide a more trauma-informed class experience for students.	Create a team of diverse stakeholders to review various social emotional learning programs and discuss pros versus cons for adopting one such program schoolwide.
FOCUS ON CO-INSTRUCTING		
Academic	Co-teachers can select one of the different regrouping strategies (Station, Parallel, Alternative) to practice weekly.	Instructors who teach the same subject and/or grade level can identify ways to collaborate for specific projects and activities.
Social Emotional	Classroom teachers can invite specialists to share strategies related to social emotional learning through Station Teaching.	Bring larger groups of students together for a "catch them being good" assembly and have teachers share positive actions they've seen students employ with peers.
FOCUS ON CO-ASSESSING		
Academic	Co-teachers can put 20 minutes aside weekly to discuss, create, or adapt upcoming formative and summative assessments.	Create a Co-Teaching Professional Learning Community to review academic outcomes and compare with solo-taught teams.
Social Emotional	Classroom teachers can ask behavioral specialists to visit their classes and help identify areas for ongoing support and data collection.	Have the administrative team review disciplinary referrals and suspensions before and after implementing a Positive Behavioral Interventions and Supports program schoolwide.

Creating a Personalized IEP for Inclusion

In *Leading the Co-teaching Dance*, a book geared toward supporting administrators and school leaders in their creation and management of co-teaching teams, Murawski and Dieker (2013) recommend using an IEP format for goal setting. Let's use this technique when setting our own goals for collaborating to improve inclusive practices in academics and social emotional learning. Most educators are familiar with the basic IEP structure. First, we must identify the "present level of performance." This is where our data collection and analysis come in. How are we doing? What are our inclusive strengths and areas of challenge? How collaborative are we, really? Would everyone concur, and if not, why not? If we are not sure of our present level of performance as it relates to inclusion and collaboration, what data might we examine? The list below offers some ideas for figuring it out.

Identifying Present Level of Performance for Inclusion and Collaboration

- What percentage of students with IEPs are taught with their non-disabled peers?

- Do we have any other populations who tend to be segregated (e.g., English learners, gifted)?

- How many co-teaching teams currently exist at our school?

- What collaborative teams are in place, what are their goals, and do they feel productive?

- How do teachers rate themselves in terms of comfort and ability to differentiate, make accommodations, and universally design instruction?

- What assessment data already exist for us to look at (e.g., IEPs, referrals, grades, test scores)?

The next step in basic IEP structure is to identify where we want to be in a year or so. This is our general goal. Obviously, we first need our baseline (i.e., present level of performance) in order to know what a reasonable goal or objective might be. Feel free to go back to Figure 12.1 to determine if you want to narrow your goal to an area of academics or social emotional learning. The overarching goal is to have more improved inclusive practices, and the methodology is to do it through collaboration, but you'll need to be more specific than that! We do not want anyone overwhelmed, but the concept of "baby steps" still involves taking steps. What would you like to see in a year? Would you like 90% of your co-teaching teams to stay together (unlike this year's 30%)? Are you ready to address the goal of having 80% of your students with IEPs in general education classes for 80% of the day? Would you like all teachers to have participated in professional development around Positive Behavioral Interventions and Supports as part of a schoolwide social emotional learning initiative, or around co-teaching as a schoolwide academic initiative? Talk to your team and identify a few possible goals.

Before you go out and take action that results in an incredible change for students, the third and final step involves determining how you are going to make this change happen. What are some measurable objectives or benchmarks that you can set along the way to make sure you are making appropriate progress? It is essential to set *smart* goals, but nowadays we have an opportunity to make them even SMARTER.

Clarifying Concepts

Each of the letters in the SMARTER acronym can represent a variety of terms related to goal setting. Collaborate to choose the terms that most accurately reflect your team's SMARTER goals.

S – specific, strategic, significant

M – meaningful, measurable, motivational

A – achievable, adjustable, actionable, ambitious, attainable, assignable, aligned, agreed-upon

R – realistic, relevant, results-oriented, risky

T – timely, time-related, time-bound, time-keyed, triggered, tangible

E – evaluative, emotional, exciting

R – re-evaluative, revised, re-adjusted, rewarded, reality-checked, relevant

You may be familiar with a specific set of terminology associated with the SMARTER acronym. A quick search of the internet reveals multiple variations. In the spirit of choice, feel free to create your own SMARTER goals by selecting the terms from the Clarifying Concepts box that make the most sense to you and your team. Create your overarching primary goal(s) for the year and then use the SMARTER acronym to also help determine some benchmark objectives at regular intervals. The SMARTER goals worksheet in Table 12.3 provides a template for starting to determine your collaborative and inclusive goals and benchmarks. Don't forget to discuss roles and responsibilities for ensuring that this work happens!

TABLE 12.3   Establishing SMARTER Goals for Collaboration and Inclusion

Our Inclusive Area of Focus: _____

Write what each letter of the SMARTER acronym means to your team here:

_____

_____

_____

Our overarching SMARTER goal for one year from now:

_____

_____

_____

Use the check boxes below to evaluate your overarching goal for SMARTER elements.

Check each component (✓ or ⊗)	S	M	A	R	T	E	R

Our SMARTER benchmarks:

1. _____

_____

Use the check boxes below to evaluate your first benchmark objective for SMARTER elements.

Check each component (✓ or ⊗)	S	M	A	R	T	E	R

2. _____

_____

Use the check boxes below to evaluate your second benchmark objective for SMARTER elements.

Check each component (✓ or ⊗)	S	M	A	R	T	E	R

Closing Thoughts

As we leave you to write your goals and make your change, we encourage you to review the various resources and strategies connected to high-leverage practices throughout this volume. We know you have ample free time as an educator (just kidding!), so we encourage you to pick one strategy and begin to take action. With that, we wish you well. Go forth, collaborate, play nicely with others, and make a positive change in the world.

Appendix A

High-Leverage Practices for General Education

GENERAL EDUCATION HLPs FROM TEACHINGWORKS (2019)	FOCUS CHAPTERS AND COLLABORATIVE PRACTICES DISCUSSED	RELATED HLPs
1. Lead a discussion [GE_HLP1]	Chapter 4 – Engage in group discussions with professionals, family members, and students to co-assess academic needs Chapter 9 – Use restorative circles to engage students in discussions	GE_HLP3 SE_HLP4
2. Explain and model content [GE_HLP2]	Chapter 6 – Provide specially designed instruction (SDI) with explicit instruction and metacognitive strategies	GE_HLP14 SE_HLP14 SE_HLP16 SE_HLP20 SE_HLP21
3. Elicit and interpret individual students' thinking [GE_HLP3]	Chapter 4 – Engage students in group discussions or use interest inventories to understand their preferences and experiences Chapter 10 – Interview students as part of the Functional Behavior Assessment (FBA) process	GE_HLP1 GE_HLP4 SE_HLP6 SE_HLP10
4. Diagnose patterns of student thinking [GE_HLP4]	Chapter 8 – Analyze school-level data to identify patterns and trends Chapter 10 – Conduct Functional Behavior Assessments to identify patterns of student thinking related to behaviors Chapter 11 – Collect and analyze social emotional learning (SEL) data to identify patterns in student thinking and behavior	GE_HLP1 GE_HLP12 GE_HLP17 SE_HLP6 SE_HLP10

(Continued)

(Continued)

GENERAL EDUCATION HLPs FROM TEACHINGWORKS (2019)	FOCUS CHAPTERS AND COLLABORATIVE PRACTICES DISCUSSED	RELATED HLPs
5. Implement norms and routines for discourse and work [GE_HLP5]	Chapter 1 – Develop team norms to guide collaboration Chapter 3 – Establish and model norms and respectful discourse in professional relationships using tools such as the SHARE worksheet Chapter 9 – Use responsive practices to identify and teach norms and routines	GE_HLP8 SE_HLP7 SE_HLP9
6. Coordinate and adjust instruction [GE_HLP6]	Chapter 5 – Use co-teaching models (Alternative, Parallel, and Station Teaching) to meet learning needs	GE_HLP15 SE_HLP6 SE_HLP15 SE_HLP19
7. Establish and maintain community expectations [GE_HLP7]	Chapter 9 – Integrate community values into schoolwide and classroom behavior expectations Chapter 10 – Develop and implement Behavior Intervention Plans to define and support expected behaviors	GE_HLP3 GE_HLP5 GE_HLP10 SE_HLP7 SE_HLP8
8. Implement organizational routines [GE_HLP8]	Chapter 9 – Develop, teach, and reinforce routines to organize time, space, and materials	GE_HLP5 SE_HLP7 SE_HLP9
9. Set up and manage small-group work [GE_HLP9]	Chapter 2 – Pair co-teaching models with evidence-based practices such as Classwide Peer Tutoring	GE_HLP5 GE_HLP8 GE_HLP14 SE_HLP17
10. Build respectful relationships with students [GE_HLP10]	Chapter 1 – Demonstrate respect and collaboration in relationships with professionals and family members to model for students Chapter 3 – Model respectful collaboration when defining roles and responsibilities among professionals Chapter 8 – Develop understanding of student and community identity to promote a positive classroom climate	GE_HLP1 GE_HLP12 SE_HLP7 SE_HLP8/22 SE_HLP9
11. Communicate with families [GE_HLP11]	Chapter 1 – Include family members in collaborative teams Chapter 3 – Share feedback and use problem-solving strategies Chapter 8 – Engage family members in establishing goals for classroom climate	GE_HLP7 GE_HLP12 SE_HLP2 SE_HLP3

GENERAL EDUCATION HLPs FROM TEACHINGWORKS (2019)	FOCUS CHAPTERS AND COLLABORATIVE PRACTICES DISCUSSED	RELATED HLPs
12. Learn about students [GE-HLP12]	Chapter 8 – Learn about student identity through co-assessment with students, family members, and other stakeholders	GE_HLP1 GE_HLP10 GE_HLP11 GE_HLP16 SE_HLP10
13. Set learning goals [GE_HLP13]	Chapter 6 – Collaborate with IEP team members to develop standards-based goals through task analysis	GE_HLP14 SE_HLP12
14. Design lessons [GE_HLP14]	Chapter 5 – Incorporate Universal Design for Learning into lesson plans and delivery to increase accessibility for all learners	GE_HLP2 GE_HLP13 SE_HLP12 SE_HLP16 SE_HLP17
15. Check student understanding [GE_HLP15]	Chapter 5 – Integrate formative assessment into co-instruction with Opportunities to Respond (OTR)	GE_HLP3 GE_HLP16 GE_HLP17 SE_HLP6
16. Select and design assessments [GE_HLP16]	Chapter 7 – Collaborate to select and design equitable assessments aligned that are aligned with learning objectives	GE_HLP15 SE_HLP4 SE_HLP6 SE_HLP19
17. Interpret student work [GE_HLP17]	Chapter 7 – Co-analyze summative assessments using rubrics and responsive feedback strategies Chapter 11 – Establish collaborative processes for evaluating group and individual progress toward social emotional learning goals	GE_HLP3 GE_HLP4 SE_HLP4 SE_HLP5 SE_HLP6
18. Provide feedback to students [GE_HLP18]	Chapter 7 – Develop and utilize responsive and objective feedback systems for academic assessments Chapter 11 – Provide feedback to students regarding behavioral expectations through positive reinforcement systems	GE_HLP3 GE_HLP4 SE_HLP5 SE_HLP8 SE_HLP22
19. Analyze instruction [GE_HLP19]	Chapter 12 – Reflect upon academic and social emotional outcomes using a structured process such as CTIME	GE_HLP6 SE_HLP4 SE_HLP5 SE_HLP6

Appendix B

High-Leverage Practices for Special Education

SPECIAL EDUCATION HLPs FROM MCLESKEY ET AL. (2017)	FOCUS CHAPTERS AND COLLABORATIVE PRACTICES DISCUSSED	RELATED HLPs
1. Collaborate with professionals to increase student success [SE_HLP1]	**Chapter 7** – Engage stakeholders with diverse backgrounds to select and design summative assessments **Chapter 11** – Involve varied professionals in co-assessing social emotional learning (SEL) outcomes	GE_HLP1 GE_HLP6 SE_HLP2 SE_HLP5 SE_HLP10
2. Organize and facilitate effective meetings with professionals and families [SE_HLP2]	**Chapter 1** – Create organizational structures and norms for collaborative teaming **Chapter 3** – Co-plan Back-to-School night, parent–teacher conferences, and IEP meetings	GE_HLP1 GE_HLP5 GE_HLP11 SE_HLP3
3. Collaborate with families to support learning and secure needed services [SE_HLP3]	**Chapter 8** – Include family members in multi-disciplinary teams focused on school and classroom climate	GE_HLP11 GE_HLP13 SE_HLP2 SE_HLP5 SE_HLP10
4. Use multiple sources of information to develop a comprehensive understanding of a student's strengths and needs [SE_HLP4]	**Chapter 4** – Seek information from a variety of stakeholders to understand student strengths, needs, and preferences **Chapter 7** – Use a variety of summative assessment formats to evaluate student learning **Chapter 8** – Analyze formal and informal sources of information to co-assess student identity	GE_HLP1 GE_HLP3 GE_HLP12 GE_HLP17 SE_HLP10

(Continued)

(Continued)

SPECIAL EDUCATION HLPs FROM MCLESKEY ET AL. (2017)	FOCUS CHAPTERS AND COLLABORATIVE PRACTICES DISCUSSED	RELATED HLPs
5. Interpret and communicate assessment information with stakeholders to collaboratively design and implement educational programs [SE_HLP5]	**Chapter 4** – Co-analyze student data to understand student strengths and needs in preparation for academic instruction; share student assessment information with professionals and family members **Chapter 12** – Critically reflect and act upon assessment data to improve programs	GE_HLP3 GE_HLP4 GE_HLP19 SE_HLP4
6. Use student assessment data, analyze instructional practices, and make necessary adjustments that improve student outcomes [SE_HLP6]	**Chapter 5** – Adjust instruction based on formative assessment **Chapter 11** – Collect, analyze, and interpret outcomes from social, emotional, and behavioral measures to inform Positive Behavioral Interventions and Supports	GE_HLP3 GE_HLP4 SE_HLP4
7. Establish a consistent, organized, and respectful learning environment [SE_HLP7]	**Chapter 1** – Use collaborative teaming to establish a positive and responsive learning environment **Chapter 3** – Establish trust and parity in professional relationships **Chapter 9** – Identify, teach, and reinforce expected behaviors and routines	GE_HLP5 GE_HLP7 SE_HLP8 SE_HLP9
8. Provide positive and constructive feedback to guide students' learning and behavior [SE_HLP8]	**Chapter 10** – Incorporate evidence-based practices such as Check-In, Check-Out to provide constructive feedback for behavior	GE_HLP5 GE_HLP7 GE_HLP10 SE_HLP9 SE_HLP10
9. Teach social behaviors [SE_HLP9]	**Chapter 3** – Model productive social behaviors when defining roles and responsibilities among professionals **Chapter 9** – Systematically teach expected behaviors	GE_HLP7 GE_HLP10 SE_HLP7
10. Conduct Functional Behavioral Assessments to develop individual student behavior support plans [SE_HLP10]	**Chapter 10** – Engage collaborative teams to define the functions of student behavior and develop individualized behavior supports	GE_HLP3 GE_HLP7 SE_HLP6 SE_HLP8 SE_HLP9
11. Identify and prioritize long- and short-term goals [SE_HLP11]	**Chapter 6** – Collaborate with IEP team members to establish standards-based learning goals **Chapter 11** – Establish and monitor progress toward social emotional learning goals	GE_HLP13 GE_HLP14 SE_HLP10 SE_HLP12

SPECIAL EDUCATION HLPs FROM MCLESKEY ET AL. (2017)	FOCUS CHAPTERS AND COLLABORATIVE PRACTICES DISCUSSED	RELATED HLPs
12. Systematically design instruction toward a specific learning goal [SE_HLP12]	**Chapter 5** – Incorporate Universal Design for Learning into instruction to increase access for all learners **Chapter 6** – Deliver specially designed instruction in alignment with standards-based IEP goals	GE_HLP13 GE_HLP14 SE_HLP10 SE_HLP11
13. Adapt curriculum tasks and materials for specific learning goals [SE_HLP13]	**Chapter 5** – Utilize accommodations and modifications to provide differentiated instruction	GE_HLP6 GE_HLP13 GE_HLP16 SE_HLP19
14. Teach cognitive and metacognitive strategies to support learning and independence [SE_HLP14]	**Chapter 6** – Integrate cognitive and metacognitive strategy instruction into specially designed instruction (SDI)	GE_HLP3 GE_HLP14 SE_HLP13 SE_HLP15
15. Provide scaffolded supports [SE_HLP15]	**Chapter 5** – Co-instruct with UDL, accommodations, and modifications	GE_HLP14 SE_HLP13 SE_HLP19
16. Use explicit instruction [SE_HLP16]	**Chapter 6** – Provide explicit and intensive instruction as academic intervention	GE_HLP2 GE_PHLP14 SE_HLP15 SE_HLP20
17. Use flexible grouping [SE_HLP17]	**Chapter 2** – Use varied co-teaching models to group students in ways that address content, engagement, or differentiation needs **Chapter 5** – Co-instruct with purposeful student groupings	GE_HLP5 GE_HLP6 GE_HLP9
18. Use strategies to promote active student engagement [SE_HLP18]	**Chapter 5** – Co-teach with multiple means of engagement using UDL	GE_HLP1 GE_HLP3 GE_HLP9 SE_HLP19
19. Use assistive and instructional technologies [SE_HLP19]	**Chapter 3** – Identify assistive technologies used as accommodations including AAC and positioning equipment **Chapter 5** – Use assistive and instructional technology for formative assessment during co-instruction	GE_HLP13 SE_HLP18

(Continued)

(Continued)

SPECIAL EDUCATION HLPs FROM MCLESKEY ET AL. (2017)	FOCUS CHAPTERS AND COLLABORATIVE PRACTICES DISCUSSED	RELATED HLPs
20. Provide intensive instruction [SE_HLP20]	**Chapter 6** – Provide intensive and explicit instruction as academic intervention	GE_HLP13 SE_HLP12 SE_HLP16
21. Teach students to maintain and generalize new learning across time and settings [SE_HLP21]	**Chapter 6** – Use co-teaching models and cognitive strategy instruction to promote generalization	GE_HLP12 SE_HLP12 SE_HLP14 SE_HLP15
22. Provide positive and constructive feedback to guide students' learning and behavior [SE_HLP22]	**Chapter 7** – Use co-assessment strategies to provide meaningful and responsive academic feedback	GE_HLP3 GE_HLP17 GEP_HLP18 SE_HLP5

References

Aceves, T. C., & Orosco, M. J. (2014). *Culturally responsive teaching* (Document No. IC-2). https://ceedar.education.ufl.edu/wp-content/uploads/2014/08/culturally-responsive.pdf

Alawamleh, M., Al-Twait, L. M., & Al-Saht, G. R. (2022). The effect of online learning on communication between instructors and students during Covid-19 pandemic. *Asian Education and Development Studies, 11*(2), 380–400. https://doi.org/10.1108/AEDS-06-2020-0131

Allday, R. A., Nelson, J. R., & Russel, C. S. (2011). Classroom-based functional behavioral assessment: Does the literature support high fidelity implementation? *Journal of Disability Policy Studies, 22*, 140–149. https://doi.org/10.1177/1044207311399380

Americans With Disabilities Act of 1990, 42 U.S.C. § 12101 *et seq.* (1990).

Anderson, C. M., Martin, M. M., & Infante, D. A. (1993). *Willingness to collaborate as a new communication trait: Scale development and a predictive model of related communication traits* [Paper presentation]. Joint Meeting of the Southern States Communication Association and the Central States Communication Association. https://files.eric.ed.gov/fulltext/ED359582.pdf

Arao, B., & Clemens, K. (2013). From safe spaces to brave spaces: A new way to frame dialogue around diversity and social justice. In L. M. Landreman (Ed.), *The art of effective facilitation* (pp. 135–150). Stylus.

Atkinson, A., Watling, C. J., & Brand, P. L. P. (2021). Feedback and coaching. *European Journal of Pediatrics, 181*, 441–446. https://doi.org/10.1007/s00431-021-04118-8

Ball, D. L., & Forzani, F. M. (2011). Building a common core for learning to teach: And connecting professional learning to practice. *American Educator, 35*(2), 17–21, 38–39.

Barrio, B. L., Hott, B. L., & Randolph, K. M. (2021). Developing an individualized education program. In J. A. Rodriguez & W. W. Murawski (Eds.), *Special education law and policy: From foundation to application* (pp. 227–262). Plural.

Bastable, E., Falcon, S. F., Nese, R., Meng, P., & McIntosh, K. (2021). Enhancing school-wide positive behavioral interventions and supports: Tier 1 core practices to improve disciplinary equity. *Preventing School Failure, 65*(4), 283–290. https://doi.org/10.1080/1045988X.2021.1937020

Beauchamp, C. (2015). Reflection in teacher education: Issues emerging from a review of current literature. *Reflective Practice, 16*(1), 123–141. https://doi.org/10.1080/14623943.2014.982525

Benade, L. (2012). Challenging the domestication of critical reflection and practitioner reflectivity. *Educational Philosophy and Theory, 44*(4), 337–342.

Bennouna, C., Brumbaum, H., McLay, M. M., Allaf, C., Wessells, M., & Stark, L. (2021). The role of culturally responsive social and emotional learning in supporting refugee inclusion and belonging: A thematic analysis of service provider perspectives. *PLoS ONE, 16*(8), 1–19. https://doi.org/10.1371/journal.pone.0256743

Black, P., & Wiliam, D. (2009). Developing the theory of formative assessment. *Educational Assessment, Evaluation and Accountability, 21*(1), 5–31. https://doi.org/10.1007/s11092-008-9068-5

Blackley, A. (2019, April 5). 8 things successful co-teachers do. *We Are Teachers*. https://www.weareteachers.com/co-teaching-tips

Blaich, C., & Wise, K. (2011). *From gathering to using assessment results: Lessons from the Wabash National Study*. National Institute for Learning Outcomes Assessment. https://www.bu.edu/provost/files/2015/09/From-Gathering-to-Using-Assessment-Results_Lessons-from-the-Wabash-Study-C.-Blaich-K.-Wise1.pdf

Bojic, A. (2022, February 9). Collaborative communication: Why it matters and how to improve it. *Pumble Blog*. https://pumble.com/blog/collaborative-communication

Botsas, G. (2017). Differences in strategy use in the reading comprehension of narrative and science texts among students with and without learning disabilities. *Learning Disabilities: A Contemporary Journal*, *15*(1), 139–162.

Brookhart, S. M. (2011). Starting the conversation about grading. *Educational Leadership*, *69*(3), 10–14. https://www.greatschoolspartnership.org/wp-content/uploads/2016/11/Starting-the-Conversation-about- Grading-2.pdf

Browder, D. M., Wood, L., Thompson, L., & Ribuffo, C. (2014). *Evidence-based practices for students with severe disabilities* (Document No. IC-3). https://ceedar.education.ufl.edu/wp-content/uploads/2014/09/IC-3_FINAL_03-03-15.pdf

Brown, F., McDonnell, J., & Snell, M. E. (2020). *Instruction of students with severe disabilities: Meeting the needs of children and youth with intellectual disabilities, multiple disabilities, and autism spectrum disorders*. Pearson Education.

Brown, J. E., & Sanford, A. (2011). *RTI for English language learners: Appropriately using screening and progress monitoring tools to improve instructional outcomes*. National Center on Response to Intervention. https://mtss4success.org/sites/default/files/2020-07/rtiforells.pdf

Brown, M. R., Dennis, J. P., & Matute-Chavarria, M. (2019). Cultural relevance in special education: Current status and future directions. *Intervention in School and Clinic*, *54*(5), 304–310. https://doi.org/10.1177/1053451218819252

Bullock, J. (2018). CEC needs assessment identifies preferences in professional development. *TEACHING Exceptional Children*, *50*(6), 396–398. https://doi.org//10.1177/0040059918776509

Caparas, R. (2021). *Spotlighting whole-person success: A guide for using statewide data to identify exemplar districts in SEL and school climate*. WestEd.

Carello, J., & Butler, L. D. (2015). Practicing what we teach: Trauma-informed educational practice. *Journal of Teaching in Social Work*, *35*, 262–278. https://doi.org/10.1080/08841233.2015.1030059

Carroll, L. (1986). *Alice's adventures in Wonderland*. Chancellor Press. (Original work published 1865)

Caruana, V. (2015). Accessing the common core standards for students with learning disabilities: Strategies for writing standards-based IEP goals. *Preventing School Failure*, *59*(4), 237–243. https://doi.org/10.1080/1045988X.2014.924088

Casserly, A. M., & Padden, A. (2018). Teachers' views of co-teaching approaches in addressing pupils with special educational needs (SEN) in multi-grade classrooms. *European Journal of Special Needs Education*, *33*(4), 555–571. https://doi.org/10.1080/08856257.2017.1386315

CAST. (2018). *Universal design for learning guidelines 2.2 [graphic organizer]*. https://udlguidelines.cast.org/binaries/content/assets/udlguidelines/udlg-v2-2/udlg_graphicorganizer_v2-2_num bers-no.pdf

CEEDAR Center. (2014). *The CEEDAR center evidence standards*. https://ceedar.education.ufl.edu/wp-content/uploads/2014/08/Evidence-Based-Practices-guide.pdf

Center on PBIS. (n.d.). *Classroom PBIS*. https://www.pbis.org/topics/classroom-pbis

Centers for Disease Control and Prevention. (2019). *Youth Risk Behavior Survey: Data Summary & Trends Report 2009–2019*. https://www.cdc.gov/healthyyouth/data/yrbs/yrbs_data_summary_and_trends.htm

Centers for Disease Control and Prevention. (2021). Managing chronic health conditions. *CDC Healthy Schools*. https://www.cdc.gov/healthyschools/chroniccondi tions.htm

Chafouleas, S. M., Briesch, A. M., Riley-Tillman, C., Christ, T. J., Black, A. C., & Kilgus, S. P. (2012). An investigation of the generalizability and dependability of the Direct Behavior Rating Single Item Scales (DBR-SIS) to measure academic engagement and disruptive behavior of middle school students. *Journal of School Psychology, 48*(3), 219–246. http://doi.org/10.1016/j .jsp.2010.02.001

Chang, B. (2019). Reflection in learning. *Online Learning, 23*(1), 95–110. https://doi.org/ 10.24059/olj.v23il.1447

Cheney, D., Lynass, L., Flower, A., Waugh, M., Iwaszuk, W., Mielenz, C., & Hawken, L. (2010). The check, connect, and expect program: A targeted Tier 2 intervention in the schoolwide positive behavior support model. *Preventing School Failure, 53*(3), 152–158.

Cherasaro, T. L., Reale, M. L., Haystead, M., & Marzano, R. J. (2015). *Instructional improvement cycle: A teacher's toolkit for collecting and analyzing data on instructional strategies* (REL 2015–080). National Center for Education Evaluation and Regional Assistance. https://ies .ed.gov/ncee/rel/regions/central/pdf/ REL_2015080.pdf

Civil Rights Data Collection. (2018). *2017-2018 state and national estimations.* https:// ocrdata.ed.gov/estimations/2017-2018

Collaborative for Academic, Social, and Emotional Learning. (2020). *CASEL's SEL framework: What are the core competence areas and where are they promoted?* https://casel.org/ casel-sel-framework-11-2020/

Common Core State Standards Initiative. (2010). *Common Core State Standards for English language arts & literacy in history/ social studies, science, and technical subjects.* http://www.cor estandards.org/ assets/CCSSI_ELA%20Standards.pdf

Common, E. A., Lane, K. L., Cantwell, E. D., Brunsting, N. C., Oakes, W. P., Germer, K. A., & Bross, L. A. (2020). Teacher-delivered strategies to increase students' opportunities to respond: A systematic methodological review. *Behavioral Disorders, 45*(2), 67–84. https://doi .org/10.1177/0198742919828310

Conderman, G., & Hedin, L. (2012). Purposeful assessment practices for co-teachers. *TEACHING Exceptional Children, 44*(4), 18–27.

Conderman, G., & Hedin, L. (2017). Two co-teaching applications: Suggestions for school administrators. *Kappa Delta Pi Record, 53*(1), 18–23. https://doi.org/10.1 080/00228958.2017.1264815

Cook, L., & Friend, M. (1995). Co-teaching: Guidelines for creating effective practices. *Focus on Exceptional Children, 28*(3), 1–16.

Council of Chief State School Officers. (2013). *InTASC model core teaching standards and learning progressions for teachers 1.0.* https://ccsso.org/sites/default/ files/2017-12/2013_INTASC_Learning_ Progressions_for_Teachers.pdf

Darling-Hammond, L., & Cook-Harvey, C. M. (2018). *Educating the whole child: Improving school climate to support student success* [Research brief]. Learning Policy Institute.

Day, C., Sammons, P., Leithwood, K., Hopkins, D., Harris, A., Gu, Q., & Brown, E. (2010). *Ten strong claims about successful school leadership.* National College for School Leadership.

Dillon, S., Armstrong, A., Goudy, L., Reynolds, H., & Scurry, S. (2021). Improving special education service delivery through interdisciplinary collaboration. *TEACHING Exceptional Children, 54*(1), 36–43. https:// doi.org/10.1177/00400599211029671

Dixon, D. D., & Worrell, F. C. (2016). Formative and summative assessment in the classroom. *Theory Into Practice, 55*, 153–159. https://doi.org/10.1080/00405841.2016.1 148989

Donaldson, K., & Park, A. (2019, December 5). Trauma informed & restorative practices [Blog]. *Prime Center.* https://www .sluprime.org/prime-blog/trauma-informed

Drevon, D. D., Hixon, M. D., Wyse, R. D., & Rigney, A. M. (2019). A meta-analytic review of the evidence for check-in checkout. *Psychology in the Schools, 56*, 393–412. https://doi.org/10.1002/pits.22195

Dubek, M., & Doyle-Jones, C. (2021). Faculty co-teaching with their teacher candidates in the field: Co-planning, co-instructing, and co-reflecting for STEM education teacher preparation. *The Teacher Educator, 56*(4),

445–465. https://doi.org/10.1080/088787 30.2021.1930310

Durlak, J. A., Weissburg, R. P., Dymnicki, A. B., Taylor, R. D., & Schellinger, K. B. (2011). The impact of enhancing students' social and emotional learning: A meta-analysis of school-based universal interventions. *Child Development, 82*(1), 405–432. https://doi.10.1111/j.1467-8624.2010.01564.x

Egeci, I. S., & Gençöz, T. (2006). Factors associated with relationship satisfaction: Importance of communication skills. *Contemporary Family Therapy, 28*, 383–391.

Egolf, D. B., & Chester, S. L. (2013). *Forming, storming, norming, performing: Successful communication in groups and teams* (3rd ed.). iUniverse.

El Mallah, S. (2022). Toward equity-oriented assessment of social and emotional learning: Examining equivalence of concepts and measures. *Urban Education, 57*(2), 289–317. https://doi.org/10.1177/0042085920933335

Elkhart County Parks. (2020). *One room schoolhouse: Rules for behavior* [Video]. https://www.youtube.com/watch?v=8QntHohQ2LA

Elliott, S. N., & Gresham, F. M. (2008). *Social skills improvement system performance screening guide*. Pearson.

Espin, C. A., Förster, N., & Mol, S. E. (2021). International perspectives on understanding and improving teachers' data-based instruction and decision making: Introduction to the special series. *Journal of Learning Disabilities, 54*(4), 239–242. https://doi.org/10.1177/00222194211017531

Esteban-Guitart, M., & Moll, L. C. (2014). Funds of identity: A new concept based on the funds of knowledge approach. *Culture & Psychology, 20*(1), 31–48.

Evans, C. (2021). *A culturally responsive classroom assessment framework: The intersections of equity pedagogy, and sociocultural assessment*. Center for Assessment. https://www.nciea.org/blog/a-culturally-responsive-classroom-assessment-framework

Every Student Succeeds Act., 20 U.S.C. § 6301. (2015). https://www.congress.gov/114/plaws/publ95/PLAW-114publ95.pdf

Fallah, S., Reynolds, B., & Murawski, W. (2020). *Learning challenges for culturally and linguistically diverse (CLD) students with disabilities*. IGI Global.

Filter, F. J., Johnson, L. D., Ford, A. L. B., Sowle, C. A., Bullard, S. J., Cook, C. R., Kloos, E., & Dupuis, D. (2022). An expert consensus process to distill Tier 1 PBIS into core practice elements essential to frontline implementation. *Education and Treatment of Children, 45*, 51–67. https://doi.org/10.1007/s43494-021000066-y

Flower, A., McKenna, J. W., & Haring, C. D. (2017). Behavior and classroom management: Are teacher preparation programs really preparing our teachers? *Preventing School Failure, 61*(2), 163–169. https://doi.org//10.1080/1045988X.2016.1231109

Fook, J. (2015). Reflective practice and critical reflection. In J. Lishman (Ed.), *Handbook for practice learning in social work and social care* (pp. 440–454). Jessica Kingsley.

Fook, J., & Askeland, G. A. (2007). Challenges of critical reflection: "Nothing ventured, nothing gained." *Social Work Education, 26*(5), 520–533.

Foster, M., Halliday, L., Baize, H., & Chisholm, J. (2020). The heuristic for thinking about culturally responsive teaching (HiTCRiT). *Multicultural Perspectives, 22*(2), 68–78. https://doi.org/10.1080/15210960.2020.1741370

Friend, M. (2016). Welcome to co-teaching 2.0. *Educational Leadership, 73*(4), 9–14.

Friend, M., & Barron, T. (2016). Co-teaching as a special education service: Is classroom collaboration a sustainable practice? *Educational Practice & Reform, 2*, 1–12.

Friend, M., & Cook, L. (2021). *Interactions: Collaboration skills for school professionals* (8th ed.). Longman.

Friend, M., Cook, L., Hurley-Chamberlain, D., & Shamberger, C. (2010). Co-teaching: An illustration of the complexity of collaboration in special education. *Journal of Educational and Psychological Consultation, 20*, 9–27. https://doi.org/10.100/10474410903535380

Fröjd, K., Murawski, W. W., & Austin, J. (2023). Lärearens verktygslåda: Praktiska strategier för att hantera mångfalden i klassrummet. (*The Teachers' toolkit: Thirty tools for your top ten challenges. Practical strategies to manage the diverse classroom*). Stockholm, Sweden: Studentliteratur.

Gable, R. A., Tonelson, S. W., Sheth, M., Wilson, C., & Park, K. L. (2012). Importance, usage, and preparedness to implement evidence-based practices for students with emotional disabilities: A comparison of knowledge and skills of special education and general education teachers. *Education and Treatment of Children, 35*(4), 499–519.

Gage, N. A., Lewis, T. J., & Stichter, J. P. (2012). Functional behavioral assessment-based interventions for students with or at risk for emotional and/or behavioral disorders in school: A hierarchical linear modeling analysis. *Behavioral Disorders, 37*, 55–77.

Gaines, A. I., & Murawski, W. W. (in press). HLP 1: Collaborating with school professionals to improve student outcomes. In K. Cornelius & R. Owiny (Eds.), *The practical guide to high-leverage practices in special education.* Slack.

Gajda, R., & Koliba, C. (2007). Evaluating the imperative of intraorganizational collaboration: A school improvement perspective. *American Journal of Evaluation, 28*(1), 26–44. https://doi.org/10.1177/109821400 6296198

Garnett, B. R., Kervick, C. T., Moore, M., Ballysingh, T. A., & Smith, L. C. (2022). School staff and youth perspectives of Tier 1 restorative practices classroom circles. *School Psychology Review, 51*(1), 112–126. https://doi.org/10.1080/23729 66X.2020.1795557

Ghedin, E., & Aquario, D. (2020). Collaborative teaching in mainstream schools: Research with general education and support teachers. *International Journal of Whole Schooling, 16*(2), 1–34.

Gillies, R. M. (2016). Cooperative learning: Review of research and practice. *Australian Journal of Teacher Education, 41*(3), 39–54. http://doi.org/10.14221/ajte.2016v41n3.3

Greer, L. L., & Dannals, J. E. (2017). Conflict in teams. In E. Salas, R. Rico, & J. Passmore (Eds.), *The Wiley Blackwell handbook of the psychology of team working and collaborative processes* (pp. 317–343). John Wiley & Sons. https://doi .org/10.1002/9781118909997.ch14

Guskey, T. R., & Jung, L. A. (2009). Grading and reporting in a standards-based environment: Implications for students with special needs. *Theory Into Practice, 48*, 53–62. https://files.eric.ed.gov/fulltext/ED509343.pdf

Hackett, J., Kruzich, J., Goulter, A., & Battista, M. (2021). Tearing down invisible walls: Designing, implementing, and theorizing psychologically safer co-teaching for inclusion. *Journal of Educational Change, 22*, 103–130. https://doi.org/10.1007/s10833-020-09401-3

Hallinger, P., & Heck, R. H. (2011). Exploring the journey of school improvement: Classifying and analyzing patterns of change in school improvement processes and learning outcomes. *School Effectiveness and School Improvement, 22*(1), 1–27.

Hammond, Z. (2015). *Culturally responsive teaching and the brain: Promoting authentic engagement and rigor among culturally and linguistically diverse students.* Corwin.

Hang, Q., & Rabren, K. (2009). An examination of co-teaching: Perspectives and efficacy indicators. *Remedial and Special Education, 20*(5), 259–268.

Hanover Research. (2012). *The effectiveness of the co-teaching model: Literature review.* https://www.ousd.org/cms/lib/CA01001176/Centricity/Shared/The%20Effectiveness%20of%20the%20Co-Teaching%20Model-Inclusion%20Material.pdf

Hershfeldt, P. A., Rosenberg, M. S., & Bradshaw, C. P. (2010). Function-based thinking: A systematic way of thinking about function and its role in changing student behavior problems. *Beyond Behavior, 19*(3), 12–21.

Hindman, A. H., Miller, A. L., Froyen, L. C., & Skibbe, L. E. (2012). A portrait of family involvement during Head Start: Nature, extent, and predictors. *Early Childhood Research Quarterly, 27*, 654–667.

Hollett, A. (2022). Socio-emotional learning and justice: Against control, beyond triage. *TCARE Newsletter, 12*, 8. https://www .csun.edu/sites/default/files/TCARE%20 Spring%202022_0.pdf

Hughes, C. E., & Murawski, W. W. (2001). Lessons from another field: Applying co-teaching strategies to gifted education. *Gifted Child Quarterly, 45*(3), 195–204.

Hunt, P., McDonnell, J., & Crockett, M. A. (2012). Reconciling an ecological curricular framework focusing on quality of life outcomes with the development and instruction of standards-based academic goals. *Research & Practice for Persons With Severe Disabilities, 37*(3), 139–152.

Hutchison, J. (2020, April 8). *Psychological safety and transparent communication at work: Strengthening collaboration and innovation.* [Video]. https://mediaspace.msu .edu/media/Psychological+Safety+and+ Transparent+Communication+at+WorkA+ Strengthening+Collaboration+and+Inno vation/1_fqkk7m2f

IDEA. (2004). Individuals with Disabilities Education Act of 2004, 20 U.S.C. §1400. http://idea.ed.gov/download/statute.html

IRIS Center. (2022). *Serving students with visual impairments: The importance of collaboration.* https://iris.peabody.vanderbilt .edu/module/v03-focusplay

Israel, M., Marino, M., Delisio, L., & Serianni, B. (2014). *Supporting content learning through technology for K-12 students with disabilities* (Document No. IC-10). https://ceedar.educa tion.ufl.edu/wp-content/uploads/2014/09/ IC-10_FINAL_09-10-14.pdf

Jackson, K. M., Willis, K., Giles, L., Lastrapes, R. E., & Mooney, P. (2017). How to meaningfully incorporate co-teaching into programs for middle school students with emotional and behavioral disorders. *Beyond Behavior*, 26(1), 11–18. https:// doi.org/10.1177/1074295617694408

Jacques, C., & Villegas, A. (2018). *Strategies for equitable family engagement.* State Support Network. https://oese.ed.gov/ files/2020/10/equitable_family_engag_ 508.pdf

Jung, L. A., & Guskey, T. R. (2010). Grading exceptional learners. *Educational Leadership*, 67(5), 31–35.

Kansas State Board of Education. (2018). *Kansas social, emotional, and character development model standards.* https://www.ksde .org/Portals/0/CSAS/Content%20Area%20 (M-Z)/School%20Counseling/Soc_Emot_ Char_Dev/Standards%20-%20SECD%20 -%20Instructional%20Examples%20-%20 K-12.pdf?ver=2019-04-08-150531-770

Karadimou, M., & Tsioumis, K. (2021). Willingness to communicate and collaborate: The key role of educational leadership in primary education. *European Journal of Educational Management*, 4(2), 141–155.

Karten, T. J., & Murawski, W. W. (2020). *Co-teaching do's, don'ts, and do betters.* ASCD.

Kelty, N. E., & Wakabayashi, T. (2020). Family engagement in schools: Parent, educator, and community perspectives. *SAGE Open*, 10(4), 1–13. https://doi .org/10.1177/2158244020973024

Kilgus, S. P., Bonifay, W. E., von der Embse, N. P., Allen, A. N., & Eklund, K. (2018). Evidence for the interpretation of Social, Academic, and Emotional Behavior Risk Screener (SAEBRS) scores: An argument-based approach to screener validation. *Journal of School Psychology*, 68, 129–141. https:// doi.org/10.1016/j.jsp.2018.03.002

King, A. H. (2022). Synchronizing and amending: A conversion analytic account of the "co-ness" in co-teaching. *Linguistics and Education*, 67, 1–12. https://doi .org/10.1016/j.linged.2022.101015

King, M. L. (1947). The purpose of education. *Maroon Tiger*. http://okra.stanford .edu/transcription/document_images/ Vol01Scans/123_Jan-Feb1947_The%20 Purpose%20of%20Education.pdf

King-Sears, M. E., Brawand, A. E., Jenkins, M. C., & Preston-Smith, S. (2014). Co-teaching perspectives from secondary science co-teachers and their students with disabilities. *Journal of Science Teacher Education*, 25, 651–680. https://doi.org/10.1007/ s10972-014-9391-2

King-Sears, M. E., Janney, R., & Snell, M. E. (2015). *Collaborative teaming* (3rd ed.). Brookes.

King-Sears, M. E., & Jenkins, M. (2020). Active instruction for co-teachers in a support role. *Intervention in School & Clinic*, 55(5), 301–306. https://doi .org/10.1177/1053451219881729

Klevan, S. (2021, October 28). *Building a positive school climate through restorative practices.* Learning Policy Institute. https://learningpolicyinstitute.org/prod uct/wce-positive-school-climate-restor ative-practices-brief

Klingner, J., Vaughn, S., Boardman, A., & Swanson, E. (2012). *Now we get it! Boosting comprehension with collaborative strategic reading.* Jossey-Bass.

Knackendoffel, E. A. (2005). Collaborative teaming in the secondary school. *Focus on Exceptional Children*, 37(5), 1–16.

Koenka, A. (2022). Grade expectations: The motivational consequences of performance feedback on a summative assessment. *Journal of Experimental Education*, 90(1),

88–111. https://doi.org/10.1080/0022097
3.2020.1777069

Kohli, R. (2019). Lessons for teacher education: The role of critical professional development in teacher of color retention. *Journal of Teacher Education, 70*(1), 39–50.

Lane, K. L., Oakes, W. P., Cantwell, E. D., Schatschneider, C., Menzies, H., Crittenden, M., & Messenger, M. (2016). Student risk screening scale for internalizing and externalizing behaviors: Preliminary cut scores to support data-informed decision making in middle and high schools. *Behavioral Disorders, 42*(1), 271–284. https://doi.org/10.17988/bd-16-115.1

Lane, K. L., Oakes, W. P., Royer, D. J., Cantwell, E. D., Menzies, H. M., Jenkins, A. B., & Hicks, T. (2019). Using schoolwide expectations survey for specific settings to build expectations matrices. *Remedial and Special Education, 40*(1), 51–62. https://doi.org/10.1177/0741932518786787

Lester, R. R., Allanson, P. B., & Notar, C. E. (2017). Routines are the foundation of classroom management. *Education, 137*(4), 398–412.

Leverson, M., Smith, K., McIntosh, K., Rose, J., & Pinkelman, S. (2021). *PBIS cultural responsiveness field guide: Resources for trainers and coaches.* Center on PBIS. https://www.pbis.org/resource/pbis-cultural-responsiveness-field-guide-resources-for-trainers-and-coaches

Lochner, G. (2021). Students' standpoint: How COVID leveled the playing field. *TCARE, 11*, 12. https://www.csun.edu/sites/default/files/Vol.%20XI%2C%20Fall%202021.pdf

Maier, A., Adams, J., Burns, D., Kaul, M., Saunders, M., & Thompson, C. (2020, October 13). *Using performance assessments to support student learning.* Learning Policy Institute. https://learningpolicyinstitute.org/product/cpac-performance-assessments-support-student-learning-brief?gclid=CjoKC-QjwtvqVBhCVARIsAFUxcRvEE3WyWQir-C2i8zQGjw7Y8mMHFdQAlFLiOl6zZi_XT5dWM7dhSHEcaAg5KEALw_wcB

Maras, M. A., Thompson, A. M., Lewis, C., Thornburg, K., & Hawks, J. (2015). Developing a tiered response model for social-emotional learning through interdisciplinary collaboration. *Journal of Educational and Psychological Consultation, 25,* 198–223. https://doi.org/10.1080/1047441 2.2014.929954

Massafra, A., Gershwin, T., & Gosselin, K. (2020). Policy, preparation, and practice . . . Oh my! Current policy regarding the paraprofessional role and preparation for working with students with disabilities. *Journal of Disability Policy Studies, 31*(3), 164–172. https://doi.org/10.1177/1044207320920004

Mathes, N. E., Witmer, S. E., & Volker, M. A. (2020). Middle school teachers' perceptions of academic and behavioral support testing accommodations. *Journal of Applied School Psychology, 36*(3), 293–323. https://doi.org/10.1080/15377903.2 020.1749202

McKown, C. (2019). Challenges and opportunities in the applied assessment of student social and emotional learning. *Educational Psychologist, 54*(3), 205–221. https://doi.org/10.1080/00461520.2019.1614446

McLeskey, J., Barringer, M.-D., Billingsley, B., Brownell, M., Jackson, D., Kennedy, M., Lewis, T., Maheady, L., Rodrigues, J., Scheeler, M. C., Winn, J., & Ziegler, D. (2017). *High-leverage practices in special education: Instruction research syntheses.* Council for Exceptional Children & CEEDAR Center.

McLeskey, J., & Waldron, N. L. (2007). Making differences ordinary in inclusive classrooms. *Intervention in School and Clinic, 42*(3), 162–168. https://doi.org/10.1177/10534512070420030501

McTighe, J. (2015, June 30). How can educators design authentic performance tasks? (Part 3) [Blog]. *Defined Learning.* https://medium.com/performance-task-pd-with-jay-mctighe-blog/how-can-educators-design-authentic-performance-tasks-part-3-5817561ae422

McTighe, J. (2016, March 2). How will we evaluate student performance on tasks? (Part 6) [Blog]. *Defined Learning.* https://blog.performancetask.com/how-will-we-evaluate-student-performance-on-tasks-part-6-946c82deee02

McTighe, J., & Wiggins, G. (2004). *The understanding by design professional development workbook.* ASCD.

Miller, F. G., Chafouleas, S. M., Riley-Tillman, T. C., & Fabiano, G. A. (2014). Teacher perceptions of the usability of school-based behavior assessments. *Behavior Disorders*, *39*(4), 201–210.

Miller, G. E. (1990). The assessment of clinical skills/competence/performance. *Academic Medicine*, *65*(5), S63–S67. http://doi .org/10.1097/00001888-199009000-00045

Missouri Department of Elementary and Secondary Education. (2017). *Missouri schoolwide positive behavior support: Tier 2 team workbook 2017-2018.* https://pbismissouri.org/wp-content/ uploads/2017/08/0.-MO-SW-PBS-Tier-2-2017-2.pdf?x30198

Missouri Positive Behavior Supports. (2014). *MO SW-PBS teacher tool: Classroom procedures and routines.* https://pbismissouri .org/wp-content/uploads/2017/06/ECP2 .3-Teacher-Tool-ClassroomProcedures-and-Routines-1.pdf

Mofield, E. L. (2020). Benefits and barriers to collaboration and co-teaching: Examining perspectives of gifted education teachers and general education teachers. *Gifted Child Today*, *43*(1), 20–33. https://doi .org/10.1177/1076217519880588

Montenegro, E., & Jankowski, N. A. (2020). *A new decade for assessment: Embedding equity into assessment praxis* (Occasional Paper No. 42). National Institute for Learning Outcomes Assessment.

Moore, S. (2018). The evolution of inclusion: The past and future of education [Video]. *Five Moore Minutes.* https://www.you tube.com/watch?v=PQgXBhPh5Zo&t=4s

Moreno, G. (2021). Stemming exclusionary school discipline: Implementing culturally attuned positive behavior practices. *Emotional and Behavioural Difficulties*, *26*(2), 17–186. https://doi.org/10.1080/13 632752.2021.1930907

Murawski, W. W. (2003). *Co-teaching in the inclusive classroom: Working together to help all your students find success (grades 6–12).* Institute for Educational Development.

Murawski, W. W. (2010). *Collaborative teaching in elementary schools: Making the co-teaching marriage work!* Corwin.

Murawski, W. W., & Dieker, L. A. (2004). Tips and strategies for co-teaching at the secondary level. *TEACHING Exceptional Children*, *36*(5), 52–58.

Murawski, W. W., & Dieker, L. A. (2013). *Leading the co-teaching dance: Leadership strategies to enhance team outcomes.* Council for Exceptional Children.

Murawski, W. W., & Lochner, W. W. (2011). Observing co-teaching: What to ask for, look for, and listen for. *Intervention in School and Clinic*, *46*(3), 174–183.

Murawski, W. W., & Lochner, W. W. (2018). *Beyond co-teaching basics: A data-driven, no fail model for continuous improvement* ASCD.

Murawski, W. W., & Scott, K. L. (Eds.). (2019). *What really works with universal design for learning.* Corwin.

Murawski, W. W., & Spencer, S. A. (2011). *Collaborate, communicate, and differentiate! How to increase student learning in today's diverse schools.* Corwin.

National Center for Education Statistics. (2021). *Back-to-school statistics.* https://nces .ed.gov/fastfacts/display.asp?id=372#:~:- text=Using%20preliminary%20data%20 for%20fall,students%20

National Center for Education Statistics. (2022, May). *Students with disabilities.* https:// nces.ed.gov/programs/coe/indicator/cgg/ students-with-disabilities#:~:text=In%20 2020%E2%80%9321%2C%20the%20num-ber,of%20all%20public%20school%20 students

National Center for Learning Disabilities. (2020). *Significant disproportionality in special education: Current trends and actions for impact.* https://www.ncld.org/wp-content/ uploads/2020/10/2020-NCLD-Dispropor tionality_Trends-and-Actions-for-Impact_ FINAL-1.pdf

Nese, R. N. T., Nese, J. F. T., McCroskey, C., Meng, P., Triplett, D., & Bastable, E. (2021). Moving away from disproportionate exclusionary discipline: Developing and utilizing a continuum of preventative and instructional supports. *Preventing School Failure*, *65*(4), 301–311. https://doi.org/10.1080/ 1045988X.2021.1937019

Ohio Department of Education. (2018). *Implementing the operating standards for identifying and serving students who are gifted: A guide for Ohio school districts and educators.* https://education.ohio.gov/ getattachment/Topics/Other-Resources/

Gifted-Education/Rules-Regulations-and-Policies-for-Gifted-Educatio/Implementing-the-Operating-Standards-for-Identifying-and-Serving-Students-Who-are-Gifted.pdf.aspx

O'Neill, R. E., Albin, R. W., Storey, K., Horner, R. H., & Sprague, J. R. (2015). *Functional assessment and program development for problem behavior: A practical handbook.* Cengage Learning.

O'Neill, R. E., Horner, R. H., Albin, R. W., Sprague, J. R., Storey, K., & Newton, J. S. (1997). *Functional assessment and program development for problem behavior: A practical handbook.* Brooks/Cole.

Overton, T. (2015). *Assessing learners with special needs: An applied approach.* Pearson.

Park, S., & Paulick, J. (2021). An inquiry into home visits as a practice of culturally sustaining pedagogy in urban schools. *Urban Education.* https://doi.org/10.1177/0042085921998416

Pierson, R. (2013). Every kid needs a champion [Video]. *TED Talks Education.* https://www.ted.com/talks/rita_pierson_every_kid_needs_a_champion/transcript?language=en

Powell, D. R., Son, S. H., File, N., & San Juan, R. R. (2010). Parent–school relationships and children's academic and social outcomes in public school pre-kindergarten. *Journal of School Psychology, 48,* 269–292. https://doi.org/10.1016/j.jsp.2010.03.002

Pratt, S. (2014). Achieving symbiosis: Working through challenges found in co-teaching to achieve effective co-teaching relationships. *Teaching and Teacher Education, 41,* 1–12. https://doi.org/10.1016/j.tate.2014.02.006

Regan, K. (2003). Using dialogue journals in the classroom: Forming relationships with students with emotional disturbance. *TEACHING Exceptional Children, 36*(2), 34–39. https://doi.org/10.1177/004005990303600205

Richards-Tutor, C., Aceves, T., & Reese, L. (2016). *Evidence-based practices for English learners* (Document No. IC-18). https://ceedar.education.ufl.edu/wp-content/uploads/2016/11/EBP-for-english-learners.pdf

Richardson, B. G., & Shupe, M. J. (2003). The importance of teacher self-awareness in working with students with emotional and behavioral disorders. *TEACHING Exceptional Children, 36*(2), 8–13. https://doi.org/10.1177/004005990303600201

Riley, D., San Juan, R. R., Klinkner, J., & Ramminger, A. (2008). *Social and emotional development: Connecting science and practice in early childhood settings.* NAEYC.

Rishel, C. W., Tabone, J. K., Hartnett, H. P., & Szafran, K. F. (2019). Trauma-informed elementary schools: Evaluation of school-based early intervention for young children. *Children & Schools, 41*(4), 239–248. https://doi.org/10.1093/cs/cdz017

Rodgers, W. J., Weiss, M. P., & Aal Ismail, H. (2021). Defining specially designed instruction: A systematic literature review. *Learning Disabilities Research & Practice, 36*(2), 96–109. https://doi.org/10.1111/ldrp.12247

Rodrigues, A. (2013). *Perceptions of co-teaching by content area and special education teachers with and without experience* [Doctoral dissertation, Northeastern University]. https://repository.library.northeastern.edu/files/neu:336517/fulltext.pdf

Rodriguez, J. A., & Murawski, W. W. (2021). *Special education law and policy: From foundation to application.* Plural.

Ronfeldt, M., Farmer, S. O., McQueen, K., & Grissom, J. A. (2015). Teacher collaboration in instructional teams and student achievement. *American Educational Research Journal, 52,* 475–514. https://doi.org/10.3102/0002831215585562

Royer, D. J., Lane, K. L., Dunlap, K. D., & Ennis, R. P. (2019). A systematic review of teacher-delivered behavior-specific praise on K-12 student performance. *Remedial and Special Education, 40*(2), 112–128. https://doi.org/10.1177/0741932517751054

Ruble, L. A., McGrew, J. H., Wong, W. H., & Missal, K. N. (2018). Special education teachers' perceptions and intentions toward data collection. *Journal of Early Intervention, 40*(2), 177–191. https://doi.org/10.1177/1053815118771391

Russell, T. (2013). Has reflective practice done more harm than good in teacher education? *Phronesis, 2*(1), 80–88.

Ryoo, K., & Linn, M. C. (2015). Designing and validating assessments of complex thinking in science. *Theory Into Practice, 54*, 238–254. https://doi.org/10.1080/00405841.2015.1044374

Rytivaara, A., Pulkkinen, J., & de Bruin C. (2019). Committing, engaging and negotiating: Teachers' stories about creating shared spaces for co-teaching. *Teaching and Teacher Education, 83*, 225–235. https://doi.org/10.1016/j.tate.2019.04.013

Sandomierski, T., Martinez, S., Webster, R., Winneker, A., & Minch, D. (2022). From "quick fix" to lasting commitment: Using root cause analysis to address disproportionate discipline outcomes. *Preventing School Failure, 66*(1), 1–13.

Scruggs, T. E., & Mastropieri, M. A. (2017). Making inclusion work with co-teaching. *TEACHING Exceptional Children, 49*(4), 284–293.

Shandomo, H. M. (2010). The role of critical reflection in teacher education. *School–University Partnerships, 4*(1), 101–113.

Shepherd, K. G., Fowler, S., McCormick, J., Wilson, C. L., & Morgan, D. (2016). The search for role clarity: Challenges and implications for special education teacher preparation. *Teacher Education and Special Education, 39*(2), 83–97. https://doi.org/10.1177/0888406416637904

Shuster, K. (n.d.). Civil discourse in the classroom. *Learning for Justice.* https://www.learn ingforjustice.org/magazine/publica tions/civil-discourse-in-the-classroom

Solis, M., Vaughn, S., Swanson, E., & McCulley, L. (2012). Collaborative models of instruction: The empirical foundations of inclusion and coteaching. *Psychology in the Schools, 49*, 498–510.

Steele, J. S., Cook, L., & Ok, M. W. (2021). What makes co-teaching work in higher education? Perspectives from a merged teacher preparation program. *Issues in Teacher Education, 30*(1&2), 4–31.

Sprick, J., Sprick, R., Edwards, J., & Coughlin, C. (2021). *CHAMPS: A proactive and positive approach to classroom management.* Ancora.

Stiggins, R., & DuFour, R. (2009). Maximizing the power of formative assessments. *Phi Delta Kappan, 90*(9), 640–644. https://doi.org/10.1177/003172170909000907

Stillman, J., Anderson, L., & Struthers, K. (2014). Returning to reciprocity: Using dialogue journals to teach and learn. *Language Arts, 91*(3), 146–160.

Stillman, S. B., Stillman, P., Martinez, L., Freedman, J., Jensen, A. L., & Leet, C. (2018). Strengthening social emotional learning with student, teacher, and school-wide assessments. *Journal of Applied Developmental Psychology, 55*, 71–92. http://doi.org/10.1016/j.ppdev.2017.07.010

Stoll, L., Bolam, R., McMahon, A., Wallace, M., & Thomas, S. (2006). Professional learning communities: A review of the literature. *Journal of Educational Change, 7*, 221–258.

Strickland-Cohen, M. K., Kennedy, P. C., Berg, T. A., Bateman, L. J., & Horner, R. H. (2016). Building school district capacity to conduct functional behavioral assessment. *Journal of Emotional and Behavioral Disorders, 24*(4), 235–246. https://doi.org//10.1177/1063426615623769

Strogilos, V., Stefanidis, A., & Tragoulia, E. (2016). Co-teachers' attitudes toward planning and instructional activities for students with disabilities. *European Journal of Special Needs Education, 31*(3), 344–359.

Suter, E., Arndt, N. A., Parboosingh, J., Taylor, E., & Deutschlander, S. (2009). Role understanding and effective communication as core competencies for collaborative practice. *Journal of Interprofessional Care, 1*, 41–51. https://doi.org/10.1080/13561820802338579

TeachingWorks. (2019). *High-leverage practices.* https://library.teachingworks.org/curriculum-resources/high-leverage-practices

Tomlinson, C. A., Brighton, C., Hertberg, H., Callahan, C. M., Moon, T. R., Brimijoin, K. I., Conover, L. A., & Reynolds, T. (2003). Differentiating instruction in response to student readiness, interest, and learning profile in academically diverse classrooms: A review of literature. *Journal for the Education of the Gifted, 27*(2/3), 119–145.

Topor, D. R., Keane, S. P., Shelton, T. L., & Calkins, S. D. (2010). Parent involvement and student performance: A multiple mediational analysis. *Journal of Prevention & Intervention in the Community, 38,* 183–197. https://doi.org/10.1080/10852352.2010.486297

Tschannen-Moran, M., & Gareis, C. R. (2017). Principals, trust, and cultivating vibrant schools. In K. Leithwood, J. Sun, & K. Pollock (Eds.), *How school leaders contribute to student success* (pp. 153–174). Springer.

U.S. Department of Education. (2007a). *Questions and answers on response to intervention and early intervening services (EIS).* https://sites.ed.gov/idea/files/07-0021.RTI_-1.pdf

U.S. Department of Education. (2007b). *WWC intervention report: ClassWide peer tutoring.* https://ies.ed.gov/ncee/wwc/Docs/InterventionReports/WWC_CWPT_070907.pdf

U.S. Department of Education. (2016a). *Issue brief: Early warning systems.* https://www2.ed.gov/rschstat/eval/high-school/early-warning-systems-brief.pdf

U.S. Department of Education. (2016b). *Universal Design for Learning in ESSA: Policies and practices for every student.* https://www.bie.edu/sites/default/files/documents/idc2-089460.pdf

U.S. Department of Education. (2017). *Reimagining the role of technology in education: 2017 national education technology plan update.* https://tech.ed.gov/files/2017/01/NETP17.pdf

U.S. Department of Education. (2019). *Parent and educator guide to school climate resources.* https://www2.ed.gov/policy/elsec/leg/essa/essa guidetoschoolclimate041019.pdf

U.S. Department of Education. (2021a). *Federal Educational Rights and Privacy Act (FERPA).* https://www2.ed.gov/policy/gen/guid/fpco/ferpa/index.html

U.S. Department of Education. (2021b). *Supporting child and student social, emotional, behavioral, and mental health needs.* https://www2.ed.gov/documents/students/supporting-child-student-social-emotional-behav ioral-mental-health.pdf

U.S. Department of Education, Office of English Language Acquisition. (2021). *English learner population by local education agency.* https://ncela.ed.gov/files/fast_facts/20210315-FactSheet-ELPopulation-byLEA-508.pdf

Venkateswaran, N., Laird, J., Robles, J., & Jeffries, J. (2018). *Parent teacher home visits implementation study.* RTI International. https://pthvp.org/wp-content/uploads/2022/03/parent-teacher-home-visits-implementation-study.pdf

Villarroel, V., Boud, D., Bloxham, S., Bruna, D., & Bruna, C. (2020). Using principles of authentic assessment to redesign written examinations and tests. *Innovations in Education and Teaching International, 57*(1), 38–49. https://doi.org/10.1080/14703297.2018.1564882

Vincent, C., Inglish, J., Girvan, E., Van Ryzin, M., Svanks, R., Springer, S., & Ivey, A. (2021). Introducing restorative practices into high schools' multi-tiered systems of support: Successes and challenges. *Contemporary Justice Review, 24*(4), 409–435. https://doi.org/10.1080/10282580.2021.1969522

Wakefield, C., Adi, J., Pitt, E., & Owens, T. (2014). Feeding forward from summative assessment: The essay feedback checklist as a learning tool. *Assessment & Evaluation in Higher Education, 39*(2), 253–262. http://doi.org/10.1080/02602938.2013.822845

Walker, J. D., & Barry, C. (2017). Improving outcomes of behavioral intervention plans. *Intervention in School and Clinic, 53*(1), 12–18. https://doi.org//10.1177/1053451217692566

Wang, J., Cheng, G. H.-L., Chen, T., & Leung, K. (2019). Team creativity/innovation in culturally diverse teams: A meta-analysis. *Journal of Organizational Behavior, 40*(6), 693–708. https://doi.org/10.1002/job.2362

Wehmeyer, M. L., Shogren, K. A., & Kurth, J. (2021). The state of inclusion of students with intellectual and developmental disabilities in the United States. *Journal of Policy and Practice in Intellectual Disabilities, 18*(1), 36–43. https://doi.org/10.1111/jppi.12332

Weiss, M. P., & Rodgers, W. P. (2019). Instruction in secondary cotaught classrooms: Three elements, two teachers, one unique approach. *Psychology in Schools, 57,* 959–972. https://doi.org//10.1002/pits.22376

Westbroek, H. B., van Rens, L., van den Berg, E., & Janseen, F. (2020). A practical approach to assessment for learning and differentiated instruction. *International Journal of Science Education, 42*(6), 955–976. https://doi.org/10.1080/09500693.2020.1744044

Whittaker, C. R., Salend, S. J., & Duhaney, D. (2001). Creating instructional rubrics for inclusive classrooms. *TEACHING Exceptional Children, 34*(2), 8–13.

Wiggins, G., & McTighe, J. (2005). *Understanding by design.* ASCD.

Wiggins, G., & McTighe, J. (2012). *The understanding by design guide to creating high-quality units.* ASCD.

Wiliam, D., & Leahy, S. (2015). *Embedding formative assessment: Practical techniques for K-12 classrooms.* Learning Sciences International.

Woods, A. D., Morrison, F. J., & Palincsar, A. S. (2018). Perceptions of communication practices among stakeholders in special education. *Journal of Emotional and Behavioral Disorders, 26*(4), 209–224.

Zablotsky, B., Boswell, K., & Smith, C. (2012). An evaluation of school involvement and satisfaction for parents of children with autism spectrum disorders. *American Journal on Intellectual and Developmental Disabilities, 117,* 316–330. https://doi.org/10.1352/1944-7558-117.4.316

Zimmerman, K. N., Chow, J. C., Majeika, C., & Senter, R. (2022). Applying co-teaching models to enhance partnerships between teachers and speech-language pathologists. *Intervention in School and Clinic, 58*(3), 146–154. https://doi.org/10.1177/10534512221081255

Index

A Sage Company

CORWIN HAS ONE MISSION: to enhance education through intentional professional learning.

We build long-term relationships with our authors, educators, clients, and associations who partner with us to develop and continuously improve the best evidence-based practices that establish and support lifelong learning.